Divide and Dissent

DIVIDE
AND
DISSENT

KENTUCKY POLITICS
1930-1963

JOHN ED PEARCE

THE UNIVERSITY PRESS OF KENTUCKY

Editorial and Sales Offices: Lexington, Kentucky 40506-0024

Library of Congress Cataloging-in-Publication Data

Pearce, John Ed.
  Divide and dissent.

  Bibliography:p.
  Includes index.
    1. Kentucky—Politics and government—1865-1950.
  2. Kentucky—Politics and government—1951-   .
  3. Kentucky—Governors—History—20th century.
  I. Title.
  F456.P42   1987   976.9′043   86-28978
  ISBN 0-8131-1613-9

CONTENTS

Photographs follow pages 24 and 120

PREFACE

The reader will note that this volume has not been footnoted, a lack which will probably be a red flag to historians and other scholars, even if a mercy to readers. But this is not really a scholarly work, nor is it intended as such. Actually, I began it as a brief review of the Bert Combs administration in Frankfort, and it somehow grew on me. Everyone to whom I showed the first draft (and then the second, and the third) had suggestions to make about needed additions. I had neglected this or that political figure, this episode, that squabble. Before I knew it, I had a full-length book on my hands, and a project that took years instead of the months that I had planned. But that is all right. I have had a good time writing it. I only hope that someone will have as much fun reading it.

In that regard, I want to thank such people as Thomas Clark, John Kleber, Al Smith, and Barry Bingham for reading the manuscript of this book and for their criticism and advice. It was invaluable. So were the objections and suggestions and criticisms of the people who read the manuscript for the University Press of Kentucky.

I am indebted to the many officials of the Combs, Wetherby, Clements, Chandler, and Breathitt administrations who were kind and patient enough to furnish me with documents and recollections; and to such men as Bill May, John Crimmins, Ed Prichard, Ed Farris, Henry Ward, and Robert Bell, who granted me interviews. I also want to thank Kimberly Lady of the Kentucky Oral History Commission and Terry Birdwhistell of the University of Kentucky Library and Archives for their considerable time and patience in helping me with the tapes and papers of some of the figures treated in this book. Bob Bender of the Department of Parks furnished me with a raft of facts concerning the parks and the tourist industry. I benefited greatly from conversations with James Klotter of the Kentucky Historical Society, Louisville historian George Yater, author and longtime friend Philip Ardery, author and archivist Sam Thomas, and publisher Tyler Munford of Morganfield.

Of course, many of the people to whom I refer in the book are dead now, and I have been obliged to depend to an unfortunate extent on my own recollection of events when I was not able to find newspaper clippings or official papers to fill in the blank spots. By all measures, my chief source of information about the years from 1920 to 1963 was the files of the *Courier-Journal* in Louisville, and I want to thank librarian Sonny Tharp and his assistants for helping me in this regard. I also had the advantage of copies of the *Legislative Record* in Frankfort, limited files of the Lexington *Herald* and *Leader,* and records of the Kentucky Court of Appeals.

But a great deal of the material in this book, especially the personal and intimate references that would not be likely to show up in official records, are just from my own memory. I have known most of these people fairly well. I was never a favorite of Governor Chandler; I can understand this, since I was an editorial writer for the *Courier-Journal* during Mr. Chandler's second race and administration, when the paper did not support him and was often critical. There were periods when Earle Clements was cool toward me (to indulge in some massive understatement). I regretted this. As a newsman, as a student of politics, and as an ordinary onlooker, I liked and respected Clements. He was a great personality.

I had better explain something of my relationship with Bert Combs, since it is inevitable that some people will consider this book biased in his favor because we have long been friends. As an editorial writer for the *Courier-Journal* in 1955, when Combs first ran for governor, I got to know him casually. I met him again when he began to run in 1959. We were supporting Wilson Wyatt at the time but switched to Combs when he and Wyatt merged their campaigns. But I did not get to know him well until, in 1960, he appointed me to the newly created Parks Board. I was permitted to take the post by the *Courier-Journal* management only with the provision that the job would be nonpaying, and it was so stipulated (a provision that did not leave my fellow board members overjoyed). It was after that that I really came to know and admire Combs. I regret that I have not had occasion for much association with him since his most recent (and unsuccessful) try for office and now see him infrequently.

At the same time I think I can, and have shown that I can, view him and his administration objectively. During his term in office I was the author of many editorials that were critical of him and his policies. I would be less than honest, however, if I did not admit that I thought then and think now that his administration was outstanding. I hope I have not let this approval distort my reporting of his years.

INTRODUCTION

The governors of Kentucky have not been an exceptional lot. While there have been few outright rogues or scoundrels among them, there also have been relatively few outstanding performers, partly because of the nature of the job. It has never paid much. The state constitution won't let governors succeed themselves (though they may run again after a term has elapsed), and in the four years' term they do not have much chance to design or carry out long-range programs. For the past century Kentucky has been one of the poorer states, and poverty tends to feed on poverty, limiting what a governor can accomplish. By the time the average governor leaves office, he has had to say no so often that he enjoys little popularity.

The ferocity with which Kentuckians play politics and the corruption that so often marks the average courthouse—the vote buying, the patronage, the selling of public services for political loyalty—have their roots in that poverty. Political power is sought for the financial gain it offers; corruption is accepted, if not condoned, since the outs intend to do the same when they get in; and spoils, not service or progress, become the point of the political process.

People made cynical by such a process are often suspicious also of reform, modernization, and necessary taxation. To lead them out of the resulting poverty and ignorance requires capable, determined, and courageous leaders, willing to risk the political price of telling people the unpleasant truth. It is the lack of such leadership, more than any other factor, that accounts for Kentucky's troubles today.

Furthermore, it is hard to design laws that will meet both the needs of the moment and the multitude of restrictions contained in the cumbersome state constitution. Yet the people and usually their governors have persisted in refusing to revise and modernize the constitution, a destructive attitude that, again, results in part from a lack of positive leadership. It is a self-defeating cycle: the lack of good leadership perpetuates the handicaps that discourage good people from seeking positions of leadership. Perhaps it is remarkable that Kentucky has had governors as good as they have been.

The record is spotty. Modern government in Kentucky can be said to have begun with the governmental reorganization effected during the 1935–39 administration of Governor A. B. Chandler. But if there has been a particular era when the state got consistently better than average government, it was during the middle of the current century when, beginning with Governor Earle C. Clements and extending through the administration of Edward Breathitt, the performance of state government enabled Kentucky to break with a generally backward past. In some respects, especially in education, it did not have enough money to keep abreast of its sister states. Perhaps it never will. But those who remember the roads, colleges, hospitals, mental institutions, and welfare services of the years before World War II can appreciate the progress made since.

The peak of this 20-year period was probably reached during the 1959–63 term of Governor Bert T. Combs, who is becoming recognized as one of the key figures in Kentucky history. A major reason for his success was the passage, at the beginning of his term in office, of the sales tax that has since produced revenue without which Kentucky could not have operated on modern levels. With revenue from the tax and innovative use of a bonding mechanism approved by Kentucky courts, Combs was able to push and haul a reluctant state a significant distance along the road to modern governmental services.

Combs suffered one major setback: he almost persuaded the people to approve a convention to revise their constitution but, strangely enough, lost the effort because the people of Louisville—the state's only metropolis and usually considered a center of some enlightenment—failed to go along. That failure was significant. Kentucky's refusal to scrap its archaic charter and give its government a new beginning, though every student of government and every political scientist of the past half-century has urged such reform, is typical of the attitude that has helped to keep Kentucky backward. And wherever Combs turned, he ran into one stubborn fact: Kentuckians are to a harmful extent a cautious, conservative people. They are suspicious of change, and while not all change is progress, all progress involves change. And though Kentuckians are devoted to democracy, they are suspicious of the dirty engine of politics that powers the vehicle of democratic government, and they are above all suspicious of taxes of all kinds, for all purposes.

Despite the evidence and lessons of a century of disappointment, Kentuckians persist in believing that there is such a thing as a free lunch. They persist in following candidates who promise to give them good government through such alchemy as "sober government," "common sense," and "cutting out the fat." Ironically, leaders who have bellowed their hatred of taxes most loudly have often been the heaviest taxers. There is, after all, a price for the free lunch.

Many political observers and some people in government argue that Kentuckians have seldom been politically progressive because they have seldom been offered progressive leadership. It is true that Kentucky's rich soil seems to sprout pseudopopulists as thickly as it yields burley and bluegrass. Such people, luring the voter with assurances that they can run government without taxes, make it difficult for honest candidates to win—and, if they do get into office, make it hard for them to achieve progressive goals. But there is no denying that even when they have been given good leadership, Kentucky voters have often balked at needed reforms.

While these are the most evident drawbacks to the governor's job, they are not necessarily the most crippling. Kentucky is and has always been a divided state—divided by geography, politics, history, folkways, speech patterns, and economics. The history of eastern Kentucky, like its accents, differs from that of the Bluegrass, which differs from that of western Kentucky, and all are different from those of Louisville and the river cities. These differences make it a difficult state to govern, to unite in common cause and effort, to persuade to give a little in one place in order to help a little in another. It is not surprising that for a century political factions were one of the great dividing and retarding forces in the state, complicating the work of governors and diluting the quality of government. Time after time, as soon as one faction took office, the other—instead of uniting behind a party program—launched an attack based not on philosophy but on politics, designed not to create but to cripple. For generations, the leaders of the losing faction preferred to see the state suffer rather than see the winning faction succeed. The willingness of candidates to appeal to the voters' historic resentment of taxes, urban culture, and higher education has made it difficult and politically risky for those winning office to impose taxes and effect changes that would let Kentucky keep pace with her sister states.

The more we examine the history of Kentucky, the more it seems the state was, like the hero of a Greek tragedy, doomed by the circumstances of its beginnings. The political history of the state is the story of a people struggling against handicaps largely the result of things beyond their control. It is ironic that the state seal bears the words "United We Stand, Divided We Fall," for no state has ever been more a house divided against itself. Even before Kentucky became a state, the seeds of division were being planted, and they were to bear bitter fruit. All of these divisions—cultural, political, economic, geographic, and historic—have imposed an incalculable burden. According to legend, Dragging Canoe, the son of the Cherokee chief who sold most of eastern and southern Kentucky to Colonel Richard Henderson of North Carolina, warned the buyers that "a dark cloud hangs over that land," supposedly a warning from which the term "dark and bloody ground" derived. The name of the cloud was surely division, and it is still overhead.

Kentucky was never able, for one grisly example, to unite on the issue of slavery, for or against; the resulting division caused lingering hatreds. Perhaps more serious, the division and violence following the Civil War bred poverty and party factionalism, which in turn proved roadblocks to progress. Since before the turn of the century, the dominant Democratic party has itself been so torn into warring factions that it has been unable to shape and develop a coherent, enduring philosophy of government. Few state administrations have managed to overcome these handicaps. Backwardness and provincialism have proved too great a burden.

In the experience of one administration that succeeded to an unusual degree may lie some indications of how progressive government may be attained, as well as regret for the opportunity not seized. And in the public service of three men—Albert Benjamin Chandler, Earle Chester Clements, and Bert Thomas Combs—one can see the effects of the factional division and reaction that have so handicapped the state.

1

Dividing the Bloody Ground

The history of Kentucky is the story of missed opportunity. In colonial days explorers, hunters, and surveyors who pushed westward took back to the colonies along the eastern seaboard glowing tales of an Eden beyond the mysterious mountains, and people along the seaboard soon believed that if a man could acquire a few acres of Kentucky land he would be rich. The place had—indeed, it still has—natural advantages that made their exaggerated expectations understandable: fertile soil, a mild climate, a varied terrain offering heavily forested mountains, numerous navigable rivers, rich and rolling land for farming, and a favorable location at the north-south and east-west crossroads of the country. But 200 years later, Kentuckians are waiting for Eden to take shape and the dream to come true.

The trouble started before Kentucky became a state, when the English, tired of the expense of defending the long western frontier, made a treaty with the Indians that said, in effect, you stay on your side of the mountains, we'll stay on ours. The Indians were agreeable for the most part, though some tribes had already been embittered by colonist incursions into their territory. The colonists, on the other hand, simply ignored the treaty and pushed beyond the mountains as fast as conditions would allow, surveying and staking out land, claiming and squatting on it. Many titles were based on surveys in which boundary lines ran from trees or rocks to creeks or springs; these tended to shift or disappear, making it impossible to determine boundaries later. Colonel Richard Henderson of North Carolina bought most of eastern and southern Kentucky from the Cherokees and started selling acreage to anyone who would buy. When Virginia, with the Revolution, assumed authority over the territory, it invalidated his claim, thus putting in jeopardy the titles of all who had bought from him. The Virginia legislature, concerned primarily with the loyalty of the settlers and their willingness to defend the frontier against the Indians, passed laws in 1777 and 1779 giving settlers who had improved their land up to 1,400 acres. It also used the promise of Kentucky land to get men into the military and to reward them for their service, giving grants ranging from 100 acres for common soldiers to 5,000 acres for colonels. Unfortunately, it did this without requiring surveys and issued warrants for more land than was there, resulting in overlapping boundaries and a hopeless tangle of disputed claims.

Soldiers, afraid that they were to be cheated out of their holdings, demanded that a territory be set aside for them; for this purpose Virginia created a vast "Green River Military District," composed roughly of what is today known as the Pennyroyal. That helped but did not prevent land speculators from getting control of vast acreages. And generous grants to officers, who were usually Virginia aristocrats, encouraged the creation of big plantations in the richer central area of Kentucky, dividing the settlers into classes and opening the door to the importation of slaves.

The great migration to Kentucky began in the winter of 1778–79, as surveyors, farmers, merchants, lawyers, criminals, political refugees, and just ordinary people swarmed into the territory seeking a new life. Some were obvious adventurers and cutthroats, but most were willing to work for the wealth they hoped to gain, and these were embittered when they found, as they often did, that the land they had claimed and were working was already owned by someone else.

The Virginia Assembly then passed a law declaring that squatters who had built and farmed on the land could keep it. This created chaos, not to mention a paradise for lawyers. It has been said, with some truth, that there is not a property line in eastern Kentucky that has not been "lawed over or fought over." By 1785 there were claims for 50 percent more land than existed, and the resulting lawsuits ran for generations. Historian Joan Coward has estimated that by 1790 a majority of Kentucky householders were landless, many of them tenants.

Generally speaking, the wealthy and influential got the better land, especially in central Kentucky; the poor and latecomers got shoved back into the hills and hollows. Many, including old settlers, got no land at all. This produced sullen divisions between rich and poor (a division not uncommon on the frontier farther west) and a cultural blight that persisted for more than a century. Stuck back on their mud roads, when they had any roads at all, with little or no access to the political, cultural, and commercial mainstream, Kentucky agrarians developed a narrow, provincial view of life. They had a tight suspicion of culture, manners, and refinement, all of which they saw as the marks of the town and corruptive of honest farm life. They developed a distrust of schools, which in their view existed only to teach farm boys book learning they did not need to raise a crop, and to take them away from the plow when they were needed.

This was not just meanness or ignorance; the rural dwellers, in the hills of eastern Kentucky or on the river farms of the west, sensed that formal, institutional education constituted a threat to their native cultural values; they saw that those who managed to get an education put a barrier between themselves and the culture they had known and with which they had once been comfortable. The only thing a farm boy could do with an education was to leave. The agrarian also had a stubborn resistance to taxes of all kinds, for whatever purpose, seeing them as the invention of politicians to help the decadent town at the expense of the honest farmer. Tragically, but perhaps inevitably, there have always been politicians willing to appeal to these class, cultural, and regional prejudices in order to gain votes, thus aggravating the problem.

Kentuckians have always been inordinately willing to believe their own myths. Just as they have clung to the distorted legend of Daniel Boone, so have they nurtured the image of the rugged, proud, self-dependent Kentuckian, and the image has been a burden. The spirit of fierce independence that was salvation to the frontiersman and proud legacy to successive generations of agrarians became a lingering handicap, and remains so today, impelling Kentuckians to resist or regard with suspicion the cooperation and collective action through which society progresses in the modern world.

Conditions for progressive government were not improved when, during the early decades of the nineteenth century, the legislature spewed out counties as though on a prolonged drunk. Counties were created for any reason. Real estate dealers, eager to sell lots in the town that would grow up around a courthouse, would offer to donate land for a courthouse and jail and, on the day when the referendum on forming the county was held, would put out barrels of whiskey to influence the voters. Many counties were formed through the efforts of men who wanted only to hold the office of judge, sheriff, or jailer. Once the citizens had voted to petition the General Assembly to make them a county, representatives curried favor in Frankfort by proposing to name the new county for the governor or lieutenant governor. A splitoff from Floyd and Letcher counties in 1884 was named Knott County to gain the support of Governor Proctor Knott, and the county seat was diplomatically named Hindman in honor of Lieutenant Governor John Hindman. Thus Kentucky was jigsawed into 120 counties, more per capita than any other state; only Georgia and Texas have more in number.

The existence of these "Little Kingdoms," as historian Robert Ireland dubbed them, made some sense at the time. The crumpled terrain of Kentucky, especially its eastern and southern sections, made it hard for the country dweller to get in to the county seat to conduct necessary business. Because of the sprawling shape of the early counties, residents often had to walk or ride 100 miles to the courthouse, a terrible undertaking in a territory with few roads. Therefore, new county seats were located when possible in spots that could be reached from all sections in a day's ride. (Even so, distance and bad roads made it almost impossible for the sheriff to enforce the law effectively in the far reaches of the county. Isolated families necessarily turned to self-defense, adding to a feeling of alienation from the law and a distrust of it, and laying the groundwork for feuds.)

Unfortunately, the counties continued to exist after the need for them had vanished, saddling Kentucky, apparently forever, with a multitude of unnecessary, burdensome governments. Their very existence bred provincialism and xenophobia, increasing the difficulty of persuading Kentuckians to cooperate and take concerted action for their mutual benefit. Not surprisingly, inefficient and often corrupt courthouse operations compounded the suspicion of the rural taxpayers that all politicians were crooks and all politics crooked. This attitude, in turn, was reflected in the state constitution of 1891, which provided another handicap to responsive government.

Opposition to taxes and distrust of government in general were inevitably reflected in Frankfort, helping to keep Kentucky on the back roads of progress. Until 1950, it was a detour state: travelers would go to great lengths to avoid passing through Kentucky, with its bad roads and the small-town speed traps that preyed on outsiders. Inadequate roads also perpetuated stubborn provincialism, since they kept Kentuckians from knowing even their own state. And bad roads crippled efforts to consolidate schools and do away with the primitive one-room schools, since buses could not run over many of the roads. Before 1960, when the Mountain Parkway was built into the mountains, eastern Kentucky had 17,000 miles of roads but not one mile of four-lane, limited-access highway; in fact, 9,000 of those miles were mud or gravel. It was not until 1928 that Harlan County, one of the most mineral-rich counties in America, had a hard-surfaced road to the outside.

The lack of social contact made the frontier Kentuckian susceptible to the emotional, open-air revivals where crowds of thousands were pilloried with fiery sermons by dozens of preachers, threats of hell and damnation so moving that the men were said to chew grass and bark like dogs, while the women jerked so violently that their long hair cracked like whips. These revivals helped to implant in early Kentuckians an emotional fundamentalism that for years regarded public, nonchurch schools with suspicion and hampered the development of a public school system until the current century. Transylvania University, once called "the Harvard of the West," had an outstanding faculty and drew students from across the South until churchmen and religious students attacked the school's nationally respected president, Horace Holley, for attending races and balls while neglecting his students' religious instruction. Holley was forced to leave the state, and Transylvania never recovered its national standing or its position of dominance within the state, though in this century it has achieved considerable stature. (Neither did higher education in general recover during the nineteenth century. Years later, after the University of Kentucky was founded, its development was hampered by church opposition to the spending of tax money on secular education, or as some put it, "the Godless university." It took a fevered mind to depict the struggling, underfinanced Lexington school as "the country club of the south.")

Transylvania did not suffer alone. Public education was almost nonexistent. Kentucky had inherited from Virginia one of its worst institutions, the private academy, the influence of which is still strong. Across the state these private schools sprang up, many of them boarding schools, often church-related or taught by a minister and supported by fees paid by the parents of students. The more well-to-do townsmen and planters sent their children to these academies, some of which offered surprisingly good classical training. (As late as the 1890s, the father of novelist John Fox, Jr., conducted an academy for both boys and girls near Paris.) Most rural dwellers, on the other hand, did not care that there were no tax-supported public schools for their sons and daughters.

It was at this time, too, that Kentucky became the only state to have two courts of appeal, a matter of no public pride. With so little hard currency on the post-Revolutionary frontier, the need for banks soon resulted in a rash of state and national banks, some of them totally unsound and offering banknotes unsupported by anything but hope. At the same time, the Napoleonic wars were taking European farmers from the plow and causing a great inflation of farm prices in America, especially in the rich farming country of Kentucky. Bluegrass farmers, giddy with profits from goods shipped downriver and across the seas, rushed to borrow money to buy more land and plant more crops; when the wars ended in Europe—as wars will—and farm prices collapsed, they were stuck with loans they could not repay.

The legislature, responding to demands for relief, passed a law creating a new currency to be issued by the state bank to repay these loans; creditors unwilling to accept this questionable currency were forbidden to demand payment for at least two years. The creditors, naturally, sued, charging that the law was unconstitutional. The Court of Appeals, the state's highest court at the time, naturally ruled in their favor. This outraged both the debtors and the legislature, which solved the problem brilliantly by abolishing the old court and creating a new "relief" court. The relief court upheld the relief law, but the old court ruled that the relief court, as well as its rulings, was unconstitutional. The legislature directed the relief court to occupy the court chambers and seize, if necessary, court records. The old court refused to surrender them or even to open the door. In the legislature, fist fights erupted between advocates of the two courts. One prominent supporter of the old court was knocked down with a club as he left the capitol building. Mobs marched and howled through Frankfort and county-seat towns. Eventually, prosperity and sanity returned, the old court was upheld, the relief court was abolished, and the farmers had to pay their debts; but the episode did nothing to dignify Kentucky's image nationally.

The dueling fever that swept Kentucky in these years was not so comical. The most picayune disputes became cause for fatal gunfights. The slightest disagreement might end in a duel, the smallest jest result in death. The toll in human life finally became so high that the next state constitution, written in 1849, specifically forbade state office to anyone who had been involved in a duel, effectively ending the custom. You can accomplish a lot in Kentucky by threatening to keep people from the public payroll.

Why the code duello struck with such virulence in Kentucky is hard to understand. Kentucky pride has often reached a stage that would have been ridiculous had it not been so lethal. But it was becoming apparent that there was a strong strain of violence in Kentuckians. They rushed by the thousands to volunteer to fight the British, the Indians, the Spanish—any excuse seemed sufficient. Perhaps some of this reflected the old frontier dependence on and love for the rifle, and the frontier necessity of self-defense and protection. But the penchant for killing was fast tarnishing the image of the "paradise beyond the mountains." Even before the Civil War, eastern publications ridiculed Kentucky with cartoons of addled colonels brandishing smoking pistols. And the tendency toward violence would later sharpen the divisions between regions, parties, and classes.

Fundamentalist opposition to legal liquor would likewise give Kentucky one of the finest and most corrupt bootlegging networks in the country, as Kentuckians persisted in "drinking wet and voting dry." Though Kentucky is the world's largest producer of bourbon whiskey, 91 of its 120 counties forbid the sale, use, or transportation of liquor. The "drys" of the state find no irony in the fact that Christian County is wet while Bourbon County (except for Paris) is dry. The collusion—unintended, perhaps, but effective—among bootleggers, ministers, and public officials has kept the great majority of Kentucky counties legally dry though actually wet; the right to carry on illegal liquor sales from under counters and in taxicabs is one of the spoils of election victory in many counties, while much time and expense is devoted by law enforcement officers to the pursuit and prosecution of other bootleggers. And all the while the revenue-hungry county coffers are deprived of the taxes that legal sales of the same liquor would produce.

But a force was at work on the Kentucky frontier that would prove far more divisive, and the effects of which would linger for more than a century. The institution of slavery from the beginning drove wedges between groups and regions. The trouble sprang, significantly, from a failure of leadership. The aristocrats around George Nicholas, who dominated the convention that wrote Kentucky's first constitution, were nearly all slaveowners and strongly proslavery. Not that they lacked opposition: such men as James Garrard, who would become second governor of the state, and the Reverend "Father David" Rice, the stubborn frontier Presbyterian, argued and begged for a constitutional bar to the importation of slaves; Nicholas was able to beat back their efforts by only a 26 to 16 vote in the convention.

But the proslavery stand of the first constitution was a signal. By 1792, when Kentucky achieved statehood, almost 23 percent of Kentucky households kept slaves, and the average slaveholder owned only four—giving aristocratic planters a wide base of middle-class support for their proslavery stance. But most small farmers and merchants opposed the institution, as did most churches, especially Presbyterian and Methodist. Legend maintains that slavery in Kentucky was relatively benign and that Kentucky slaves were happy and well treated compared with those of Deep South states. George Nicholas, who declared that "the Negro is fit only for bondage," insisted that Kentucky slaves were fortunate in their work and treatment, giving rise to a myth still reflected in the state song. But the facts do not support this rosy recollection. At the time of the Civil War, Kentucky was the sixth most populous state in the Union, and almost one-fourth of its population was slave. Slaves were bought and sold on the block; families were split apart regardless of their anguished screams and wails. Those helping slaves escape were whipped in public or thrown into prison. The peculiar institution was not pretty.

During his historic tour of America, the great French social critic Alexis de Toqueville insisted that the villages along the northern banks of the Ohio River were bright, busy, and attractive, while the southern shores appeared to be less industrious, moody, and poor. The reason, he declared, was that Ohio was free, Kentucky enslaved by its slavery. This was, of course, ridiculous exaggeration: Ohio at the time was no more progressive than Kentucky, and its per capita income was less; most of the Kentucky region past which de Toqueville sailed actually contained few slaves, and much of it was stubbornly antislavery. It is also a fact that the section of the state most opposed to slavery and loyal to the Union, eastern Kentucky, was the least prosperous and progressive.

Yet no one can dispute the terrible effects of slavery on the state's economy, its government, and its sense of statehood. If they were not divided enough, the issue further divided Kentuckians along moral as well as geographical and political lines. Other states argued over the issue and went either free or slave; Kentucky brawled about it for more than 50 years and split down the middle. There is more than casual symbolism in the fact that Kentucky was the birthplace of both Abraham Lincoln, president of the United States, and Jefferson Davis, president of the Confederate States of America.

The Presbyterian church fought stubbornly and courageously against slavery. Abolitionists such as Cassius Clay joined the crusade with pistols and Bowie knives. Movements to buy and free slaves arose and went broke. The recolonizing movement to send the blacks back to Africa struggled with the problem for a while, but the task was too great; only 661 blacks were sent from Kentucky to Liberia, the African land set aside for them, and only about 16,000 from the entire country. The investment in and dependence on slave labor made owners unwilling to free their slaves, and the abolitionists did not have enough money to buy them. (Sturdy Methodists behind John Fee founded at Berea a racially integrated school but were threatened and beaten for their efforts, and their school closed during the Civil War. After the war it reopened and flourished for a while, only to have its activities curtailed in 1912 by the state's infamous Day Law, which forbade instruction of white and black students under the same roof.)

In pulpit, courtroom, and underground railway the sour quarrel over the right to own human beings swirled. The results were disastrous. Symbolically, it was Kentucky's great senator, Henry Clay, who most persistently and futilely sought a compromise on the slavery question. Symbolically, Kentucky Senator John Crittenden pleaded with tears on his cheeks for a decent compromise, but lived to see one of his sons become an officer in the Confederate Army and another an officer with the Union. Two of Mary Todd Lincoln's half brothers were officers in the Union Army, two in the Army of the Confederacy.

No state was more torn by the Civil War than Kentucky, and no state was more torn during the years following. The states to the south were united in defeat and misery, and in the knowledge that they had fought well; those to the north were united in victory and the promise of prosperity. Poor Kentucky had succeeded, at hideous cost, only in tearing itself apart and planting the seeds of enduring hatreds, and now it turned and tore at itself again. Having stuck to the Union throughout the war, once the fighting was over it embraced the Confederate cause with an addled passion (partly because of the shortsighted and punitive policies of Union military commanders), leading one historian to remark that it was the only government in history to join the loser after the loss. Rhett Butler, in *Gone with the Wind*, said when he enlisted in the Confederate Army, "I always was a sucker for a losing cause." Kentucky was a sucker for one already lost.

Instead of peace, violence took over as the war ended. Night riders and "regulators" harassed blacks and their sympathizers. Veterans returning from the opposing armies often clashed, helping to spark feuds throughout eastern Kentucky that lasted into the present century, further weakening inept county governments and bringing ridicule to the region and to the state. A dislike for cities along the Ohio—especially Louisville—that had stuck with the Union (partly because of recent immigration from the North, partly because of superior northern markets for river traffic) flourished in areas where the Confederacy had been strong.

This dislike of Louisville was not new. Ever since the days of the Revolution, when George Rogers Clark anchored his defenses at the falls of the Ohio rather than in central Kentucky, people in the central and eastern parts of the state had resented Louisville. Following the Civil War, the resentment grew. The town attracted thousands of Irish and German Catholic immigrants. Business and civic leaders of Louisville in the early years were often Germans and the remnants of Old South gentry, an unlikely combination which, it was said, would benefit Louisville with the industry of the Germans and the hospitality and gracious manners of the South. Many people in the rest of the state jeered that, instead, Louisville had inherited German arrogance and southern laziness.

Worse, the city was headquarters for the Louisville and Nashville

Railroad. The city for years owned a large block of L&N stock, and
Louisville legislators helped to fight for the L&N cause in the legislature. During the 1870s and into the 1880s the influence of the railroad
in the legislature managed to keep forces in Cincinnati, Lexington,
Chattanooga, and Atlanta from building north-south rail lines through
central Kentucky, giving the L&N a virtual monopoly and denying
much of the state the benefit of north-south rail connections.
Eventually, the Southern Railway built its lines through Lexington
southward, but the bitterness between Louisville and much of the rest
of the state continued for years afterward. Following the tragic assassination of Governor William Goebel at the turn of the century, the
L&N again intruded into state affairs, bringing in hundreds of eastern
Kentucky riflemen to aid the Republican cause in Frankfort. Its power
had begun to wane by then; still, it remained an influence in Kentucky
politics until the 1930s, and although its headquarters are no longer in
Louisville and its participation in state affairs is minimal, the anti-
Louisville feeling it helped to generate survives.

   During the post–Civil War years a strong Bourbonism arose,
chiefly in central Kentucky, its leaders generally the rich and reactionary gentry who clung to visions of the Old South, resisted indus-
trialization, despised blacks, and distrusted government in general,
preferring local arbitration of local matters by local gentlemen. The
Bourbon influence was strongly resisted by New Departure Democrats, whose spokesman, the noted Louisville editor Henry Watterson,
begged the state to forget the war and join in the industrial boom in
process. The coming of a modest prosperity in and around Louisville
because of North-South trade had an effect on the rest of Kentucky, and
by the middle 1880s the hard-line Bourbon influence was easing. But
diehard Bourbons still disliked cities, regarded rural and mountain
residents of the state as inferior, and tended to view public education,
taxes, and much of progress with suspicion if not outright hostility.
The better class of people, they maintained, could and would educate
its own in private schools, and there was little need to educate the rest.
From their patrician perch they joined the uneducated agrarian in
regarding the education of farm boys as worse than useless, serving
only to make them dissatisfied with their rightful lot. Taxes, they felt,
were the tool of villains, money taken from the rich to buy support of
the poor. The poor, at the same time, tended to see taxes as the work of
villains, money taken from the poor to placate and enrich the gentry.
   In this atmosphere of violence and division, the constitution of
1891 was written. It is significant of their mood that the framers, with
the federal Constitution to guide them, could produce a charter so at

variance with it. The genius of the federal Constitution lies not in the meaning it might have had in days long past but in the adaptability of its principles to current problems and current needs. Yet it was less the work of genius than of intelligent adherence to principle.

The 55 men who met in Philadelphia in 1787 did not convene in an atmosphere of euphoria. The Revolutionary War had been over for some time; economic realities were closing in on the inexperienced men attempting to guide the new and competitive states; and there was widespread disagreement over the eventual nature of the new government. Indeed, the framers met not with the clear intention of writing a new constitution but to shore up the Articles of Confederation, which, compiled in 1781, had sought and failed to unify the former colonies.

In the soft glow of patriotic hindsight, all of the men at Philadelphia during that hot and crucial summer have become saints and geniuses. They were not. Indeed, fewer than a dozen proved to be of more than average intelligence or possessed of admirable qualities. Most sought to protect their own interests or those of their states. Thomas Jefferson, probably the greatest intellect of his era, was not even there. Benjamin Franklin contributed little beyond jokes and drolleries. There were, however, such men as Madison, Mason, Dickinson; they wrote a document that changed history, that permitted a vast continent to become a great nation and varied peoples to become a people. Kentucky's charter only hardened the lines of division. One possible explanation may be that the men in Philadelphia were guided by principle, the men in Frankfort by suspicion.

Kentucky's constitution is a narrow, rambling document designed to curb government rather than to guide it, a collection of restrictive statutes rather than an outline of principles. Kentucky's constitution is seven times longer than the Constitution of the United States, and is marked by neither its wisdom nor its grace. It contains such trivia as the requirement that all public officials take an oath that they have not been involved in a duel. It forbade women the vote. It even imposes a limit on the number of doorkeepers the General Assembly may hire— two for the Senate, two for the House. This may have made some vague sense at the time: guarding the doors was thought necessary to prevent irate citizens from invading the chambers to join debates (though its inclusion in a constitution boggles the mind). But it has made no earthly sense since the legislature moved from the "Old Capitol," where each chamber had two doors, to the new capitol building, where both House and Senate have three. Every time the Assembly meets, the constitution is automatically violated.

Incidentally, the constitution was never actually approved by the people of Kentucky. The draft as originally written by the convention was ratified by the people. But in the meantime the leaders of the convention realized that the first draft was simply not workable, so they reconvened and substantially rewrote it. The revised draft was never ratified.

The atmosphere of unsettled, angry division contributed to, if it did not actually cause, the assassination of Democratic Governor William Goebel in the first days of 1900, launching the state into the twentieth century on a wave of anger and bitterness.

For the first time, Kentucky in 1895 had elected a Republican Governor, W. O. Bradley, as factional fights split the Democrats. The dominant Democrats had been, since the Civil War, divided into factions loosely based on economic interests: Bourbons who longed for the past and fought for the status quo, and the advocates of New Departure, who wanted to forget the war and rebuild. Beginning in the 1890s, William Jennings Bryan and the issue of free silver split the party into new factions; in 1895, when the pro-Bryan Free Silver Democrats refused to support the conservative Parker Watkins Hardin (nicknamed "Polly Wolly" Hardin) of Harrodsburg, the Democratic nominee for governor, the Republican Bradley won.

William O'Connell Bradley ("Billy O B") was no newcomer to politics. He had run and lost races for Congress, the U.S. Senate, and the governorship and had declined nomination for state attorney general. A hard-money Republican, he followed most of the conservative policies of his party, although he differed from many in favoring legal (but not social) equality for the Negro. An eloquent speaker of impressive manner, Bradley was in many respects ahead of his times. Historians have often spoken of Kentucky's failure to grasp the chance available in 1900 for a new beginning; actually, the state might well have found a promising new direction in 1895 had the legislature enacted the enlightened and progressive program put forward by Bradley.

He proposed, for instance, a constitutional amendment giving Louisville home rule, asked that the legislature abolish the offices of commissioner of agriculture and commonwealth attorney, called for a vote on a new capitol building and mansion, and proposed the establishment of houses of reform for first offenders, an end to the fee system for attorneys, and fair and uniform assessment of property for tax purposes. In his second session, he asked for sweeping reforms in education, including an end to the district board system, adoption of uniform textbooks, and tests for school board officers and members; stiffer examinations for lawyers and stiffer penalties for unethical conduct by them; and repeal of the law requiring separate railway coaches for whites and blacks. It was, in brief, a radical and farsighted program. But the Democrats, whose split had elected him, at once turned against him, and the legislature spent most of its time squabbling over selection of a U.S. senator.

Those bills that were passed provided for two houses of reform, authorized free turnpikes and gravel roads, and required all children to attend school not less than 12 weeks a year, a law widely ignored. Unfortunately, the lawmakers failed to pass a revenue bill, with the result that there was no money with which to run the state. Bradley was bitterly disappointed by the failure of the Assembly even to consider seriously his proposed reform measures.

In its second session under Bradley, the legislature at least provided for a bond issue to give the state operating money. It also passed the famous Goebel Law, which paved the way for one of the most hurtful episodes in Kentucky history.

The split in the Democratic party gave impetus to the rise of the law's author, William Goebel. In the years following the Civil War, impolitic administration of federal laws and regulations by military commanders had led the state pell-mell into the pro-southern Democratic camp, and for a generation it was difficult, indeed almost impossible, for candidates without some Confederate or agrarian ties to win public office. Goebel was of another mold. The dour son of German immigrants and a state senator from Covington, Goebel came from a pro-Union family. He gained attention during the Bradley administration by shaping and winning passage of the so-called Goebel Election Law, a distorted piece of legislation designed to prevent the kind of corruption which, Democrats charged, caused the victories of Bradley and McKinley. The Goebel Law set up a state Board of Election Commissioners to appoint boards to oversee elections and decide disputes and contests. Unfortunately, it stipulated that the commission would have three members, which made equal representation of the two parties impossible and gave tremendous election-day power to the party with a majority in the legislature.

Goebel hoped to use his support of Bryan, his labor record, and his opposition to the L&N Railroad to win the Democratic nomination for governor. ("The L&N Railroad," he preached across the state, "must be made the servant, not the master of the people." This struck a responsive chord with a lot of people. The L&N had become so domineering that, according to legend, a legislator from Lexington arose in the House toward the end of a session of the General Assembly and said, "If the L&N Railroad has no other business to conduct, I move we adjourn.") Goebel went into the Democratic convention of 1899 the third choice of most politicians but, through shrewd jockeying, came out the nominee for governor. Thirty-year-old J.C.W. Beckham, the personable scion of a prominent Bardstown family, was chosen to run for second spot.

But Goebel's selection again split the Democrats, who by this time were so accustomed to factional divisions that another split seemed normal. In a rump convention in Lexington, conservatives calling themselves the Honest Election Democrats nominated ex-Governor John Young Brown, who called up the ghost of Robert E. Lee; spoke of beautiful homes, wives, and daughters; and challenged his listeners to refuse to be voted "like dumb, driven cattle." The floundering Populist Party made its last real effort to gain a foothold in Kentucky, nominating John G. Blair of Carlisle. As the campaign for governor became a four-sided affair, Goebel rode out to challenge Republican nominee W.S. Taylor, Bradley's well-meaning but relatively ineffectual attorney general. A western Kentuckian of unprepossessing appearance, Taylor was considered "lily white" or anti-Negro, so much so that Bradley at first refused to support him. Taylor had as his running mate John Marshall, a young Louisville lawyer; and to run for secretary of state, the convention picked slender, intellectual Caleb Powers, at 30 the superintendent of Knox County schools, who was destined to play a central and tragic role in the disastrous events to follow.

It was a tangled campaign, with both parties seeming to ride off in all directions. Goebel actively courted the black vote, the first time a Democrat had openly done so since the Civil War. When it appeared that he was faltering, he brought into the state William Jennings Bryan, the old orator who showed that he could still influence the voters. Despite these maneuvers, Taylor at first appeared to have won by a slender margin of 2,383 votes, receiving 193,714 votes to 191,331 for Goebel, with Brown picking up only 12,140 and Blair 2,936. On December 12, 1899, Taylor was duly sworn in as Kentucky's thirty-third governor.

Although he was at first bitter toward the factions that had brought about his defeat, Goebel soon accepted the outcome with surprisingly good grace for a man of his temper, though he explained in a letter to his brother that, win or lose, he would be the dominant force in the Democratic party and a certain favorite for election to the Senate. He announced that he planned to visit his brother in the West. But the Democrats were not ready to give up. They charged that there had been numerous voting irregularities (as there usually were, on both sides) and immediately contested the election. The action ushered in one of the most tragic episodes in Kentucky history.

When it became obvious that the Board of Election Commissioners formed under the Goebel Election Law would decide the election, bands of Republicans from the mountains of eastern Kentucky began sifting into the capital, many of them openly armed and all warning that they were not going to have the election stolen from them by the Democratic board. Eastern Kentucky newspapers declared that Goebel was a serpent, a tyrant, and a monster, and thundered that before "this ring of looters" is allowed to steal the victory, "we will shoulder our guns." The Kentucky penchant for violence was again boiling to the surface.

To the surprise of almost everyone, the election board quickly ruled in Taylor's favor but added that it had no powers in a governor's race; the dispute could be decided only by the legislature. On December 14, 1899, the Democrats met in Frankfort and adopted a resolution calling on Goebel and Beckham to contest the election. Goebel assented, and when the legislature convened, the election was formally contested. Committees were chosen by lot to conduct hearings into the election of governor and lieutenant governor. Names were written on slips of paper and placed in a box from which a blindfolded designee drew 11 names for each contest. Strangely, the names of ten Democrats and one Republican were pulled for the governor's hearing, nine Democrats and two Republicans for the lieutenant governor's. The men in charge insisted that the drawing had been fair, but others whispered that the slips placed in the box were of tissue paper, and that those bearing Democratic names had been crinkled so that the blindfolded official could be sure he was drawing the right ones.

The contest committee hearings began on January 15 in the Capital Hotel ballroom, but after the first day prominent Republicans met in Louisville's Galt House and charged that the hearings were being run by and for the Democrats. This was a signal for the men from the mountains again to descend on Frankfort, and more than 1,000 of them poured into the capital—all of them, it was rumored, brought in by the L&N without charge. For a while it appeared that open warfare might erupt, but Taylor urged all to put down their guns, and the following day most of the mountain men went home. Still, some 300 remained, armed and ominous, to await the outcome of the election decision. The board ended its hearings on January 29 and announced that it would have a decision within a few days.

On the morning of January 30, Goebel, with Colonel Jack Chinn and Eph Lillard, warden of the state penitentiary, left the Capital Hotel, crossed the railroad tracks, and started across the capitol lawn. Ordinarily, the lawn and the walkways leading to the capitol were crowded; this morning they were almost deserted. The three men apparently took no notice of that fact, however, and were talking casually as they approached the fountain outside the building. Lillard went ahead to check the lobby, to make sure that Goebel would encounter no trouble. Then suddenly a shot blasted the strange quiet. Goebel fell. Chinn rushed to his side. "Goebel!" he cried. "They have killed you!" Other, muffled shots were heard. "Lie down," Chinn cried, "or they will shoot you again."

"That's right," said Goebel.

Goebel later said he saw someone in a third-story window, but Chinn said the shot came from the first-floor office of Secretary of State Caleb Powers. Lillard rushed out, and he and Chinn helped several men carry Goebel to his room in the Capital Hotel. There a doctor found that he had been shot through his right lung, the bullet exiting near the spine. It was immediately evident that his condition was grave.

Outside, mobs milled through the streets. There were rumors that Taylor would be shot in retaliation. Troops hurried to the capitol and tried to seal off the mountain men, who still threatened violence. In this confused atmosphere, the legislators tried to convene at midafternoon but were barred from the Capitol by troops under orders to let no one enter or leave the building. Eventually, they met at Frankfort City Hall, where former governor Bradley and other Republicans asked the committee members to postpone action because of the explosive atmosphere. They did, but an hour later they met again, threw out some of the contested votes, and declared that Goebel and Beckham had received the highest number of votes and were therefore duly elected. An hour later Governor Taylor, indicating no intention of surrendering the office, declared a state of insurrection and ordered the legislature to meet in safely Republican London, seat of Laurel County. Republicans agreed; Democrats refused.

On January 31 the Democratic members of the legislature marched to the capitol, hoping to adopt the majority report and declare Goebel governor. Troops turned them back. Still in a body, they marched to the Opera House, where they were again turned away by troops. They tried City Hall and then the courthouse. Everywhere, troops blocked the way. Finally (some claim while they were trotting down the street followed by troops intent on keeping them from convening), a motion was made and adopted to meet in the Capital Hotel. There they went singly or by twos, to avoid attracting attention, to a second-floor room where 19 senators and 57 representatives declared Goebel and Beckham elected. A few minutes later the two were sworn in by Chief

Justice James H. Hazelrigg of the Court of Appeals. In his first action, Goebel commanded the troops to return home. The troops refused. The Democrats met again at the hotel and, apparently unsure of the validity of their first decision, again declared Goebel elected; again he was given the oath of office, this time by Judge J.C. Cantrill, although Republicans afterward insisted that Goebel was dead by the time the oath was administered.

The Democrats were obviously gearing up to make a case for Beckham in the event Goebel died, though W.S. Taylor remained in the governor's office, refusing to accept the decision of the Democratic majority in the legislature and trying to conduct the affairs of state.

While Goebel lay fatally wounded in the Capital Hotel, he is said to have asked for some oysters, a favorite food, and to have eaten them with a good appetite. They did not, of course, save him. As he was dying, he is supposed to have uttered the words now engraved on his statue: "Be brave and true and loyal to the great common people." Some, however, say his last words were, "Those oysters were no damned good" (or, alternatively, "Doc, that was a damn poor oyster").

Goebel died early in the evening of February 3, 1900. Taylor refused to yield the governor's office and filed suit to prevent Beckham from assuming it. Beckham responded by asking the court to grant his right to the capitol and executive offices, and on March 10, Judge Emmett Field of the Jefferson Circuit Court ruled in his favor. On April 6 the Court of Appeals declared the offices of governor and lieutenant governor vacant, and on May 21 the Supreme Court refused to overturn its decision. Taylor lost his nerve and fled to Indiana. Beckham was declared governor; he took office, and things began to settle into some sort of routine.

The nightmare of Goebel's assassination, however, was not ended. It was established that the shot that killed Goebel had been fired from the office of Caleb Powers, elected attorney general with Taylor. Powers later insisted that he was on the train to Louisville when the fatal shot was fired, and he had witnesses to that effect. But Democrats contended that Powers got off the train in Shelbyville and asked a man at the station, "Anything happened yet in Frankfort?" indicating that he was aware of the plan to kill Goebel and had left town until the deed was done. In any event, two days later, dressed in an army uniform, he was arrested on a train between Frankfort and Lexington. Since Powers had not previously been accustomed to wearing army clothes, his outfit seemed suggestive of guilt. At the time of his arrest, he was reported to have in his pocket a pardon from Taylor for "any complicity" in Goebel's death.

Powers was jailed and tried as an accomplice in the murder of Goebel, a charge to which he pleaded innocent. He did, however, admit that he had helped to arrange with the L&N to bring the mountain riflemen to Frankfort. Three times he was convicted—once sentenced to death—and once won a hung jury; all the verdicts were handed down by juries that were almost solidly Democratic, though impaneled in a county that was 40 percent Republican. He was still being held in jail when he was finally pardoned, in 1908, by Republican Governor Augustus Willson. He was later elected to Congress from his mountain district, and it was his boast that he served as many years in Congress as he had served in jail. The story is told that during his first congressional campaign he was approached by a voter who asked, "You killed Goebel, didn't you?" "No, I didn't," Powers replied, to which the voter responded, "I'm sorry to hear that. I had intended to vote for you."

Another Republican, Henry Youtsey, was also jailed and convicted, but the man who was widely believed to have fired the fatal shot was "Big Jim" Howard of Clay County. At the time he was arrested, Howard was free on appeal after having been convicted in Clay County of killing George Baker, victim in a notorious Clay County feud. When arrested, Howard was also said to have in his pocket a pardon signed by Governor Taylor, this one for his role in the killing of George Baker; it was widely assumed that Taylor had offered Big Jim his freedom if he would remove Goebel. Howard was also pardoned by Willson, as was Youtsey, in 1908.

Once more Kentucky's image was blackened in the nation's eyes. The incident lent credence to the caricature of the one-gallused, bearded, homicidal Kentucky hillbilly; it discredited the Republican party and crippled the Republican mountain counties, contributing directly to their lack of influence in Frankfort and thus their inability to gain needed state money for roads and schools. Kentucky's shackles were still largely self-imposed. And once more the seeds of lingering bitterness between Kentuckians had been planted. Republicans insisted for years that "they stole the election." Democrats retorted that "they killed our governor." Both were probably right.

Young John Crepps Wyckliffe Beckham, of Bardstown, elected lieutenant governor with Goebel, was now governor. It was to be the start of a long though not always distinguished career.

"My father [Judge Robert Worth Bingham, publisher of the Louisville *Courier-Journal* and *Louisville Times*] always supported Beckham" said Barry Bingham, "not for any particular policy reason but because he felt that Beckham was a gentleman, an honorable man, and would do the right thing. I don't think Beckham ever had any burning convictions, actually. It was more a matter of what was popular at the time."

The description is apt. If Beckham had any resounding convictions, they changed frequently. His policy decisions were based largely on the advice of Percy Haly, a tough, wily Irishman whose father ran a saloon in North Frankfort and who had enjoyed a brief political career as House sergeant-at-arms. He was also, incidentally, a trusted adviser of Judge Bingham, perhaps accounting for the Bingham-Beckham alliance. Haly was what we might today term a pragmatist, a practical man. But he was a man of few overriding convictions, and Beckham lacked the philosophic principles or the firmness of purpose to keep together the Democratic party that was, for the moment, united by the death of Goebel.

In all, not the best possible way to begin a new century.

2

Happy Days Begin

Despite the pleas of New Departure progressives such as Marse Henry Watterson, editor of the *Courier-Journal*, that they forget their differences and help create a new industrial South, Kentuckians remained divided, backward, poor, and largely resentful of culture as the state entered the twentieth century. It is remarkable how enduring these traits proved to be. The factions, the isolation of eastern Kentucky, the sectional differences, the dislike of urban Louisville, the state's failure to provide sufficient tax money to develop modern roads and schools, and the relative poverty that made the state consistently susceptible to opposition to taxes—these handicaps clung like leeches to Kentucky throughout the first half of the current century, handicaps worsened by the Depression and lessened only by the relative prosperity following World War II.

Even good leaders have had trouble leading Kentuckians very far. Henry Clay could not get them to modernize or compromise. Neither Father David Rice nor John Fee nor old Cassius Clay could persuade them to give up the immoral profit from the odious practice of slavery. Watterson could not persuade them to forget the Civil War and go forward into the twentieth century. From the early decades of the nineteenth century to the second decade of the twentieth, educators tried to persuade Kentucky to establish a real public school system, with almost no success. For over half a century various leaders have called for revision of the state's burdensome constitution, but in vain. And just as consistently have Kentuckians resisted taxes to support the improvements they have demanded.

With the assassination of Goebel, Kentucky became in effect a state of three factions, two Democratic and one Republican. Had the Republicans been stronger, the Democrats would have had to unite to beat them. But Republican weakness tempted the Democrats to squabble among themselves for power, though they several times lost important general elections when disgruntled primary losers bolted to the op-

Resplendent in morning coat, top hat, and cane is newly-inaugurated Lieutenant Governor A. B. "Happy" Chandler, who has already taken center stage from Governor Ruby Laffoon, to his right in this 1931 photo. *Courier-Journal Magazine.*

Happy Chandler and his mother, reunited for the first time since his infancy. He had grown up thinking she was dead. After his election as lieutenant governor in 1931, he went to Florida to find her grave but instead found her alive and overjoyed to see him. International News Service.

Except where otherwise indicated, all photos are courtesy of the *Courier-Journal* and *Louisville Times.*

The face of Ruby Laffoon shows the pain of defeat as he attends the December 1935 inauguration of Happy Chandler. Laffoon had chosen Democratic boss Thomas S. Rhea of Russellville (below) as his successor, only to see him beaten in a run-off primary that Laffoon had dreamed up as a way to stop Chandler.

Governor Chandler confers with J. Dan Talbott, often called the conscience of his administration, in 1938. Chandler was trying to unseat Alben Barkley in the U.S. Senate. He failed.

When President Franklin D. Roosevelt came to Covington to support Alben Barkley's reelection bid, Governor Chandler, Barkley's opponent, hopped aboard the presidential car, causing some to wonder which man FDR favored. Roosevelt dispelled the confusion with a strong endorsement of Barkley.

Baseball Commissioner Chandler and Congressman Earle C. Clements could laugh together in 1947. They weren't running against each other.

A friendly group of Kentucky Democrats—left to right, Earle C. Clements, Ben Kilgore, Thomas Underwood, and Harry Lee Waterfield—smile at the prospect of burying each other's hopes in the 1947 Democratic gubernatorial primary. Clements beat Waterfield and launched a notable Frankfort career.

Governor Clements and Conservation Commissioner Henry Ward enjoy
a conversation with Look photographer Bob Sandburg at the 1948
Derby Breakfast. Kentucky Department of Highways.   Below, Governor
Clements and Lieutenant Governor Lawrence Wetherby, sleeves rolled
up, tackle the job of drawing up a new state budget, 1948.

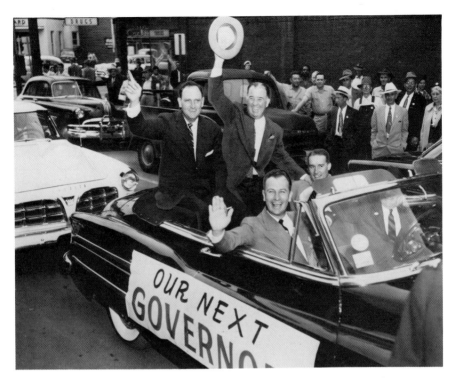

Happy Chandler where he was happiest—on the campaign trail, this time running for governor in Owensboro in 1955. He is flanked by his running mate, Harry Lee Waterfield (left), and Owensboro Mayor Casper "Cap" Gardner, later a legislative supporter (right). Smiling in the front seat is Daviess County Judge Norris Vincent.

A gathering of grinning governors at the Kentucky State Fair. Left to right, Flem D. Sampson, Keen Johnson, Happy Chandler, Fair Board chairman Smith Broadbent, Lawrence Wetherby, and Earle Clements.

Gathered in Hazard in spring 1957 to discuss flood control—after floods have already swept the town—are (left to right) Governor Chandler, Former Governor Flem Sampson, the Reverend Virgil Miller, U.S. Senator John Sherman Cooper, Congressman Carl Perkins, U.S. Senator Thruston Morton, and Hazard businessman Lawrence Davis.

Below, Happy Chandler was not a candidate in the 1959 race, but he was an issue and the object of a lot of undignified clowning. He had been accused—falsely—of killing a crippled goose in Ballard Wildlife Conservation Area.

Frequently enemies but here temporary allies in the 1965 Constitution
Revision Assembly are political sage and adviser to governors Edward
F. Prichard and an aging Happy Chandler.

Home to the victors of the gubernatorial wars—the governor's mansion
in Frankfort. Kentucky Department of Public Information.

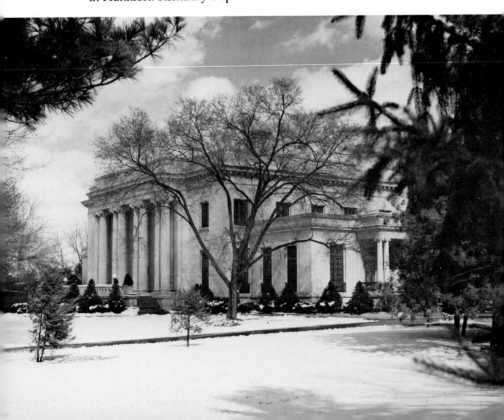

position Republicans. It was not concern for party principles that bound the factions to the party or kept them divided against each other. In a poor state the prize of political patronage, even as poorly paid as are most political jobs, kept the factions tearing at each other, and politicians tended to switch back and forth from one faction to another as self-interest dictated.

Bolting, or deserting one's party rather than supporting the other faction, became the curse and trademark of Kentucky Democrats. The ability of defeated politicians to jump from one party to the other showed not only a lack of loyalty but the absence of a unifying philosophy. Yet so persistent were the Democratic divisions that in the first three decades of the current century, Republicans won the governorship as often as did the Democrats (four each; five Republicans if Taylor is counted) and elected four U.S. senators, an impressive showing for a minority party. They did not, however, have to contend with the Goebel Election Law; on August 28, 1900, Governor Beckham called a special session of the legislature and got the law repealed.

Republican Edwin Morrow's race against Augustus Owsley Stanley for the governorship in 1915 was long remembered for the uninhibited speaking campaign of the two men, who traveled together and often roomed together—to save money, some claimed—and debated almost daily from the same platform. Both were orators of the old school, given to volume and hyperbole, and both were known to take a drink. Morrow's campaign focused on his opposition to the law requiring dog owners to buy dog tags. A man's right to own a dog, he implied, was God-given, and his attachment to his mutt was not much less important than his ties to wife and children. Thus to force a man to license his dog was to intrude upon a relationship sanctioned by the Almighty, and Morrow could wring tears from his rural listeners by describing the tender devotion of the noble dog to his master and the manly pleasures of hunting on frosty mornings behind a good and trusted canine, and would wind up his long-winded orations with a bellowed demand that the state "Free old Ring!"

On one sizzling late-summer afternoon, while Morrow tugged and hauled at the heartstrings of his dog-loving listeners, Stanley dulled the pain of the event with more liquor than his stomach could accommodate. As the heat bore down he gave up the fight for self-control, walked solemnly to the back of the platform, and vomited enthusiastically, to the shocked surprise of all concerned. "I realize that was a terrible thing to do," he calmly admitted to his astonished audience, "but when I hear a Republican talking, it just makes me sick to my stomach."

Stanley won. He was not only an intelligent and able politician but a liberal and progressive governor. But he was a "wet," and his political fortunes declined with the coming of prohibition. In his later days he said there were two things he did not want again, "the clap [gonorrhea] and the governorship of Kentucky." Stanley won election to the U.S. Senate and resigned the governorship to his lieutenant governor, J.D. Black. Morrow, who had only narrowly lost the race to Stanley in 1915, came back in 1919 and beat Black for the office. He then freed "Old Ring," a grand victory for the Grand Old Party.

Stanley and Morrow remained on curious terms. There is a story that after Stanley left office, he was walking down the street when he spotted Morrow, who started to walk the other way. "Ed," called out Stanley, "why are you dodging me? You mad at me?" "Well, yes," said Morrow sourly. "I'm tired of hearing the stories you've been telling about me." "Hell, Ed," said Stanley, "I never told anything about you but the truth." "Yes," said Morrow, "and it's ruining me!"

After the Bryan fever abated in the first decade of the new century, the Democrats divided into factions headed for a while by Seventh District Congressman J.C. Cantrill, who was felt to represent the more conservative elements of the party, and J.C.W. Beckham, the more liberal elements. The primary concerns of both men actually centered on political survival; Cantrill, however, was the darling of the Jockey Club and was generally considered the favorite of the bipartisan combine. By 1920 the combine, composed principally of racing, coal, textbook, and whiskey interests and led by the Jockey Club, was operating under full steam. From World War I until the Depression, this loose bipartisan group was more integral to Kentucky's political operation than were the political parties. It backed Cantrill against First District Congressman Alben Barkley in his try for the nomination for governor in 1923, chiefly because Barkley had been a leading advocate of prohibition, and was then opposing racetrack gambling and proposing a severance tax on coal. Cantrill beat Barkley, but then died, and the Democratic state executive committee hurriedly named William J. Fields of Carter County ("Honest Bill from Olive Hill") as the Democratic nominee. He won, beating Republican Charles Dawson. The combine then turned around and supported Barkley in his successful 1926 race for the U.S. Senate, figuring that he would do less harm in Washington than in Frankfort. It also helped elect the Republican Flem Sampson in 1927 by backing J.C. Cantrill against Beckham, who opposed parimutuel betting, in the Democratic primary; Beckham won the nomination, but droves of Democrats—allegedly including Honest Bill— bolted, causing Sampson to be elected by a margin of 32,131 votes.

Beckham's defeat had a tinge of poetic justice about it. Parimutuel betting had been sanctioned under his administration in 1906. But by 1927 he and Barkley had become symbols of opposition to the bipartisan combine, of which the Jockey Club (under the leadership of such canny horsemen as Maurice Galvin, Polk Laffoon, and Senator Johnston Camden) was an important part. The Jockey Club had generated opposition because it not only controlled all of the racetracks in the state but could enforce its monopoly through the Racing Commission, which it controlled and which had to approve any additional tracks. More basically, it was seen as the source of corruption, threatening candidates and buying votes in the legislature with brazen openness. "My father opposed the Jockey Club," Barry Bingham said years later, "not because he disliked racing; on the contrary he liked racing very much, and was very fond of Churchill Downs. But he couldn't countenance the open corruption that the Club people engaged in."

Flem Sampson's term was not a happy one. He was a governor with the opposition party in control of the legislature and many of the elective offices, for the combine had decided to punish only Beckham. Sampson had plans for textbook reform and better roads, but the bipartisan Highway Commission got credit for what few roads were built, and Sampson got caught in a minor scandal when he became identified with textbook publishers.

After supporting Sampson during most of his first legislative session, the Democrats controlling the legislature turned on him in the spring of 1930 with a "ripper" law (a ripper was a law depriving an official of powers) that vested practically all power, including the power to name the Highway Commission, in a three-man board consisting of the governor, the lieutenant governor, and the attorney general. This was fatal to Sampson, for the commission controlled construction of roads in the post–World War I years when the automobile was coming into its own, and good roads were every American's dream and demand. Kentuckians were no exception. They wanted roads to the point where they even accepted road-user taxes. The Highway Commission was created to oversee the spending of those taxes, and to make sure they were spent where they would do the most political good. Everyone who wanted a road went hat-in-hand to the commission, and everyone wanted a road. Thus, whoever controlled the Highway Commission controlled not just contracts and purchases but a political organization with a base in every county. When the legislature deprived Sampson of his control of the commission, said the Lexington *Herald*, it "left Sampson shorn of his locks." In the words of a subsequent governor, it also left Sampson, who had a wide reputation as a ladies' man, with nothing to do but "produce Kentucky Colonels and seduce Kentucky women."

In 1931 the Democrats gathered in Lexington's Woodland Park Auditorium to nominate a governor. It would be their last convention; they had for years nominated by primary elections, and in the future they would again choose by primary, thanks to an outgrowth of the convention they were attending. But with its last gasp, this final convention produced divisions that would plague the Democratic party for the next half-century.

The Democrats had reason to be optimistic as they headed for Lexington. Historic forces were at work, and great changes were in the offing. The factional divisions of the party seemed to have weakened, if they had not entirely disappeared, with the death of Cantrill in 1923 and the defeat of Beckham in 1927. A coalition of Democrats—among them Thomas S. Rhea, Benjamin "Uncle Ben" Johnson, J. Dan Talbott, William Klair, Seldon Glenn, and A.B. Chandler—had cooperated in passing the legislation depriving Governor Sampson of much of his power, and there were hopes that such cooperation might continue, that unity might be achieved and harmony prevail.

The Republicans seemed almost hopeless. "Flim Flam Flem" Sampson's Republican administration had been a debacle. With the Depression engulfing the country, Herbert Hoover's Republican administration in Washington was in even worse repute. Two years of plummeting prices and a year of crippling drought had left Kentucky farmers crying for help, and Hoover showed no inclination to help them. The eastern Kentucky coalfields were gripped in a bitter war between miners and coal operators; indeed, on the day the Democrats convened in Lexington, a pitched battle was reported between union miners and mine guards in the Harlan County town of Evarts, leaving at least six people dead. For the first time, mountain voters were beginning to turn to the Democratic party.

Louisville had been strongly Republican since 1917, partly because of resentment of President Woodrow Wilson for getting the country into World War I. But the Democratic machine of Michael Brennan was gaining strength that would put the city and Jefferson County in the Democratic column for three decades. The Democratic organization, later called the Fourth Street Organization because of its headquarters location at 113 South Fourth Street, had seen rocky days. Louisville had been pro-Union during the Civil War. Much of the Democratic strength was made up of Irish, German, and other immigrants, most of them Catholic and considered somewhat raffish if not actually disloyal by the older, more conservative and staunchly Protestant ruling clique. But following the war, Democratic boss Colonel John Whallen, a former Confederate officer who had amassed a fortune, seized control of the Louisville Democratic organization and built it into a state power to reckon with. Whallen, who ran his organization from plush quarters in his burlesque theater, the Buckingham, was the classic Irish politician who rewarded obedience and punished opposition, was dutiful to the Catholic church and saw that the faithful got their cut. He also controlled the Louisville police and many of the local officeholders, and usually had at least the limited cooperation of the L&N Railroad.

But during the 1890s, Whallen overreached himself. In the congressional elections of 1894 he had a compliant county judge purge the names of 4,000 Republicans from the rolls, a bit of corruption so blatant that even Democrats rebelled. The Republicans won, and Whallen's organization was dealt a crippling blow. The Democratic torch was passed to Michael Brennan, variously called "Colonel Mike" or "Colonel Mickey," who moved headquarters to the Tyler Building and made the organization a far more respectable and efficient operation. It also became more powerful, as New Deal programs brought more blacks and workers into the fold during the hard days of the Depression, and as Brennan learned the finer points of patronage. Brennan died in 1938, and his protégé, Lennie McLaughlin, assumed control and moved party headquarters to Fourth Street, where it acquired its familiar soubriquet.

As long as Brennan and McLaughlin held the reins, the powerful organization tended to support the Democratic faction that grew up around Thomas Rhea and was later headed by Earle C. Clements. Although Brennan was a Rhea-Laffoon man and at first supported Jack Howard in his 1931 contest with A.B. Chandler, many pro-Howard people insist that it was Brennan's shift to Chandler that doomed Howard; Chandler himself said that "Mr. Ben [Johnson] got Brennan to be for me." But when Earle Clements dropped by to test the water in 1947, he found a welcome mat.

"I remember that we met with Earl in the Seelbach," said John Crimmins (for half a century a Fourth Street stalwart) in a 1985 interview with the author. "Miss Lennie, McKay [Reed], and I, as I remember. What we wanted to know, first, was who would handle patronage. It was that simple. And Earle said, why, there wasn't any question; he would depend on Democratic headquarters to do that. Well, you know, that sounded good to us. Now Waterfield, running against Earle, he never did answer us. So Lennie later on let it be known that we'd go with Earle. Leland Taylor and some other people in City Hall were for Harry Lee. [So were the *Courier-Journal* and *Louisville Times*.] We beat them. Later, Earle had us in and we talked politics. What he said stayed that way. We were always close after that. He was a good man. Strong. You could talk to him."

Combs, like Clements, had a solid regard for the Fourth Street Organization. "Earle had a lot of respect for Miss Lennie," Combs recalled. "He believed, and I believed, that the organization generally thought that good government was good politics. And generally speaking, governors didn't mess in Louisville affairs much except through the organization."

Personality and mutual interests always bound Clements and Fourth Street more than any issue. For the same reasons, relations between the Louisville newspapers and the organization blew hot and cold. Judge Robert Worth Bingham was known from the beginning as a reformer, a quality not always popular on Fourth Street, but his relations with the organization frequently were good—possibly because his political adviser was the wily Percy Haly, who also was not famous for reformist tendencies. Both Judge Bingham and, later, his son Barry felt that the organization was too concerned with patronage, but they often backed organization candidates. And organization leaders, especially Miss Lennie McLaughlin, always advised her people to "keep the papers in mind."

Both Fourth Street and the papers opposed Chandler after his first term. Both supported Neville Miller and Wilson Wyatt in their races for mayor, and Wyatt in his abortive Democratic gubernatorial primary against Bert Combs, though they supported Combs gainst Chandler in 1959. After the death of Percy Haly in 1937, relations between the newspapers and the Fourth Street Organization deteriorated, possibly because Barry Bingham, upon assuming direction of the papers, brought in "outsiders" such as Mark Ethridge, who seemed to distrust most urban political machines, including Louisville's. (This also explains in part why Earle Clements and the Louisville papers were cool toward each other, though Clements in his congressional years was a definite liberal and a sturdy supporter of President Franklin Roosevelt, as were the papers.)

After the shock of losing the governorship to Sampson, the Democrats in 1931 were in a mood to unite for victory, and the Lexington convention was marked at first by a degree of harmony. Ruby Laffoon—a genial, honest circuit judge from Madisonville who was backed by Thomas Rhea, the powerful western Kentucky boss from Russellville—was the overwhelming favorite to take the nomination for governor. Lieutenant Governor James Breathitt, Jr., of Hopkinsville and Judge W.R. Shackleford of Richmond were considered his most serious opposition, though there was regional support for Rainey T. Wells, president of Murray State Teachers College (later Murray State University), and state representative William B. Ardery of Paris. None of them, however, was given much chance to block Laffoon; the critical contest of the convention was for lieutenant governor.

Rhea, like Laffoon, was said to favor J. Woodford (Jack) Howard, a young lawyer and state senator from Morgan County, in eastern Kentucky. But Ben Johnson had other ideas. The wily 73-year-old former congressman from Bardstown had already carved out a position of considerable power within the Democratic party, partly by surviving ten terms in Congress, partly by a flexibility that let him operate in any political sphere. He had bolted Beckham and supported Sampson in 1927, and had been appointed to the Highway Commission as reward. Sampson later managed to fire him, but when the legislature stripped Sampson of his power over the commission and created a new eight-man advisory commission, Johnson was chosen chairman. (His job carried power, but it included headaches, too. Dan Talbott told the story of how a delegation from Estill County, led by a Judge Redwine, called on Johnson to ask for a road. Uncle Ben couldn't see his way clear to build the road, and tried to get that message across as best he could without flatly saying no. But Redwine and his group stood stubbornly waiting for a definite answer, and finally Johnson, in an effort to change the subject, mentioned the insect infestation that was threatening the state's bean crop, an important Depression-era commodity. "How are the bean-bugs up your way?" he asked, but Redwine just looked at him. "They don't bother us none," he said. "The roads are so damn bad, they can't get in.")

Johnson was allied with his son-in-law, J. (John) Dan Talbott, a shrewd and somewhat self-righteous but painfully honest Bardstown druggist who previously had moved quietly and efficiently behind the scenes. Johnson and Talbott had become friends with 33-year-old Albert Benjamin Chandler, a Henderson County native and then state senator from Woodford County, who had been cooperative in the previous session of the legislature, helping with the legislation that ripped Sampson. Johnson decided that Chandler could be useful. If he could be elected lieutenant governor, for instance, and Johnson's bloc could elect its man, Bailey Wooten, to the post of attorney general, his group would continue its hold over the Highway Commission and thus, for all practical purposes, control patronage and the dominant faction of the party. Talbott was less materialistic than Johnson in his approach, but he had definite ideas for improving the tenor and operation of state government, and he saw in Chandler a young and pliable instrument. To be on the safe side, Johnson and Talbott were also backing Laffoon. By the time Laffoon won the office, they had him surrounded.

Tom Rhea and Johnson were cool toward each other. Rhea had nominated Beckham for governor in 1927, only to see the prize go to Sampson, partly because of the machinations of the bipartisan combine with which Johnson was identified. Rhea had not forgotten; he looked on Chandler, the protégé of Johnson, as the tool of the Bluegrass wealthy. There is irony in this, in that Chandler became, in later years, the self-proclaimed champion of "the little fella."

Jack Howard also had powerful supporters, including Congressman Fred Vinson of Louisa (later to become Chief Justice of the United States Supreme Court) and Allie Young, Democratic boss of Morehead. Vinson had, or thought he had, lined up Billy Klair and Mike Brennan for Howard, as well as important elements of the Jockey Club; he also thought he had the support of Laffoon. But forces of which he had no warning were moving beneath the surface of the convention.

Talbott, according to his biographer Orval Baylor, feared the prospect of a lieutenant governor with whom he and Johnson had no influence. He and Johnson called on members of the Jockey Club and reminded them that Howard was allied with Laffoon and Tom Rhea, who had backed Beckham in his fight against parimutuel betting. The state, they argued, needed a man close to the center of power who was more sensitive to the needs of racing, a man such as Chandler. The horsemen tended to agree.

The glib, handsome, outgoing, and energetic Chandler, nicknamed "Happy" by his classmates at Transylvania (he was known as "Irish" as a boy in Henderson County), was not idle. Though dismissed at first by most political observers as a lightweight, he had been working the state and later the Lexington political community with energy and was beginning to make an impression. According to Earle Clements, Chandler went directly to Laffoon, whose endorsement (or approval, at the least) would be necessary. It was a conference Laffoon would never forget.

"That fellow came into my room," Laffoon told Earle Clements with great bitterness when Chandler later turned against him, "and got down on his knees, begging me to let him run with me. And he swore he would be loyal and work with me. Begged me." (Chandler, in interviews with his son Ben, in 1973, never mentioned this alleged meeting.)

Laffoon, suspicious of Chandler, withheld his support for the time, but the forces were building. Johnson and Talbott called on Mike Brennan, and though those close to Brennan say he never went for Chandler, Chandler himself said he had Brennan's support. In any event, Laffoon knuckled under and approved Chandler, partly because he wanted support of the Johnson-Talbott clique, and his support turned the tide. Fred Vinson was furious, as were the majority of eastern Kentucky delegates, who wanted a man from the mountains with influence on the Highway Commission. At one point, Vinson stood on a chair shaking his fist and shouting at chairman John Milliken and refused to sit down, despite the boos and catcalls of the 4,100 delegates jammed into the 2,200-seat hall. But the convention nominated Chandler, who was elected with Laffoon. Talbott was elected auditor, and Bailey Wooten became attorney general. Ben Johnson was restored to his place on the Highway Commission.

With Chandler's nomination the seeds of a new factionalism had been planted. Tom Rhea had not only been for Jack Howard; he had been against Happy Chandler. His successor, Earle Clements, inherited the division, and it is worth noting that Jack Howard later became a law partner of Bert Combs, who eventually brought down the Chandler machine.

Events and enemies began gnawing away the foundations of Laffoon's administration from the beginning. Two days after the election, Laffoon, Klair, Allie Young, John Milliken, and Dan Talbott went to French Lick, Indiana, where a legislative program, allegedly written by Talbott and Johnson, was worked out. Laffoon agreed to it. He had said earlier that he thought a general sales tax was the only way to pay off the state debt and get some money for the schools, but Talbott, according to Orval Baylor, told the governor that was out of the question; he said the combine could approve a few small taxes on luxuries but nothing on necessities or on important businesses. Johnson and Talbott were rumored to have chosen the legislative leaders, too.

The Laffoon administration was less than a total success; in fact, it fell just short of a fiasco. One problem was that Laffoon, like governors before him, wanted to do something about the public schools, which were regarded as among the worst in the country, but he had no money to do it with. The school system was, generally speaking, deplorable. Almost 20 percent of the state's grade school students attended classes in one- and two-room schools that usually lacked running water, indoor toilets, or eating facilities. The only heat in winter was provided by a large potbellied stove in each room; the only relief from summer heat came from open windows. Playgrounds, such as they were, were stretches of mud much of the time. One teacher often taught four or five subjects on different levels to four or five grades. Children ate what they brought from home, and usually had no more than well water to drink. There were no school buses, since the roads were too rough to accommodate them, and children living any distance from the school-house had a long walk, regardless of weather, twice a day. It is little wonder that frequent sickness caused a high rate of absenteeism, and that the state's dropout rate ranged from first to tenth in the nation.

Governor Sampson had tried to improve the situation by propos-ing free textbooks and higher teachers' salaries. But he had been elected by the combine, and he was ripped by the combine when he appeared ready to do the one thing that had to be done—raise taxes.

Laffoon did not fare much better. Part of it was his own fault. He won passage of a bill reorganizing government and adoption of a new code for support of the public schools; finally, he recommended a 2 percent sales tax. But to pass a sales tax a governor had to be powerful and popular, had to prepare his ground carefully and be sure of his backing in the legislature. Laffoon was not such a man. His tax plan was poorly designed; the proposal came just as the country was reeling from the blows of Depression; and he did not prepare his forces in the legislature for the battle. Instead, he introduced it, without much political spadework, in the final weeks of the first session. One of the first to denounce it was Ben Johnson. The legislature rebelled and defeated it, and among those rebelling most noisily was Laffoon's smiling lieutenant governor, Happy Chandler. Laffoon worked hard to mend his fences, but it was not until 1935—after two regular sessions and two special sessions of the legislature—that he was able to win passage of a sales tax. Even then, it was a flawed instrument, hard to administer, and it cost Laffoon dearly in party unity. Furthermore, it had given Chandler the opening he was looking for.

On the first day of the Laffoon term Chandler had announced that he was moving into offices on the executive floor of the capitol and would pursue his duties there full time. This was a distinct break with the past, since previous lieutenant governors had remained in Frank-fort only during legislative sessions, when they were required to preside over the Senate; the session over, they went home. Chandler saw, as others would appreciate later, that the lieutenant governor's office provided a perfect springboard to higher things. As history would show, he was right. With no official duties or obligations except to preside over the Senate when the legislature was in session, he could devote his energies and the facilities of his office to full-time politick-ing. That Chandler did, and after he had shown the way, a long line of ambitious men sought the office as a springboard to the governorship.

Keen Johnson, lieutenant governor under Chandler, went
come governor, as did Lawrence Wetherby, second man to F
ents; Wendell Ford, lieutenant governor under Louie Nunn; and ɪ⌄.
lieutenant governor, Julian Carroll. Harry Lee Waterfield, lieutenant
governor during Chandler's second term (1955–59) ran against Bert
Combs but lost, as did Thelma Stovall, who served under Carroll but
lost to John Y. Brown, Jr., in her bid for top spot. On the other hand,
Martha Layne Collins spent her four years as lieutenant governor in a
successful campaign for the governor's mansion. It is probably significant of the state's tolerance of political waste and its reluctance to effect
change, no matter how obviously needed, that the legislature has
never taken steps either to make the office useful or to abolish it. In
1986 a move was begun in the assembly to abolish the office or cut off its
funds, but it never gained momentum. The lieutenant governor con-
tinues to take up space, spend money, and do little but campaign for
office.

Had the sales tax been passed early in Laffoon's first legislative
session and efficiently administered, the revenues might have enabled
him to accomplish enough to withstand the political attacks launched
against him as the state's economy worsened with the Depression. He
tried to improve conditions by seeking federal relief funds but was
handicapped by a lean state treasury that had little money with which
to match the federal funds. An earlier sales tax might have provided the
money he needed to match the relief help from Washington.

In 1933, Laffoon was accused by federal officials of exaggerating
Kentucky's needs and overstating the state's ability to provide matching funds. The charge was probably justified; Washington had promised additional help to states lacking matching money, and Kentucky
needed all the help it could get. By his final year in office, the wolves
were attacking Laffoon openly. The legislature passed a tax on beer and
liquor, with the revenue earmarked for relief matching. Among those
declaring that this would provide enough money was A.B. Chandler,
who added that he considered Laffoon's statement of Kentucky needs
exaggerated. A federal relief inspector, Lorena Hickok, disputed
Chandler's assertion, describing conditions in Harlan, Bell, Clay,
Knox, and Leslie as "desperate." And relief administrator Harry Hopkins reported to state directors of the National Relief Council: "I tell
you, it isn't any fun. Here's the state of Kentucky. It would not put up
any money. You say, 'You put up some money, or we won't give you
any,' and what happens? They do not put it up. Who gets licked? The
unemployed. Believe me, it's a tough order to give."

Chandler had more than philosophical reasons for his break with

Laffoon. Laffoon had made it clear, in statements at party meetings, that he favored Tom Rhea as his successor, and Rhea had already persuaded Earle Clements, who was rapidly emerging as a major western Kentucky political power, to serve as his campaign chairman. (Clements said later he had no inkling that Chandler wanted to run, and that had Chandler asked him first, he might have supported him. "I could believe that," Democratic "King Maker" Bill May said later. "I don't think any of us took Chandler seriously at first.")

To underscore his position, Laffoon managed to remove Ben Johnson as chairman of the Highway Commission and replace him with Rhea. Talbott had managed to alienate Attorney General Bailey Wootten, who resented Talbott's criticism of his office methods and the combine's obvious effort to rule Laffoon or ruin him. Wootten joined Laffoon to throw out Johnson. This was an unmistakable sign to Chandler and his followers that the fight was on. Not everyone in the Laffoon wing was pleased with the selection of Rhea. "I always thought Rhea was a poor candidate," said Tyler Munford, Morganfield publisher and legislator and a staunch Clements man. "I begged Clements to look somewhere else. But he was sold on Rhea. He was a good guy, Rhea, but people didn't warm to him."

From the start, Chandler had a keen political instinct. He could sense the growing unpopularity of Laffoon's sales tax, and in the popular dislike of the tax he saw his opportunity. Furthermore, as he later told his son Ben, he considered the sales tax wrong, regressive, and resting unfairly on the small wage earner. In this he was in the great and tragic tradition. Kentucky was still—and would be until the census of 1970—a predominantly rural state. Its people still objected to taxes, even while demanding the things that only more taxes could provide. They didn't see this attitude was hypocritical as long as someone like Chandler would promise them he could do the job without the taxes. Unfortunately, the federal government, which was playing an increasing role in providing the welfare the states had failed to provide, was also taking over income and excise taxes to support the welfare area, leaving the sales tax as one of the few possible sources of income remaining available to states.

Chandler would prove to be one of the most popular and powerful politicians in the history of his state. The voters would take his word, no matter what the factual evidence to the contrary, and support him on the basis of promises, no matter how often proven empty, for the simple reason that he knew what they wanted to hear and was willing to say it.

Chandler apparently sensed that he might become governor if he could get to the voters. He also knew that, having turned against Laffoon, he would never win the nomination for governor at a party convention ruled by Laffoon and his supporters. The solution was obvious: he had to get the law changed to require a primary instead of a convention. The question: how to do it? The answer presented itself on February 6, 1935.

Laffoon needed help with Kentucky's faltering economy, and the only hope of help lay in the New Deal relief programs. On the morning of February 6, he and Tom Rhea boarded a train for Washington to beg more money for Kentucky. They also hoped to persuade Roosevelt, who opposed conventions and wanted Kentucky to return to party primaries, that Kentucky's convention system was preferable for the time being. The night before, Chandler and his closest aides and advisers had made their plans: some say Frankfort attorney Clifford Smith was the chief strategist; others credit J. Dan Talbott. In the memoir dictated to his son, Chandler seems to take credit for thinking up the scheme himself.

When a Kentucky governor leaves the state, the lieutenant governor becomes acting governor, with all the attendant powers. Chandler denied that he had previously planned to call the legislature into special session, but others say that he had a sentinel stationed in Ashland and that when Laffoon's train for Washington rolled across the Ohio River, the sentinel raced for the telephone; within minutes Chandler had issued a proclamation calling for a special session of the legislature to consider a compulsory primary law. With this bold stroke, Chandler launched one of the most remarkable political careers in state history.

In Washington, Laffoon heard of Chandler's action and raced home, arriving on the morning of February 7. He immediately issued a proclamation rescinding Chandler's call for a special session, but Chandler forces at once filed suit challenging his action, contending that the call was legal and binding and not subject to annulment. On February 26 the Court of Appeals, by a vote of four to three, agreed. Laffoon was obliged to face a special session and a primary bill that he knew would be popular, since many legislators, like their constituents back home, distrusted conventions and the "machines" that seemed to dominate them.

Laffoon, Rhea, and their advisers had to find some means to turn this adversity to their advantage. They chose a bizarre way: instead of having one primary, they proposed a second, or runoff, in case there were several candidates, none of whom received a majority. This sounded good to the legislators, who promptly voted the runoff primary into being. Why would Laffoon do this? Some people contend that he thought former governor J.C.W. Beckham would be the anti-Laffoon candidate, to face Laffoon's choice, Thomas Rhea, in the coming gubernatorial election, and while Rhea might not beat Beck-ham in a field of several candidates, he would come in second; then, with the support of the sturdy statewide Democratic organization, he would beat him in a runoff.

This analysis seems unlikely. While Laffoon may have seen Beck-ham as the probable candidate earlier, he could hardly have so re-garded him at the time. Judge Robert Bingham had urged Beckham to run, but by the time of the special legislative session Beckham had flatly taken himself out of consideration. He had not been well and his son was ill, he protested, prompting Bingham to turn to Chandler. Further-more, it is impossible to believe that Chandler and his cohorts would have gone to the risk and effort of the special session scheme in order to give Beckham the governorship. In his interviews with his son, Chandler says that he gave Beckham the courtesy of a call and asked him to run, but Beckham declined. The sincerity of such an effort must be suspect, however. It is inconceivable that Talbott would have master-minded Chandler's primary plan for the benefit of Beckham, whom he disliked, or that Ben Johnson would have countenanced the candidacy of Beckham, his old hometown enemy. It is similarly inconceivable that Chandler would have gone to so much trouble for someone else and gained such an advantage for himself in order to yield it to a man to whom he owed nothing.

In any event, Laffoon had outsmarted himself. In the following primary, Rhea and Chandler were the leading candidates for nomina-tion: the minor candidates in the lists were Frederick A. Wallis and Elam Huddleston, each hoping that the voters would tire of the Frank-fort bickering and send the lightning his way. That didn't happen, but the two minor runners did get enough votes to keep either Rhea or Chandler from obtaining a majority, though Rhea outpolled Chandler 203,010 to 189,575 (Huddleston got 15,501, Wallis 38,410). But after the first primary, Huddleston and Wallis threw their support to Chandler, who then won the runoff and the nomination, 260,573 to 234,124.

Laffoon was heartbroken, and his final days in the governor's office were lonely and bitter. Until his death in 1946, Tom Rhea never forgave or forgot. When the Republicans nominated Lexington's King Swope, Rhea openly bolted Chandler and supported Swope. Mrs. Emerson Beauchamp of Russellville, widow of longtime Democratic leader Emerson "Doc" Beauchamp, has said that on at least one occasion Rhea made a radio speech endorsing Swope. Chandler made much of Rhea's radio speech, for years insisting that Clements also bolted; he used Clements' alleged bolt to justify his own frequent desertions of the party when the Clements wing was successful. But supporters, including Tyler Munford and Doc Beauchamp, said that Clements did not bolt, and Clements himself told historian Thomas Syvertsen that he did not. Still, there is evidence that he gave Chandler's candidacy a "light ride"—that is, lip service only and not much of that.

It is interesting to note that during Chandler's campaign, he was introduced at a speech in Paris by a heavy-set young man rapidly becoming known as something of a boy genius. Edward Prichard was just finishing college at Princeton and preparing to go to law school at Harvard. He had spoken—and brilliantly—for Chandler at the Woodland Park convention, and when he came home from school in 1936, he went to work for the state department of revenue for $125 a month—a "munificent" salary, as he termed it—and he and Chandler became quite close. (Prichard's father was a Chandler supporter in the legislature, as well.) But during the 1935 race, Chandler was supported by the eastern Kentucky coal operators and the Harlan County sheriff they supported, who had become infamous for his brutal mistreatment of striking miners. Prichard objected hotly to the operators' influence in Frankfort and their ties to Chandler. By 1937 Chandler was showing an open preference for Virginia's Senator Harry Byrd over Prichard's idol, Franklin D. Roosevelt, and relations between them cooled. When Chandler challenged F.D.R.'s faithful supporter Alben Barkley for the U.S. Senate, Prichard left him, and they later became bitter enemies. (Actually, Chandler and Byrd had been friends for years, since they had met in Virginia when Chandler was courting his wife to-be, Mildred Watkins. The two men were of a similar conservative southern Democratic mold, and later, when Chandler was in the Senate, he voted with Byrd and against Roosevelt on matters of government spending.)

A continuing source of strength and stability for Chandler was J. Dan Talbott. "Talbott was a good man, and a good influence on Happy," Prichard said later. "Not much of a politician, really, but honest, and helped Happy with his fiscal program more than anyone else could have. Then, when Talbott ran into personal problems, fell out with Ben Johnson and fell on hard times, Happy abandoned him. Dan was really hard up, when Charlie Dawson, of Louisville, gave him a job."

This remark is interesting. Talbott was married to Johnson's daughter, Rebecca. Apparently during the later years of the Chandler administration, relations between the Talbotts grew strained; they later separated, and Talbott moved to Louisville. It was widely assumed that Johnson broke with Talbott because of Talbott's dispute with Rebecca, and because it was common gossip that he was involved with a tall, striking, and ambitious blonde woman from Bardstown who later became something of a celebrity in Democratic political circles. Descendants of Talbott, however, say that the opposite was true: that Talbott and Johnson fell out chiefly because Talbott questioned Johnson's rough and dictatorial management of highway affairs, and that Rebecca defended her father and finally separated from her husband. This split, they say, was partly healed, but later reopened—possibly because of the other woman—never to be resolved. This does not sound implausible. Johnson never hesitated to use the Highway Commission to build roads where they would be politically productive, nor did he object to enriching allies with purchases and construction contracts. Such flagrant abuse of the office might have led the scrupulous Talbott to insist that Chandler remove Johnson from the commission. At the same time, stories that Talbott and Rebecca parted because of his infatuation with the Bardstown woman were never put to rest. In any event, Johnson was outraged, and his break with Talbott was never healed.

3

Strong Man from Morganfield

Before Chandler's 1935 race, Kentucky campaigns had been marked by marathon oratory and practiced pomposity, designed more to impress than inform or entertain. Happy gave them something new. Introducing the sound truck, he tore through Kentucky with flags flying and loud-speakers blaring in a nonstop whirlwind of a campaign, name-calling, ridiculing, promising, sweating, hugging, kissing, speaking anywhere at any time, sweeping the crowds along with him, breaking into a rendition of "Sonny Boy" at any or no provocation. Alongside him, the staid, traditional King Swope was an aging carriage horse facing Man O' War.

It was not all hoopla, by any means. Chandler promised to repeal the sales tax, oppose any increase in property taxes, reduce the gas-oline tax, and end the practice of assessing state employees a percentage of their salaries. All of these reflect Chandler's philosophy, as he told his son Ben, that the best government is the least, and that the sales tax is the worst of all taxes. Throughout his career, Chandler believed that the duty of government was to provide roads, schools, and "charity," and little else, and it is significant that he preferred to see welfare as charity given by the rich to the poor and cause for the pulled forelock, rather than as an economic and social weapon for rebalancing an economy. He was, in brief, a southern conservative, a Republican who found himself in the Democratic camp mainly through the accident of birth and geography. The same, of course, could be said of Dan Talbott, who influenced, if he did not actually dictate, Chandler's program before and after he won office. To his credit, Chandler kept most of the promises.

The campaign was not all good-natured. When Chandler wrapped himself in the stars and stripes and referred to his service during World War I, Henry Denhardt, adjutant general under Laffoon (and later the victim in one of the state's most sensational murder cases), fired back with a circular certifying that Happy had never been an army officer, as some of his campaign literature implied, but only a cadet in the training unit at Transylvania College.

One of Chandler's most popular campaign posters showed an ebullient President Franklin D. Roosevelt smiling upon a trim, handsome, serious Chandler, and the legend read "Help Roosevelt and Chandler get things moving again"—an interesting sidelight in view of the fact that Chandler broke with F.D.R. hardly more than two years later with his race against Alben Barkley. As a matter of fact, Chandler, as he admitted later, never cared much for either Roosevelt or his New Deal policies and seldom supported his programs, even while taking advantage of them. He was strictly a "pay as you go" man and deplored the Roosevelt spending.

Chandler roared to victory in November of 1935 with a solid win over Swope—556,573 to 461,104—and surprised his critics, who considered him reactionary and shallow, by producing two of the most spectacular years in the history of the office. To his credit he brought into his cabinet a "brain trust" of University of Kentucky professors—including such recognized authorities on state finances and organization as Dr. James Martin and Dr. Clyde Reeves—and listened to the advice of Dan Talbott concerning state finances, debt, and policies in general. He reorganized the loosely run and uncoordinated departments of state government into a logical and efficient cabinet, restructured tax collection procedures, put the state on a sound financial basis, launched a modest highway-building program (including the first modern road in Kentucky, the four-lane highway from Frankfort to Lexington that critics called his "office to swimming pool road"), and tried to wrestle with the hydra-headed school problem. In January 1936, Chandler appointed his old mentor Ben Johnson highway commissioner (though eventually their relationship soured, and Johnson broke with Chandler, resigned, and retired to Bardstown).

True to his promise, Chandler repealed the sales tax, which had yielded only about $6,000,000 in its one year of life; in its place he imposed a production tax on whiskey, a progressive income tax, an inheritance tax, and an excise tax on beer and cigarettes, producing about $37,000,000. It was not enough to solve the school problem, but it gave Chandler the chance to say to the voters, "I took the tax off your food and put it on their whiskey"—good political strategy. And the Chandler luck was with him: the repeal of prohibition put Kentucky's distilling industry back into taxable operation, and the withdrawal of warehoused whiskey gave the state a windfall, which Happy used to maximum advantage. He afterward claimed that he had found a debt of $30,000,000 and paid it off; actually, the state debt totaled something over $28,000,000, and he reduced it to a little more than $4,000,000, or made arrangements for doing so before he left office. He established a department of industrial relations, investigated prison conditions, passed a minimum wage law for women and children, and started a rural road program.

But inefficiency and a shortage of money continued to plague the state, especially in its relations with the New Deal agencies that sprang up to cope with the Depression. In the summer of 1936 Washington officials complained of the inefficiency of Kentucky's Commissioner of Welfare, Frederick Wallis, and when the Old Age Assistance program was launched, only 238 Kentuckians received benefits that averaged only $7.43 a month. A.Y. Lloyd, director of the Division of Public Assistance, announced that same year that the state had anticipated 25,000 applicants for public assistance but had gotten 76,000, and warned that only the most indigent could be helped until more funds were available. By the end of the Chandler administration about 57,000 Kentuckians were receiving monthly checks, but the checks averaged only $9, less than half of the national average and less than that distributed by Virginia, Tennessee, and Indiana.

Harry Hopkins, President Roosevelt's federal relief administrator, complained during both the Laffoon and Chandler administrations that Kentucky's refusal or inability to provide matching funds posed a threat to the needy and unemployed. Robert Fechner, director of the Civilian Conservation Corps, warned Chandler in 1937 that he would pull all CCC workers out of Kentucky parks unless the state put up more money, and unless Parks Director Bailey Wootten showed more efficient management of the parks where CCC projects were underway. Kentucky also was unable to take full advantage of programs offered by the Agricultural Adjustment Act. In general, despite Chandler's government reorganization and his efforts to increase revenues, Kentuckians suffered throughout the Depression decade because of the state's inability to take full advantage of federal programs.

Chandler made a concerted drive to upgrade the state's roads but was handicapped by constitutional limits on salaries that discouraged competent engineers. This difficulty was partly overcome when Judge Robert Worth Bingham contributed $7,000 a year to the pay of Thomas Cutler, an engineer and administrator of national reputation who took over the highway department. (There is a curious footnote to this bit of history: Ben Collings, a Louisville contractor who had received considerable state business, later built a swimming pool for Chandler at the latter's Versailles home. This aroused, of course, a storm of criticism and charges of corruption and payoff. Orval Baylor, editor of

Chandler's Versailles newspaper and his unofficial historian, declared that Collings had as much moral right to give Happy the gift of a swimming pool as Bingham had to give him $7,000 a year with which to hire a highway engineer.)

Obviously, here was no flash in the political pan, nor was Chandler merely a vigorous, instinctive politician. Throughout his career he showed no great political philosophy. But he had the good sense to bring able people into key positions and, until they landed too heavily on sensitive ground, leave them alone. Critics charged, then as now, that Dan Talbott was the real architect of the administration and that Chandler, after endorsing the Talbott program, seldom worked at the job of being governor but played golf and took the bows. It is interesting to speculate on what he might have achieved had he kept the sales tax, reformed the state's business taxes, revised the constitution, and issued bonds with which to modernize state roads, as such states as North Carolina were doing. Considering his popularity at the time, he probably could have done all that, and it would have made his administration historic.

But the more basic changes of the Chandler years, 1935 to 1939, came about as a result of the New Deal programs of Franklin D. Roosevelt—ironic in that Chandler was never a New Deal man. The Works Progress Administration provided life-saving jobs by the thousands, the Public Works Administration built hundreds of schools, libraries, courthouses, playgrounds, and roads, while the Civilian Conservation Corps reclaimed and reforested hundreds of thousands of acres of cut-over and burned-over land. The Rural Electrification Administration brought electricity to farms, more than 90 percent of which had never had electrical power before. The Tennessee Valley Authority changed the face of western Kentucky with its cheap electricity, its lakes, its reforestation, and erosion control.

These New Deal measures, in a Depression atmosphere of fear and despair, helped Chandler tremendously, as did his progressive administration, and he moved to take advantage of his popularity by challenging the redoubtable Alben Barkley for his seat in the U.S. Senate in 1938. This was a move of great audacity but faulty judgment. Chandler had gauged his state and concluded that he had sufficient support. He overestimated. He had already upset party moderates by what many considered his betrayal of John Y. Brown in the 1936 Senate race. Brown, in 1935 the House Speaker and a politician of considerable influence, declared that he agreed to support Chandler for governor in 1935 in exchange for Chandler's promise to support him for the Senate in 1936. But Chandler, according to both Brown and Clements, persuaded J.C.W. Beckham to make the race, with the result that Senator M.M. Logan retained his seat in the three-way race in which Brown ran third.

Now Chandler again antagonized liberal Democrats by threatening to rob F.D.R. of Alben Barkley, a senior senator and staunch supporter. It was a tough, bitter dogfight of a campaign and a typical Chandler show. After the 1935 race, Earle Clements said that "many, including myself, were either fed up or bitter with the political abuse and vilification Happy unnecessarily leveled on Tom Rhea." This was to become a Chandler trademark—ridicule, abuse, false charges—any fight in which he was involved became a dogfight. There were no holds barred. Chandler knew the people liked a show, and he gave them one, in the most basic sense of the Roman bread and circuses.

He ripped into Barkley, ridiculing him as "Old Alben," a pointed reference to the fact that Chandler was 39, Barkley 60. He ignored Barkley's years of service to the state and his value to President Roosevelt, insisting that his opponent had been so long out of the state and in Washington that he could no longer be considered a Kentuckian. He also took credit for the New Deal programs that were easing somewhat the pains of the Depression.

Since there was no merit system to protect state employees from political manipulation, Chandler had the state payroll at his command. Barkley could fight back with WPA relief rolls. President Roosevelt, who had previously written a supporting letter to Barkley addressed to "My Dear Alben," came to Kentucky to endorse Barkley, but Happy made a remarkable effort to turn the trip to his own advantage. When, in Covington, F.D.R. and Barkley rode through the streets toward Latonia Race Track, Chandler nimbly jumped into the back seat of the president's touring car, putting himself between Roosevelt and Barkley. It was customary then, when the president usually rode in an open touring car, for him to ride on the right side of the rear seat, where he would be next to the crowds lining the street. Chandler did not make the mistake of intruding on the right side of the crippled Roosevelt, but by jumping in between him and Barkley, he conceivably caused many to wonder where the president stood. At the racetrack he mounted the speaker's platform, smiling confidently, but Roosevelt chilled him with a strong endorsement of Barkley that made Chandler appear green, uninformed, and unimpressive. As Edward Prichard said, "Roosevelt told him, 'You're a good boy, but you won't do.' "

Barkley beat Chandler 294,562 to 223,690. (This was not the humiliation it might seem; even the formidable Somerset Republican John Sherman Cooper was unable to stand against Barkley.) Chandler was obliged to wait until 1939, when Senator Mills Marvel Logan died in office. Chandler resigned; his lieutenant governor, Keen Johnson, succeeded him (and was shortly elected to a full term) and immediately appointed him to the Senate vacancy. As proof that he could still appeal to the Kentucky voter, Chandler won the 1940 election to fill the unexpired term, beating Charles P. Farnsley in the primary and Walter B. Smith in the general election, 561,151 to 401,812. In 1942 he won the right to a full term, defeating John Y. Brown in the primary and Richard J. Colbert in the general. In 1945 he resigned his Senate seat to become commissioner of baseball, a post he held until 1951, when he was forced out by club owners.

In view of his political ambition, Chandler's decision to take the baseball job is puzzling. It certainly gained him no political strength, took years out of his campaign for higher office, and deprived him of the dignity which might have been his as U.S. Senator and which, though apparently unnecessary in Kentucky, would have helped him nationally. Years later he told his son that Harry Byrd had said his decision to become baseball commissioner had been his one big mistake. "But then," said Chandler, "I leaned over and whispered the real reason to him, and he said, 'That explains it.' " He did not say what the whispered reason was.

Perhaps his decision can be traced in part to the presidential nominating convention of 1944, where Harry S. Truman was chosen to run as vice-president with F.D.R. Chandler had had hopes of winning the nomination himself—a peculiar aspiration, in view of his experience with Roosevelt in his race against Barkley—and was indignant when the Kentucky delegation, including Earle Clements, refused to support him. His ebullient personality had won him considerable favorable notice in the party, and he thought he had enough support from other states to make a serious try for the second spot if he could make the run as Kentucky's favorite son. Had he succeeded, of course, he would have become president when Roosevelt died in 1945, and he always blamed those who failed to support him for keeping him out of the White House. Some political observers believed that the convention was the start of the Chandler-Clements friction; Chandler, they said, viewed Clements' nonsupport as a bolt, too.

As the federal government took over the job of providing services that the states had not or would not provide, it also took a lot of the taxing power, making it difficult for states to finance their own improvements or to participate fully in the federal programs. Kentucky did not have the matching money or the functioning agencies to capitalize on the vast farm, welfare, and educational programs that proved the major impetus for progress after 1932. Once more, for lack of money, it fell behind other states.

Between the Chandler and Clements administrations, relatively little happened in Kentucky government, primarily because those were the years of World War II, with interests and resources focused on national survival. Governor Keen Johnson, a competent, conservative newspaper publisher from Richmond, promised honest and efficient government and boasted of his frugality, prompting one Democratic official to complain that "Old Keen frugaled here and he frugaled there till he damn near frugaled us to death." Then, in 1943, the Democrats nominated Highway Commissioner Lyter Donaldson of Carrollton for governor, to oppose a conservative and respected Republican nominee, Judge Simeon Willis of Ashland. Donaldson, a lackluster candidate at best, beat Ben Kilgore and Rodes K. Myers in the primary but lost the general election to Willis, 270,525 to 279,144. The Prohibition party candidate, Andrew Johnson, polled 3,239.

The only almost-bright spot of the campaign for the Democrats was the race made by William H. May, the handsome, gregarious nephew of Congressman Andrew Jackson May of Floyd County. Bill May had first come to public attention four years earlier when he easily won the race for agriculture commissioner. In 1943, after defeating newspaperman and state legislator Henry Ward and farmer John Whitaker in the primary, he lost the race for lieutenant governor by only 533 votes to Republican Kenneth Tuggle.

With the end of World War II, the return of servicemen, and the surprisingly rapid resurgence of the economy, the people as well as conditions were ready for change and action, and the voters decided that Earle Clements—who had gone from county judge of Union County to Congress—offered the best chance for action and change in Frankfort. Clements, the big, popular son of a substantial Union County family, had gone in 1915 from Morganfield to the University of Kentucky, where he played center on the football team and, as a member of Pi Kappa Alpha fraternity, dabbled in campus politics. During World War I he enlisted in the army, served 28 months, and emerged a captain but did not return to Lexington for his degree. Instead, he went back home to become county clerk, county judge, sheriff, and coach of the local football team—and not just coach but winning coach, an addition to the record that did not hurt him in subsequent races when he became in turn state legislator, congressman in 1944 and 1946, governor, and U.S. senator. In the process he was said to have inherited the political organization of Thomas Rhea, when the strong man from Logan County died in 1938. It might be more accurate to say that he took control of the Rhea organization because no one was able to prevent him from doing so.

The 1947 primary race between Clements and Hickman County farmer and newspaper publisher Harry Lee Waterfield was a fairly close (Clements won, 158,196 to 125,276) but not very lively contest. Clements could be warm, even charming, in small groups, but on the campaign trail his greatest virtues were energy and caution. His speeches were masterpieces of mediocrity, punctuated by lame jokes and occasional smiles that seemed to be afterthoughts. Waterfield showed more honest emotion and more rapport with the voter, but he lacked Clements' organization. Waterfield was the champion of the farmer and the Rural Electrification Administration cooperatives that served them; Clements was considered more friendly toward business and the established utilities that were then opposing the spread of the co-ops. But Clements had by far the better organized campaign. Nor could he be dismissed as a tool of business. In Congress he had been known as a supporter of the REA, conservation and wildlife programs, Social Security, and federal aid for education. Standing against many southern colleagues, he supported bills to ban lynching and the poll tax and to disband the House Un-American Activities Committee. He also voted against the Taft-Hartley Act so beloved by business.

He won rather handily in the gubernatorial election, beating Republican Eldon S. Dummit, 387,795 to 287,756, and taking with him as lieutenant governor Lawrence Wetherby, former juvenile court judge of Jefferson County. Wetherby won the nomination by defeating Bill May in a curiously significant campaign that was to have long-range repercussions. May had tried to get on the ticket with Clements, but Clements had never warmed to him—possibly because May's uncle, Congressman A.J. May, had long been an ally of John Young Brown, never a Clements supporter. In an effort to curry favor with Clements, May went to see Emerson "Doc" Beauchamp (pronounced Beechum, in the Logan County tradition), the Democratic boss of Logan County and a strong Clements man, hoping that Beauchamp would help him break the ice with Clements. He was rudely disappointed.

"Young fella," rasped the gravel-voiced Beauchamp, "I want you to know you're second on my list."

"All right," said May, "but who's first?"

"Any sonofabitch," said Beauchamp, "who'll run against you."

Wetherby nosed out May, though May carried 106 of the state's 120 counties. "Miss Lennie [then head of Louisville's Fourth Street Organization] stole it for Lawrence," May said later. "I'm not crying; that's the way things were done, and I recognized that. Later on, when Lawrence was governor and planning to build the Kentucky Turnpike from Louisville to Etown [Elizabethtown], I went to him and told him he ought to give me some of the engineering work—I had started Brighton Engineering by that time—because he had gotten to be governor by stealing that election from me. We laughed about it. I always liked Lawrence."

Clements and May later told how Wetherby came to be chosen to run with Clements. The story goes that Clements was talking with Miss Lennie McLaughlin in the sidewalk-level coffee shop of the old Kentucky Hotel at the corner of Fifth and Walnut in Louisville, and making a serious pitch for her support. "You can name the lieutenant governor," he told her. That seemed to impress her, and she said as much. "You have anyone in mind?" Clements asked, pressing for a commitment. Miss Lennie said she didn't, but about that time Wetherby, then a juvenile court judge, happened to walk by. "There," said Lennie, motioning through the window, "there's a good young man." "All right," said Clements, "he looks pretty good. Who is he?" And that, allegedly, is how Wetherby went to Frankfort. Historian John Kleeber insists that the story is not true. Whatever the facts, Lawrence Wetherby proved to be an intelligent, hard-working, and politically adroit lieutenant governor. He liked Clements, admired his political mind and his grasp of the state's many-faceted politics. He and Clements worked well together. Wetherby knew how to get along with the Louisville organization and acted as something of a liaison, which didn't hurt him when he decided to run for top spot on his own.

May never ran for office again but went on to become a wealthy and powerful man, largely through highway-building contracts with Kentucky and other state governments. He was a prime mover of a small group of Frankfort political backers known as the Kingmakers, and a principal supporter of Bert Combs. After Wetherby's term as governor ended and he was looking for a job, May made him an official of Brighton Engineering; Wetherby later became a vice-president of the firm and, with May's help, was elected to the state Senate, where he was involved in critical legislative battles in which May had an interest.

Earle Clements was an unusual governor in many respects. (He was once called "the man who dragged Kentucky into the twentieth century," although some political scientists credit Chandler with having the first truly modern administration.) For one thing, Clements was probably the hardest-working chief executive the state ever had. A man of tremendous energy, he had no hobbies, seldom took a vacation, and had almost no interests outside his work. In all fairness to his immediate predecessors, though they had been content for the most part to let the state slip further behind its sister states in education and public services while New Deal programs had eased the suffering of Kentucky's poor and unemployed, they could not remove the statutory and constitutional barriers that held Kentucky back.

Clements tried to break free of some of the restrictions imposed by the state constitution. For example, the constitution forbade the state to pay any employee—and this included the governor, presidents of colleges, doctors at state hospitals, and the like—more than $5,000 a year. A handsome salary in 1891, when the constitution was adopted, the $5,000 ceiling threatened to shut down state government in the surge of inflation following World War II. Clements set out to get rid of the salary limit.

It has been charged that Clements had his political faithful steal the referendum on repeal of the salary limit. There is the story, for instance, that on the day before the election he called his good friend Circuit Judge Ervine Turner of Breathitt County, who, with his wife Marie, superintendent of county schools, wielded considerable political control over Breathitt and surrounding counties.

"Judge," Clements is supposed to have said, "I'm hoping you can help me with this little amendment." This request put Turner on the spot. Several years before, there had been some embarrassing gunplay during a dispute over the composition of the Breathitt County school board; an opponent of the Turner faction had been shot, and threats had subsequently been made against the judge. So there had been some relief when Clements, then a member of Congress, managed to get Turner appointed to a temporary post with a federal agency in Chicago, safely out of the line of fire. So the judge owed the governor, and both men knew it. They also knew that under ordinary circumstances the voters of the tough, conservative mountain county wouldn't touch a constitutional amendment for love, money, or free whiskey—the traditional rewards in the hills for voting correctly.

"Lord, Earle," said Turner, "I could make hogs fly before I could get people here to vote for that thing, and you know it."

"Oh, now, Judge, I know you can do it if you put your mind to it," said Clements, and his voice was flat and hard. "And let me say to you I need, I say I NEED, your help."

Ervine Turner had not gained power through inability to recognize necessity. The next day the voters of Breathitt County, in an impressive display of enlightened thinking, cast a heartwarming majority of their votes for the amendment. The voters of other counties, including populous Jefferson (Louisville), likewise surprised people by their strong support of the amendment. The people had seen the light,

Clements had his victory, and this single accomplishment literally saved Kentucky government.

Clements circumvented the constitutional provision limiting state debt to $500,000 by issuing bonds with which to erect new state buildings, the bonds to be retired by rentals paid by the occupying agencies. The capitol annex, which still houses many executive departments and legislative offices, is an example of his use of this bonding power. He also converted the old highway patrol into the modernized Kentucky State Police, drew the blueprints for the state fairgrounds in Louisville, and made a start on the first modern facilities in state parks. He brought into government such men as Felix Joyner, Robert Bell, Guthrie Crowe, and Henry Ward, men whose influence would be felt in Frankfort for the next generation. And he began a long overdue rural road program, financed by earmarking two cents of the tax on each gallon of gasoline, and run by a commissioner of rural highways.

Several men have been given the title of "father of the state parks," among them Clements, Combs, and Ward. Actually, the parks were begun in 1926 by Willard Rouse Jillson, the crusty and egotistical state geologist, who was given the magnificent budget of $1,100 for his first year but managed nevertheless to incorporate four parks into the fledgling system. But it was still a clutch of undeveloped nature sites, with a couple of lodges and some cabins and roads built by the CCC, when Clements took over.

It is to his credit that he chose as commissioner of conservation (the parks department was then a division of conservation) Henry Ward, a staunch parks man but not a Clements supporter. Ward's outspoken, almost belligerent honesty had gained him more respect than friends in his years of political infighting; he could say yes to people and still make them mad. A Paducah boy who went from high school to become a reporter on the Paducah *Sun-Democrat* and then a crusading columnist, the short, stocky Ward happily took on all comers, from local gamblers to the private utilities—which, he charged, kept rates high in his part of the state and failed or refused to take power to remote farms of the region. It was largely his utility battles that got him elected to the state legislature and attracted the attention of Alben Barkley, of whom he became a devoted follower. "I loved the old man," he said, "loved him."

Ward also became an ardent New Dealer. On the strength of his western Kentucky support, he ran for lieutenant governor in 1943 but lost in the primary to Bill May. He jumped into the fight to bring REA cooperatives to western Kentucky and to make TVA power available to them. In the state Senate he introduced a bill to permit cities to deal directly with TVA for power without having to buy out the private utility already serving them, as the law then required. None of this had put him in the Clements camp. In fact, Ward had backed Harry Lee Waterfield, Clements' opponent, in the 1947 primary and was not looking forward to an easy time in the 1948 session of the legislature.

"Earle surprised a lot of people, including me, when he asked me to take the job of Conservation Commissioner," Ward said later. "And I wasn't sure I wanted it. After all, I was a newspaperman, and this meant giving up my job to become a bureaucrat. But Ed Paxton, publisher of the *Sun-Democrat*, said I could have a leave of absence if I would take it, and I was always interested in parks. I had sponsored the bill to put $800,000 into the budget for Parks just before Earle picked me; before that, Parks had gotten $35,000 a year and what receipts they took in, which wasn't much, and it was a bad way of doing business, inefficient and probably corrupt. So I took the job. And never regretted it. It gave me a chance to move into other areas that interested me—water pollution control, forestry. And it put me close to Earle Clements, and I never regretted that, either."

In 1950 Clements ran for and was elected to the Senate—after Barkley had been elected vice-president—and Wetherby became governor. Four months later, when Senator Virgil Chapman died (on March 8, 1951), Wetherby thought of going to the Senate himself, but after talking with Clements and other party powers, he decided instead to wait and run for a full term as governor. (It is interesting to speculate on what might have happened had Wetherby become a senator. He and Clements together might have been able to build a constituency that would have held off the later attacks by Republicans Thruston Morton and John Cooper.) Wetherby brushed aside Howell Vincent and Jesse Cecil in the primary and then rolled over Republican Eugene Siler by 58,000 votes in the general election.

His running mate was Doc Beauchamp, who had long had his eye on higher office and hoped that his elevation to lieutenant governor would pave the way to his selection as top runner the next time around. Beauchamp was a man who, had he had just a couple of breaks, might have gone far. Affable, shrewd, and possessed of a natural feel for politics, he was handicapped by a gravel voice and a rotund, unimpressive figure. He had a way of looking disheveled, his tie just slightly askew, his hat always crumpled. A gentle, temperate, humorous man, he resembled a slightly bottle-worn Irish ward heeler more than the home-loving, small-town businessman and farmer he was.

But he had a way with small groups. He could work a crowd. He had been in politics practically all of his life, starting as a legislative page in Frankfort at age 13. He was twice bill clerk of the state Senate, then assistant senate clerk, six years clerk of Logan County, six years sheriff, and a member of the State Tax Commission under Governor Laffoon; he was elected commissioner of agriculture and state treasurer, became director of personnel and rural highway commissioner under Governor Clements, and was for five years secretary of the state Democratic central committee. Between times, he was an army private in World War I and a captain in World War II. Asked once what the vote in a certain Logan County precinct would be, Doc said, "Oh, they ought to vote about 314 to 28." The precinct voted 314 to 28.

Doc was something of a trencherman. He also had what might be described as a commonsense view of political ethics. As governor, Bert Combs announced in 1960 that he didn't want anyone in state government accepting any gift worth more than ten dollars. The ruling sorely tried Doc's ingenuity when a friend from western Kentucky, who admittedly had had some dealings with the state, presented Doc with a fine country ham for Christmas. Doc was torn by indecision, not wanting to violate Combs's edict but determined not to give up a delicious western Kentucky ham. "What's that thing worth?" asked Doc. "Oh," said the man, "about twenty dollars." Doc thought for a minute. "Tell you what you do," he said finally. "Why don't you take that downtown and have them cut it in two and give it to me in two pieces?"

The Wetherby-Beauchamp race was not spectacular. Unless Democrats fall out, the Republicans don't have an awfully good chance, and in 1951 nobody bolted. Siler ran a slow, stubborn, unimaginative race; the Democratic victory, 346,345 to 288,014, was never in doubt.

Outwardly, Lawrence Wetherby seemed to some Frankfort observers a little too jovial, a little too casual, too easygoing. Tall, dark-haired, and handsome, Wetherby liked a few drinks after work, was fond of dancing, parties, and social life, and enjoyed hunting and fishing trips with political friends—traits that made some people regard him lightly. The appearance was deceptive. Lawrence Wetherby was a serious, determined, and hard-working governor but one who preferred diplomacy and friendly tact over confrontation. A Wetherby trademark was his booming laugh, and his rich baritone voice seemed to carry for miles. During his administration a popular (and accurate) anecdote made the rounds noting the contrasting ways in which Clements and Wetherby conducted affairs of government. When Clements wanted to confide a secret to a trusted aide—the story went—he would take him into the governor's office, then through a conference room, out a side door, and into the men's room; behind the closed door of a stall, he would whisper the information to the aide. Wetherby, on the other hand, would whisper the information across his desk—and the whisper could be heard in the corridor outside.

The accomplishments of his administration were substantial, though in the heat of attacks later launched against him by Happy Chandler, many of his achievements were for a time obscured. Wetherby generally carried on the Clements policies, and finished several projects, including the state fairgrounds, that Clements had begun. Following the Supreme Court school desegregation ruling in the 1954 case of Brown *v.* Board of Education, Wetherby issued a strong statement supporting the ruling, effectively quieting segregationist critics who were seeking to arouse opposition to school desegregation. "We will do," he declared in a brief statement, "whatever it takes to obey the law."

Wetherby founded the Department of Mental Health, and the Youth Authority, and wrote his name into history by building Kentucky's first superhighway—then called the Kentucky Turnpike—which ran from Louisville to Elizabethtown. But his administration was more distinguished by the fact that it was probably the most open administration up to that time, honest, morally and legally impeccable, with no whisper of scandal. As his term drew to a close, Wetherby joined Clements in the search for a successor. There was some logic in their choice of Appellate Judge Bert T. Combs.

4

Not a Great First Act

Bert Thomas Combs didn't become governor of Kentucky easily. Indeed, it's a wonder he made it at all. In a state accustomed to the flamboyant tactics and histrionics of a Happy Chandler, he was a sincere and likable but rather colorless judge of the Court of Appeals. At the same time, he was considered a liberal, hard-working jurist, had been praised in the press for the moral courage of his votes on the court, and had acquired a reputation for almost painful integrity. Doc Beauchamp once said that Combs had an "affidavit face." He was a handsome man, especially when he smiled, but except in small groups he seldom smiled. On the other hand, he had defeated a former governor, Simeon Willis, in his one race for public office and had shown some ability in conducting that campaign. His speeches invariably made sense and impressed thoughtful listeners with their honest approach to Kentucky's lingering problems. But in the summer of 1955, when Combs made his first try for the governorship, that may have been a handicap.

Kentucky was caught, then as now, in its historic bind: it was a poor state; its people had incomes below the national average and were consequently reluctant to support programs that cost new taxes, no matter how much they were needed. Thus starved for money, Frankfort could not deliver the services that might have brought Kentucky into the national mainstream and raised the educational level and living standards of its people. The further Kentucky lagged behind, the more money it had to have just to catch up and the less likely it was to get it. This cycle of despond—a poor people keeping poor a government that helped to keep them poor—produced repeated pleas for more progressive government. But progressive government meant more money for such things as schools; that meant higher taxes; and the voters had long ago gotten into the habit of baying along behind politicians who promised to "cut out the waste," trim the state payroll, and produce honest government—all of which would miraculously improve their lot without raising taxes.

Nothing in Bert Combs's background gave any hint that he might be the man to break this cycle. In fact, there was little to indicate that he had a political philosophy of any kind. For one thing, his background was limited. Men who run for governor usually begin by running for mayor, county judge, sheriff, or the state legislature. At the time he declared for governor, Combs had run for office just once. He had not come from a particularly political family, nor was anyone in his immediate family then involved in politics.

This does not mean that he entered the race without advantages. He had the support of Earle Clements and of the Wetherby administration. Theoretically, the Court of Appeals—at the time, Kentucky's highest tribunal—had always been above the political battle; in practice, it had always been in the thick of the fight, since its justices are elected and therefore personally interested in politics. In Combs's race for the governorship, the justices made no bones about where they stood: they stood with Combs.

Combs had a clean record. He was a member of a large family from the mountains of eastern Kentucky, though few people outside the judicial system had heard of him. Even some people who later became his most devoted followers wondered aloud, as they watched him beat the campaign trail in that long, hot summer of 1955 when he challenged the redoubtable Happy Chandler, "What is he doing here?"

It was a question to which a casual review of his life provides no persuasive answers. The family of Stephen and Martha Combs, into which Bert was born on August 13, 1911, was a solid but undistinguished mountain family, living at the time on Town Branch near Manchester, the county seat of Clay County, deep in the Cumberland Mountains of southeastern Kentucky. The Combs family was one of the oldest in Kentucky, or for that matter in the United States, John Combs having arrived in Jamestown, Virginia, on the English ship *Marigold* more than a year before the *Mayflower* brought the Pilgrims to Plymouth Rock. In 1775 a Benjamin John Combs pushed westward into what is now Clark County, Kentucky, and in 1790 three other Combs brothers followed, two of them settling in Perry and Clay counties. One of these, another John Combs known as Jack, became the grandfather of Stephen Combs, Bert's father.

In authentic political tradition, Bert lived in a log house on Beech Creek (but only while his father was bulding a home nearby). He attended the Beech Creek grade school for six years and then went to a boarding school in Oneida for high school. The Combses were experiencing lean years, and Bert was obliged to work after school and on weekends; this was not unusual, and he did not regard it as a hardship.

Isolated by bad roads and with a reputation for violence as a result of its numerous lingering feuds, Clay County was relatively poor, and there was no stigma attached to a boy who had to work; most boys did. Bert's jobs didn't prevent him from graduating first in his class, and they helped to prepare him for earning most of his way when he enrolled at Cumberland College in nearby Williamsburg in 1929.

Working as a janitor at Cumberland, though, didn't enable him to save enough to pursue his plan to become a lawyer, an ambition that had sprung from noting the influence and affluence of lawyers around the courthouse in Manchester. He wasn't sure what lawyers did, but he noticed that they talked big, wore white shirts, and drove cars. But that took money, so after two years at Cumberland, where he finished near the top of his class, he got a job as a clerk with the Department of Highways in Frankfort, making $125 a month. As a matter of curious fact, Combs, a Democrat, was able to get his highway department job because of the ripper bill that took the department away from Republican Governor Sampson and gave it to Democrat "Uncle Ben" Johnson. That was not a bad salary for a young man in 1931; the Depression was beginning to make any kind of salary look good, and Combs was able to save enough in three years to enter the University of Kentucky school of law in Lexington in the fall of 1934.

The job with the highway department had given Combs his first knowledge of Kentucky. Law school and Lexington began his introduction to people who would be important to him later. He became managing editor of the *Kentucky Law Journal* and a member of the Order of the Coif, and graduated second in his class. And at the university he began to develop from the basically quiet, shy young mountain boy into the more sociable, quietly humorous man he was to become.

Yet when he returned to Manchester in the summer of 1937, Combs was still basically a mountain man. As was said of him then and years later, he kept his own counsel and accepted stoically the workings of fate. Mountain accents clung to his speech and would for many years. He would slip into the use of "ye" instead of "you," reflecting the old English dialect of the early mountain settlers whose speech patterns had been little affected by time and outside influence. His wit was the wry, quiet type of the general store or courthouse steps rather than the back-slapping joviality of the urban politician. And his inflections, considered backwoods in the more urban areas of the state, made some people tend to take Combs lightly during his early years in public life. In a politician, a certain rustic veneer may be acceptable, even an asset, when it is obviously affected, hinting that the speaker has risen above his humble beginnings; it is likely to be a liability if it is genuine.

"Combs always had a bad case of mountain boy, you know," said Bill May. "The rest of us, we made a little money and moved down to the Bluegrass, learned how to talk and wear clothes, but Combs always had a handful of mountain boys that he had to get together with every now and then and drink a little whiskey, play a little poker, tell mountain stories."

Combs stayed in Manchester a little more than a year before moving to establish a law practice in Prestonsburg. The reason for the move, he explained later, was not the dissatisfaction of a returning son with his hometown but an understandable desire to make a living. "I had too many kinfolks and friends in Manchester," he recalled, "and they all expected me to handle little things for them as a favor. They'd say 'Go down and see cousin Bert. He's a lawyer now; he'll handle that for you.' Then they'd get their feelings hurt if I charged them. I was taking in a lot of cases, but not sending out many bills."

He had an added reason to seek greener financial pastures. He now had a wife to support: before leaving the Bluegrass he had married Mabel Hall, a Knott County girl then living in Lexington. Fortunately, the relatives were fewer and the fees more numerous in Prestonsburg, and Combs was building a respectable practice when World War II broke out. Had he been keeping a more calculating eye on his future, he might have gained a commission in the legal branch of one of the services. Instead, he enlisted as a private in the army and went through the traditional rigors of the footslogging soldier before the army spotted his legal qualifications and sent him to Officers Training School and then to the staff of General Douglas MacArthur as chief of investigation of Japanese war criminals. He emerged from the war with the rank of captain, the Bronze Star and the Philippine Medal of Merit, and a record he could build on.

Back home in Prestonsburg, things began to happen in fairly rapid order. His daughter Lois Ann had been born in 1943, and his son Thomas George two years later, while he was still in uniform. The year he came home, Combs was appointed city attorney of Prestonsburg, and two years later was appointed commonwealth's attorney of Floyd County. His reputation as a young man on the rise began to spread beyond county lines. Still, there was considerable surprise in political circles when, in 1951, the justices of the Court of Appeals, then the state's highest court, unanimously recommended to Governor Lawrence Wetherby that Combs be appointed to fill the vacancy on the court created by the death of Justice Roy Helm of Hazard. Wetherby followed the recommendation. Combs was not quite 40 years old.

Combs had climbed a good distance up the ladder without having to run a campaign for office, but now he was obliged to make a race if he wanted to fill out Judge Helm's full unexpired term, since state law requires that persons named to unexpired terms serve until the next general election. And so, in the fall of 1951, Combs decided to run, though his announced opponent was the highly respected former governor, Republican Simeon Willis. In the 27 counties of the Seventh District, Combs won, 73,298 to 69,379; by defeating the former governor, he vaulted into the public eye. But only for the moment. The court is seldom a magnet for public attention, nor has it proved a dependable springboard to political office. And Combs was not the type to attract public attention easily.

But for several reasons the campaign had been important. It had given Combs his first taste of elective politics, and he found, somewhat to his surprise, that he liked it. He also found within himself a considerable lode of political philosophy; he had more ideas about the nature and operation of the state than he was called on to reveal in a race for a judgeship, a philosophy that had been slowly forming, based more on his studies of history and his personal experiences at the courthouse level than on his legal training and practice.

Equally important, he had met politicians of the highest order the state had to offer: Governor Lawrence Wetherby, Congressman Carl Perkins (who had been a key force in getting Combs appointed to the court and whose help had been vital in the campaign for election), and Earle C. Clements. It would not be accurate to say that he had gotten to know Clements; the big, quiet man from Morganfield was too complex, too secretive, too guarded of his own counsel to be easily or quickly understood. Neither would it be correct to say that the two men had become friends; Clements made friends carefully and slowly, and Combs—always a man of reserve—was quicker to take the outstretched hand than to offer it. But each man came to see and appreciate the qualities of the other. Clements sensed the potential, the tough resiliency beneath Combs's reserve, and Combs had his first encounter with one of Kentucky's great political intellects.

Clements and Chandler were by this time recognized as the leaders of Kentucky's two Democratic factions. And they were opposites as well as rivals. Thoughtful, cautious, almost taciturn, Clements had built—through the careful use of political power to help friends and frustrate enemies—a tight, tough organization based in western Kentucky but with strongholds also in the mountains of eastern Kentucky. The Chandler faction had strong points, especially in central Kentucky, and as long as Happy remained active, he had the allegiance of able leaders in many counties. But the organization was built around his personality and tended, in cult fashion, to wither without him.

It has been said, and with considerable truth, that Clements didn't care who was governor of Kentucky as long as he could run the state, while Chandler didn't care who ran Kentucky as long as he could be governor. Clements saw campaigning as a necessary burden; Chandler gloried in it. Clements preferred to move quietly behind the scenes; Chandler fed on the applause of the crowd. He was a master of ridicule and sarcasm, of finding a wound on the body politic and rubbing salt in it. Once the campaign was over and the clash and tension of the legislative session subsided, he often appeared bored.

It is significant that throughout his peripatetic political career, Chandler was one of the stubbornest defenders of Kentucky's constitution. For the constitution was designed to curb the function of government, state and local, and Chandler maintained an emotional rapport with his fellow Kentuckians partly because, like them, he believed in limited government. Similarly, Kentuckians responded to him because, vocally at least, he opposed taxes, especially sales taxes. Indeed, while representing the traditionally conservative faction of the party, Chandler cultivated a populist image, though his was not a populist record. For these reasons and because he was a strong, personable man, Chandler never lost the affection of masses of Kentuckians, despite the fact that he regularly quit, or appeared willing to quit, offices to which Kentuckians had elected him in order to seek higher things.

For a relatively unknown judge of the Court of Appeals to enter the arena with such time-toughened fighters as Clements and Chandler seems in retrospect a rash step. Yet there was Bert Combs, a rather quiet, thoughtful mountain lawyer, without a single statewide race under his belt, preparing to run for the state's top post.

"I guess you could say I got it by a process of elimination," Combs said later in typically self-deprecating fashion, for he was not the only hopeful in the fall of 1954. Doc Beauchamp was casting about for support. So were Henry Ward, former Adjutant General Jess Lindsay, and Frankfort attorney Louis Cox. But Beauchamp opposed Ward, Clements was cool toward Lindsay, and Cox took himself out of consideration for personal reasons. And Clements told his friend Beauchamp that he could not support him "at this time."

"Lawrence Wetherby called me at my home in Prestonsburg one night about eight o'clock," Combs recalled later, "and asked me to come to the mansion next day. When I arrived I found Lawrence, Earle, and Doc sitting around a dinner table where the dishes had not been cleared, and either Lawrence or Earle, I forget which, said they had decided that I should run for governor with the support of the three of them. I told Doc I wouldn't run without his approval. It was a very painful time for him. He wanted so badly to run himself. But he finally said, with tears in his eyes, "No, go ahead and run. You were always my second choice. I was my first."

Not everyone was overjoyed at the selection of Combs. "George Kerler, who was Lawrence's press secretary, came to me and said Lawrence wanted to see me," Bill May remembered. "I'd been doing some work on the Kentucky Turnpike, you know, what's now Interstate 65, and had gotten pretty close to Wetherby, so I went to see him, and when I got there he told me they had picked Bert Combs to run. I told him he was crazy. I knew Bert had come back to Prestonsburg after the war, but he hadn't built much steam. I told Lawrence, I said, 'Wetherby, that dog ain't going to hunt.' I told him Combs didn't know anybody and, worse, nobody knew him. But he said they'd figured it out. So I worked with them, raising money."

But the irrepressible Happy Chandler was back home, fired from his job as baseball commissioner by club owners, restless and eager to get back to his search for high office. He announced that, out of the goodness of his heart, he was ready to take over the governorship again and declared that he was just in time to save the state from the chicanery of Clements and Wetherby. With customary zest, he took aim not only at Combs but at the whole Clements wing. He declared that Combs, whom he called "the Little Judge," was "an innocent bystander" brought into the picture by "Clementine and Wetherbine"—his nicknames for Clements and Wetherby—who, he hinted, had evil reasons for wanting to put the naive Combs into the governor's office. As usual, Happy was discovering hideous waste in Frankfort, and promising economy and reform as soon as he could get back in. As an example of Wetherby's criminal extravagance, Happy charged that he had bought a $20,000 rug for his office and had spent countless thousands on unnecessary air conditioning. He promised that when he regained the office he would cool it by opening the windows to the sweet Kentucky air, and he invited all Kentuckians to come to the Capitol and walk on "that $20,000 rug."

When Wetherby produced invoices showing that there was no "rug," and that carpeting for the entire first floor of the capitol had cost only $2,700, Chandler ignored the facts and continued his charges. (At the end of the campaign, *Courier-Journal* reporter Allan Trout asked Chandler why he had persisted in this charge after being shown the truth. Chandler replied that the lie "didn't hurt anybody, and people liked to hear it.") He also charged that Wetherby had gone "clear to Africa" to find "some fancy wood to panel his office with," and promised that, if elected, he would use good, honest Kentucky wood. (A minor official in the Wetherby administration had approved a contract including paneling of African mahogany, supplied by a Kentucky contractor, for the governor's office.) Ironically, after he was elected, Chandler spent $35,000 on carpeting, draperies, and other interior decoration for the capitol. It was familiar Chandler technique; before one charge could be refuted, he would launch another. He would make any charge, it appeared, that would catch the public attention. And he succeeded in making Combs appear almost a minor character in the battle by ignoring him and centering his fire on "Wetherbine and Clementine."

Combs was by no means without advantages. He had the support of the administration, strong roots in the mountains, and the backing of the Louisville organization. But on the campaign trail he was simply no match for the free-swinging Chandler, whose unsubstantiated charges kept Combs and his allies almost constantly on the defensive.

It was brilliant strategy, if distilled in demagoguery. As Allan Trout said later, "Combs was ready to discuss issues, but he wasn't prepared for a dogfight, which is what he got." Combs insisted on sticking to the high road. In his announcement of his candidacy he promised to "wage a vigorous campaign, confined to the issues," and he did just that. It was a fatal error, and one that Chandler did not make. Honesty may be the best policy, but in Kentucky political campaigns it is often poor strategy. The truth was that Kentucky schools were in trouble, and that it was going to take considerably more money than the state then had to make the improvements that both Combs and Chandler admitted were needed. That raised the specter of new taxes, a hazard for any Kentucky race.

Combs made what was a minor tactical error by failing to resign from the Court of Appeals upon announcing his candidacy, and Chandler and Harry Lee Waterfield, Chandler's running mate, lost no time in taking him to task for it. Actually, he had notified Governor Wetherby and Chief Justice Brady Stewart of his intention to resign but had not yet done so when former Attorney General Hubert Meredith, a Chandler supporter, demanded that he do it; thus, when he did resign, it appeared as though he had been forced to do so. It was a minor sensation but not a good note on which to begin.

Picking a slate to run with the candidate for governor was often a delicate business that could cost the top candidate more than it gained him. A well-known candidate for minor office was often reluctant to be aligned with a specific candidate for governor. It could lose him the votes of the other candidates' supporters without gaining him much. The gubernatorial candidate tried to pick a lieutenant governor and runners for other spots—secretary of state, treasurer, superintendent of public instruction, commissioner of agriculture, clerk of the Court of

Appeals, attorney general—who were, if not famous, at least not infamous, and who could show some vague qualification for the office desired and were from various parts of the state, so as to offer a "balanced" ticket that would presumably represent all areas of the state and as many elements of the party as possible.

The trick was to avoid slating popular incompetents who would win and then come back to haunt you, or slating seemingly sound candidates who got instant ambition and stabbed you in the back. All these officers, of course, should be in the governor's cabinet, helping him to carry out the program for which the people elect him. But as long as Kentucky clings to its constitution, which makes too many offices elective, the governor is always at the mercy of men who run for these minor posts and then are free to operate without consideration for the governor's programs, policies, or principles.

The value of a slate was uncertain. A slated candidate who was strong in his home district could wind up hurting the ticket in others. Sometimes county leaders would support an unslated local candidate and the remainder of the slated ticket. But once the primary was over, it was seldom that the lesser candidates—unless there was a truly poor runner among them—materially influenced the outcome. It has happened; so has the reverse. J.C.W. Beckham, running for governor in 1927, was the only loser on his ticket. Henry Ward lost the race for governor in 1967 to Louie Nunn; his running mate, Wendell Ford, won. One thing, however, was usually true: a relatively unknown candidate gained by being slated. He shared in the strength and the publicity of the top runner, and even if he lost, he had gotten experience and name recognition that would be of advantage in subsequent races.

Combs and his strategy people talked it over and decided not to slate anyone. As it turned out, it was probably just as well.

The formal opening of the Combs campaign took place at the Shelby County fairgrounds on the evening of June 2, 1955. It was a grand occasion in the old tradition. Almost 10,000 people were on hand, many of them state employees who had been urged to swell the crowd and lend an impression that the Combs candidacy was already hugely popular. The platform sagged with the weight of prominent party members—everyone from Wetherby and Clements, Jefferson County Judge Bert Van Arsdale and Louisville Mayor Andrew Broaddus to Congressmen Carl Perkins and John Watts, Doc Beauchamp, state party officials, wives of former officials, and even Stephen Combs, Bert's father. Bands played, people drank and ate, local officials welcomed and warm-up speakers lavished praise on the candidate. Then the candidate himself rose.

"Bert had written this speech," recalled Henry Ward, who was working in the Combs campaign, "and when I saw it, I said, 'Hell, that won't do.' It was too long. It was too heavy. And it just about called for new taxes; didn't say so exactly, but made it plain he would ask for more taxes for schools. Somebody in headquarters got it and rewrote it some, but when Bert saw it, he changed it back to the way it was. He knew what he wanted to say, no matter what the rest of us thought."

Combs spoke for 38 minutes, earnestly and intelligently. And killed his campaign.

"Combs opened and closed his campaign on the same night," said Hugh Morris, chief of the *Courier-Journal's* Frankfort bureau. Said Clay Wade Bailey, Frankfort correspondent for the United Press, "Bert really kicked himself in the ass." And in the car with Earle Clements, as they drove back toward Louisville's Seelbach Hotel, where Combs had his campaign headquarters, Doc Beauchamp leaned toward the former governor and said in his rasping whisper, "Goddamn, Earle! And you said I couldn't run because I couldn't make a speech!"

Actually, Combs's opener was not a bad speech. Anyone reading it today would probably consider it a good cut above the average. It explored issues. It suggested problems to be faced and their possible solutions. And therein lay the trouble. What Combs had done was to state the truth: to do anything substantial about state schools—the minimum foundation program (to assure a minimum per-pupil expenditure), teachers' salaries, teachers' retirement, building funds—was going to take money. The figures he quoted indicated that he would need about $25,000,000 in new money for these purposes. And if that was not enough, he then added:

"I believe the people want improvement in education, in attacks on mental illness, and in many other state services, and that they are willing to pay for these benefits . . . [which] can be made only by increasing state taxes or by finding new sources of revenue."

That was all it took. In a story in the next morning's edition of the *Courier-Journal*, Hugh Morris wrote that Combs had proposed programs calling for $25,000,000 in new taxes. This was not quite accurate; Combs had implied that he would improve education, and that education needed money. He had not proposed any specific tax or any specific amount of new tax revenues sought. But the story hurt Combs deeply, perhaps fatally.

Chandler lost no time exploiting the situation. "The taxers are after you!" he warned in an address two days later, declaring that Combs was preparing a sales tax. In an address at Greensburg on July 12, he summed up his whole campaign message and strategy:

"Do you want four more years of the tax-crazy, spend-crazy, and waste-crazy dictators, or do you want an administration that knows the value of a dollar? There must be a halting some place, some time. The people are taxed to the limit. I intend to give you some relief."

"Look at me!" Chandler would cry to his courthouse crowds. "I'm the only man in the history of Kentucky that ever cut your taxes!" The *Courier-Journal* studiously pointed out that while Chandler in his first administration had repealed a sales tax that produced $6,000,000 in its only year of collection, he had enacted 14 new or increased taxes. But Chandler had a good issue and knew it. "Combs says he's going to raise your taxes. I promise you I'll cut them," he declared in a speech in Jessamine County. "Which do you want?"

The answer was foregone. Senator Alben Barkley gave Combs a fairly strong endorsement, charging that Chandler had deserted him, had tried to undermine his campaign for the vice-presidency in 1952, and had "three times deserted his party." But Combs felt that the Barkley endorsement, coming only two weeks before the election, was too late to be of maximum help. Henry Ward hit Chandler some telling blows, flourishing checks that had been given to Chandler during the war by distillers, allegedly for getting them permission to release warehoused whiskey. Ward and the Lexington and Louisville news-papers demanded an explanation of the checks. Chandler ignored the demands. Instead of an explanation he gave a glowing account of his heroics during the war and attacked Ward, whom he called "nasty, ugly little hatchet-faced Henry."

More than 400,000 Democrats voted in the primary. Chandler won by a margin of 18,121 votes.

It was a bitter blow for Combs, who had hoped to the last that he would win. He took a few days off and went to the rustic cabin on Lake Cumberland belonging to Appellate Judge John Moremen to rest and decide about the future.

"Bert was just beat," recalled John Moremen, Jr., years later. "He would sit in a rocking chair on the porch and read, then doze off awhile, then wake up and rock awhile, and then nap again."

At the end of the brief rest, Combs went home to Prestonsburg. He had been in public life for almost ten years and had decided it was time to get back to private life and work. Strangely, he found the months following his defeat a time of relief and satisfaction.

"That was probably the happiest time of my life," he said later. "We set up a little savings and loan association, and I reestablished my law firm. Kilmer Combs was my partner. We had a pretty good practice, and it was good to be out of the tension of politics. Mabel and I had built a home. Normal living for a change."

5

Brawls in the House
of Factions

After the hurly-burly of campaigning, life in Prestonsburg was tame for Bert Combs but not entirely nonpolitical. Officeholders, politicians, and reporters continued to call on him. He was frequently asked to address civic and political clubs, and he accepted enough of the invitations to indicate that he had not completely lost interest in public life. When a Kentucky politician turns down invitations to speakings or free meals, he has either made a lot of money or lost interest in politics. Combs continued to eat and speak.

And events in Frankfort gave him plenty to talk about. It early became evident that Chandler was going to have trouble with the legislature. Again, he had won the governorship largely with his attack on the sales tax, but once in office that old bugbear, a lack of money, handicapped him. This time he could not make a big impression by reorganizing government or improving state finances. Furthermore, Clements and Wetherby had instituted programs—highways and rural roads, the state fairgrounds and exposition center, the Kentucky Turnpike, the Youth Authority, new park facilities—that had to be carried on. He had either to raise taxes or to eliminate some of the necessary functions of the state; there simply was not enough money to run an efficient government.

Chandler was obliged to cut social programs. He abolished the Youth Authority created by Lawrence Wetherby to bring all children's welfare programs under one agency, and thereby infuriated a large welfare constituency. During the campaign he had promised the Lexington community that he would build a medical school at the University of Kentucky, though he had soft-pedaled the matter in other parts of the state. Now he set in motion plans for the A.B. Chandler Medical School, despite a poll conducted among Kentucky physicians showing that they opposed a second medical school by a margin of 1,303 to 190 (there was already one at the University of Louisville) and a legislative study indicating that it would cost between $24,000,000 and $30,000,000. Chandler's support of the Lexington school was popular with people throughout the eastern and central parts of the state who were poorly served by their own hospitals. And it served again to underscore the governor's Bluegrass identity. He also found money to expand the UK College of Agriculture. To make sure the public was aware of its blessings, his public relations department published a pamphlet entitled *Kentucky on the Move,* which referred to the governor as "Kentucky's greatest living citizen" and "an unfolding genius, a rare and unusual man, thoroughly matured, God-fearing."

Happy worked hard to identify himself with Lexington, where he loved to play golf and eat lunch with friends, and with the University of Kentucky. Though he had been an undergraduate at Transylvania, he managed to become identified with the university, repeatedly getting himself appointed to both the UK and the Transylvania boards of trustees. He was also one of the most vocal supporters of UK athletic teams. He loved to sit on the bench at football games, rush to the locker room after basketball victories, and have himself photographed with the players. Once, in a beautifully timed piece of theater, he dashed onto the court and hammered a nail into the spot from which basketball star Joe Hagan had sunk a last-second shot to defeat Notre Dame. He made it seem spontaneous but did not explain why he carried a hammer and nail in his pocket to basketball games. (Bert Nelli, in *The Winning Tradition,* a history of UK basketball, says that Chandler sent for the hammer and nail. If so, he got remarkably fast service.)

When he was in his 80s, Chandler loved to appear at alumni functions and sing "My Old Kentucky Home." This may be significant, for the Kentucky of the song is of another age, no longer exists even in memory, and has little relevance to the modern Kentucky and its problems. Yet the nostalgic appeal made it good politics all the way. Far more than the University of Louisville or any of the other state colleges, the University of Kentucky is the sentimental heart of the state, just as Lexington is the sentimental heart of Kentucky for much of its population. UK alumni loom large in the political and economic life of every part of the state and are influential even in Louisville, despite its traditional rivalry with Lexington. Political hopefuls have done well to attend UK or develop a bond with it.

Early in the 1956 legislative session, it became evident that Chandler's programs were going to cost more money than the state was taking in, a fact that should have caused some slight embarrassment to a man who had assured the voters that he could carry out the promised programs without raising taxes. On June 25, 1955, he had told an Ashland audience: "I promise you I can take the money we now have, put the minimum foundation program into effect in its entirety, provide adequate support for health, welfare, old-age pensions, and other services . . . without a sales tax and still have money in the bank. We will just put aside $55,000,000 for schools first. We can live on the other $45,000,000. It will be simple." It soon became obvious that it would not be simple.

But Chandler employed an unusual technique. After getting rid of the usual departmental and technical legislation during the regular session, he called four successive special sessions. In the first, he presented his budget, which called for spending $248,350,000 for the coming two years; this was at least $48,000,000 more than he had said he would need to run the state and at least $46,000,000 more than revenue officials were estimating the state would take in. Where was the money coming from? asked the legislators. Pass the budget, Chandler said, and I'll present my tax program at the later session. It was, in its way, a rather painless method, giving the legislators a chance to approve money for any number of desirable purposes without having to impose any repulsive taxes to finance them.

But the day of reckoning arrived, and Chandler was obliged to unveil the magical tax package with which he would finance his program. It proved an eye-opener. For example, it increased personal income taxes by putting on the rolls 150,000 new taxpayers; it put a surtax on income taxes, raised corporate taxes from 4.5 percent to 5 percent, and cut tax credits; it transferred the assessment and collection of the tax on intangibles from local to state government, put new taxes on deeds and life insurance premiums, put a 5 percent production tax on whiskey, and added two cents per gallon to gasoline for trucks. Chandler also proposed a $100,000,000 bond issue for roads and promised that the first would be an improved highway from Frankfort to Versailles, his hometown. The new taxes were expected to raise an additional $40,000,000 a year.

The legislature included a lot of Democrats who had been identified with the Clements wing of the party, and rumblings of discontent grew as the first year's sessions ended. Allan Trout of the *Courier-Journal* pointed out that Chandler could not have passed several parts of his budget and tax program had he not been able to gain the support of a sizable number of the minority Republicans.

But the Eisenhower years were a time of relative calm and prosperity, in Kentucky as in the nation; an aura of good feeling prevailed. The Korean conflict had ended (though in a compromise that was alien to the American spirit); the economy, fueled by postwar demand that was again producing inflationary pressures, was humming along; and there was a general air of optimism. The most disruptive development stemmed from the 1954 Supreme Court ruling in the case of Brown *v.* Topeka Board of Education which, in effect, ended the practice of separate-but-equal school facilities for whites and blacks. Throughout the South the decision produced official as well as emotional turmoil, and though Kentucky on the whole accepted the decision calmly, there were scattered instances of resistance. On one occasion, Chandler was obliged to send National Guard troops into the town of Sturgis to compel compliance. In all his actions concerning implementation of the integration decision, Chandler refused to play the Dixiecrat, despite possible political gain and even though many of his friends from other states were making political hay with resistance to the Supreme Court ruling. While many, perhaps even a majority, of Kentuckians were not enthusiastic about racial integration, most acknowledged the moral correctness of Chandler's action.

In this, as in affairs generally, the Chandler luck was holding, as he seemed to assume it always would. It was the belief of most capital newsmen (and was borne out in his interviews with his son later) that Chandler had an almost mystical conviction that he was destined for great things, a confidence so total that he tended to view people who stood in his way as not only wrong but evil. Just as he had ridden the wave of New Deal reforms in his first term, he now profited by the relative prosperity and complacency of the Eisenhower era. Lexington, and to a lesser extent Louisville, enjoyed an industrial boom. Along the Ohio new power-generating plants were pushing smokestacks into the sky, and the state's coal industry was experiencing a modest resurgence to supply them. At the University of Kentucky in 1958, the Wildcats of Coach Adolph Rupp won another NCAA basketball championship.

But as in Bourbon France, troubling pressures were building beneath a serene surface. Kentucky's roads were bad—two thin lanes of blacktop winding up and down the hills, crumbling under heavy trucks, blocked by flooding creeks, continuing Kentucky's detour-state reputation. They were a handicap to state farmers, manufacturers, and coal operators. They complicated the task of school consolidation and efforts to develop a tourist industry. (Both Chandler and Combs employed the witticism that the roads "would crumble under a fat boy on a bicycle," and some probably would have.) The postwar "baby boom" that in a few years would swamp the nation's school systems was already crowding elementary and high schools. The state's mental hospitals were crowded and backward in their methods. A modest recession during Chandler's final years would reveal some of the state's structural weaknesses.

A revolt of "rebels," a group of chiefly younger, more liberal lawmakers, began to take shape in the final days of the first legislative session, and by the time the second session convened it had become a recognized force, led by Democrats John Breckinridge, Foster Ockerman, Paul Huddleston, Pat Tanner, and Gil Kingsbury. The session almost became a shambles, as governor and legislators snarled and bickered. Indeed, as his split with members of his own party widened, the Democratic governor was able to pass measures only through the help of Republicans. In the spring of 1958 the *Courier-Journal* reported that Chandler had been obliged to meet with the caucusing Republicans and promise to build or repair roads in their districts in return for their help in enacting his program.

Near the end of the 1958 session the Democratic rebels asked Chandler to call a special session of the Assembly to deal with several problems, including the need for more money for schools and indigent relief. Chandler agreed to do so only if the legislature would promise in advance to approve any measure he put before the special session and to consider no others. The rebels refused; the special session was not called; and Chandler went into the final year of his term at odds with some of the most influential members of his party.

The failure of Chandler, a man of such infinite persuasion on the hustings, to win the support of a legislature containing a majority from his own party is another bit of evidence of the extent of factionalism. Many of the Democrats in the Assembly were Clements-Combs people and not eager to cooperate. Others, especially the rebels, had genuine philosophical differences with Chandler over such matters as taxes, roads, welfare, and appropriation of school funds. But Chandler chose to deal with opposition Republicans rather than make the concessions or compromises that might have won him the support of his own party, chiefly because he found himself more comfortable with them. The opposition of the well-publicized and well-regarded rebels, and their support of opposition candidates, would come back to wound the governor before many months had passed.

Early in the term, Chandler made what appeared to be a remarkable gaffe for a man of his political sophistication when he bluntly told a group of Farm Bureau leaders to go home and tend to their own business. He later conceded that he had misunderstood the purpose behind their visit, and he and bureau leaders patched up their differences, at least on the surface. But he then brought the executive branch of government into direct confrontation with the judiciary when he challenged the right of the Court of Appeals to name its clerk.

Charlie O'Connell, a veteran officeholder who had served alternately as secretary of state and clerk of the Court of Appeals for two decades, died on January 10, 1957, while serving a term as clerk; the court appointed his deputy, Doris Owens, to fill the vacancy. Chandler, protesting that the constitution gave the governor power to fill all vacancies of statewide offices, named instead a Boone County farmer, Walter Ferguson, and threatened to remove State Treasurer Henry Carter from office if he paid Owens her salary. Chandler's resentment probably stemmed from the fact that the justices had supported their fellow judge, Bert Combs, against him in the primary, and feelings between governor and court became bitter—so bitter that at one point mild-mannered Appellate Judge James Milliken was said to have written Chandler a letter challenging him, or threatening to challenge him, to a duel if he persisted. Combs later said he could not believe Milliken would do such a thing, but Judge John Moremen insisted it was true.

Eventually Chandler backed down, and Owens kept the job. But she had to run in the special election called to fill the vacancy, and Chandler threw the weight of his administration and his personal prestige behind J.L. "June" Suter, a northern Kentucky car dealer. With Chandler's support, Suter was heavily favored, but then Chandler made a mistake. "We'll beat the old maid world without end!" he chortled, referring to the fact that Ms. Owens was single. This was poor judgment. Indeed, it was poor politics, which is worse. Kentuckians do not mind abusing women, but they do not like to hear others abuse them. The voters objected to this mistreatment of a woman, and in the May balloting Owens beat Suter by almost two to one. It was a stunning upset and a jarring setback for Chandler. Two years later, he would try to even the score.

Another conflict developed in Jefferson County, after Chandler threatened to cut appropriations for the state fairgrounds and exposition center (at one point he hinted that he was prepared to sell the fairgrounds if he could find a buyer, and even said he had a prospect) and moved the Health Department from Louisville to Frankfort. This latter was a defensible move; an argument can be made for grouping state offices in the capital. But to many Louisvillians it seemed a way of punishing the city for failing to vote for Chandler. There was another reason for the hostility between Louisville and Chandler: in his first administration, Chandler had bypassed the Fourth Street Organization in matters of patronage. The organization did not forget; it opposed Happy in his later races.

But perhaps Chandler's toughest fight erupted in June 1956 over control of the state Democratic party apparatus. For years, control of the party machinery had been allowed to pass quietly from the hands of one Democratic governor to his successor (as long as the successor was also a Democrat); when Chandler defeated Combs in 1955, he had reason to expect that to the victor would go the party spoils. Indeed, there had not been an all-out party fight for control since 1928, when a faction led by Thomas Rhea, Elwood Hamilton, and Seldon Glenn won over an opposition wing of Allie Young, Fred Vinson, William "Honest Bill" Fields, and Billy Klair.

But in the meantime Chandler was handed another defeat when, in the Democratic senatorial primary of May 1956, Earle Clements beat Chandler's candidate, Joe Bates, 218,353 to 136,533. It was not much of a contest. Bates was a lackluster candidate and was probably not helped by Chandler's open support, which seemed to the voters designed to assist Chandler more than Bates. Clements, on the other hand, waged a hard, careful, and skillful campaign. Encouraged by the victory, the Clements-Combs faction decided that perhaps the voters preferred them, after all, and prepared to make a fight to keep party control.

And a good old hot-summer, throat-cutting, backroom, court-house fight it turned out to be, with as many as 5,000 Democrats turning out in some counties (Fayette, for example) to choose delegates to the state convention. Chandler had a double stake in the outcome: control of the state machinery would not only ease his job for the next three years but make him almost certain to go to the national Democratic presidential nominating convention in 1956 as Kentucky's favorite son. Chandler regularly promised the voters of Kentucky that he had no earthly desire for any office other than the one he was running for at the moment, but just as regularly he felt his resolve weaken when a chance at higher office presented itself, a trait that illustrated his preference for campaigning over administering.

The party conventions across the state were unprecedented for their participation and tough infighting. At first, it appeared that the Clements-Combs forces had a majority of delegates to the state convention. But Chandler, catching his opponents off balance, got his man, Robert Humphrey—a Frankfort druggist and longtime Democratic wheelhorse—named chairman. It was a crucial victory. He began contesting every Clements delegate put forward and, with Humphrey as chairman, managed to throw out enough Clements delegates to carry the convention. Chandler thus gained the right to select the new Democratic executive committee, winning control over the delegation to the national convention.

In the meantime the party, like the nation, had been shocked by the death of Senator Alben Barkley, who dropped dead while speaking at Washington and Lee University in Lexington, Virginia, on April 30, 1956. His death did not allow time for voters to choose a successor in the May primary, and it fell to the state Democratic Central Committee to name a party candidate to run in the general election to succeed him. The committee chose Lawrence Wetherby, with explosive results.

The choice of Wetherby infuriated Chandler, who had reason to consider himself party leader and the man to be consulted in such matters. He had favored his long-time supporter and adviser Joseph Leary for the spot. So, strangely enough, had Earle Clements, according to a statement by Bert Combs some years later (in an interview with the author). Clements, said Combs, liked Leary, and while he doubted that Leary could win, he thought that having him on the ticket would keep Chandler from bolting to the Republicans.

But with his two party enemies on the ticket, Chandler launched a bolt against both Clements, who was locked in a tough battle with Republican Thruston Morton, and Lawrence Wetherby, who was facing the thankless task of running against the formidable John Sherman Cooper of Somerset.

This complicated substantially the task facing Clements and Wetherby in that critical summer of 1956. Even with a united party, Wetherby would have been an underdog against Cooper, who was becoming almost invulnerable. Under ordinary circumstances Clements would have been easily favored over Thruston Morton, a Louisville silk-stocking runner whose only experience was in the Third District Congressional seat he had won from Democrat Emmett O'Neal. But circumstances were not ordinary. Dwight D. Eisenhower was running for reelection, and it was apparent that little short of a direct act of heaven could defeat him. War hero Eisenhower had not been an outstanding president, but his inherent decency and devotion to duty and country gave him an invincible aura. A Republican tide was running.

And now Chandler was bolting. He had much to gain. At best, he would have a delegation at the national convention that might, should lightning strike, make him president. If he lost at the convention, he would have at least defeated the opposing faction, possibly removing obstacles to his control of the legislature, easing the tasks of his administration, and making it likely that he could choose his successor.

Things didn't work out quite the way he planned. True enough, he went to the convention as the state's favorite son, but the national Democrats, desperately searching for someone of sufficient stature to challenge the man sometimes referred to as "Daddy Warbucks," were not eager to choose a man who had failed to support the party in several state races, had just bolted his party's senatorial nominees, and had once quit the U.S. Senate to become involved with baseball. Neither were his policies likely to set the national party on fire. In a letter responding to a question about his beliefs, Chandler told Joel Millikan, of Oberlin, Ohio, "We need a balanced budget and lower taxes more than anything else." Then he proceeded to add, "My program calls for increased teachers' salaries, new educational buildings, better highways, more aid to the aged, and more efficient treatment of the mentally incompetent."

Yet Chandler insisted on holding onto the Kentucky delegation long after his own campaign foundered, thus depriving the state of a place in the decision-making process. Mike Barry, editor of the Louisville *Irish-American* and an inflexible Chandler foe, who regularly penned and published scathing denunciations of the man he castigated as "old blubber boy" and "the fat fraud from Versailles," wrote that "the phrase 'Kentucky's favorite son' is an unfinished sentence."

In the fall of 1956, Clements and Wetherby went down to defeat. Perhaps the revenge was sweet for Chandler, but it was costly, too. Stung by the loss of two senate seats and frustrated by the way the governor had used the state delegation at the convention, pro-Clements forces made life miserable for Chandler during his second legislative session, helped to spark the "rebel" revolt, and forced Chandler to make deals with Republicans.

For example, by any measure the most spectacular fight in the 1958 session of the legislature occurred when administration forces introduced a bill to rip State Treasurer Henry Carter of his power to choose which banks state funds would be deposited in, and to decide when they would be transferred from one bank to another. It was Chandler's chance to get even with Carter, who not only was a member of the Clements wing of the party but had sided with Doris Owens in her fight to hold her job with the Court of Appeals. And the attempt to rip him turned into one of the bitterest, loudest, and at times silliest fights of Chandler's term.

The episode offers another example of the divisive and limiting nature of the state constitution, which deprives a governor of his logical control over key figures of his administration. It can certainly be argued that Chandler, as the elected chief executive of the state, had every right to decide where state funds would be deposited. Instead, the authority rested with an official elected independently of the governor, and a member of the rival faction. So once more Chandler launched an attempt to evade—in fact, ignore—the constitution, ironic in view of his consistent support of the charter and his resistance to its revision.

Chandler did not attack Carter on the grounds of philosophy or efficiency. Rather, he accused him of drinking too much, calling him "an adulterous, drunken old man" (to which Carter replied, "Hell, I ain't fucked no more'n him"). This was characteristic of Chandler, who always made a great point of the fact that he drank sparingly, if at all. In his race against Combs, he had frequently implied that Lawrence Wetherby drank too much, and had borne down heavily on the word "sober" when he promised that "I will make you a sober governor."

In a state that hiccoughs its abhorrence of liquor, this was sound politics, though it sounded a little strange when advanced as an argument in the Assembly, where the drinking habits of many members could easily be called into question. Indeed, when one member declared that Carter drank too much, another arose to demand that he explain how much whiskey was too much, and how the accuser knew.

Actually, however, the sessions of Chandler's second term were not as rowdy as those immediately following World War II, when at least one member had to be disarmed in the House, and the old Capital Hotel was regularly the scene of fist fights and near orgies. During these years, the liquor industry kept a suite of rooms, known as the Snake Pit, in the hotel where weary legislators might find compatible company and relief from thirst at any and all hours, day or night, and frequently did. One mountain senator practically made the Snake Pit his living quarters; he would drink each night until unable to drink more, whereupon he would collapse on the sofa and sleep until his fellow lawmakers collected him next morning on their way to the Assembly. One night, for reasons never explained, he went to his own room and went to bed. Upon awakening the following day he did not recognize his surroundings, leaped up screaming, and had to be tranquilized; meanwhile, his friends, not finding him in the Pit, sent out a general alarm and had the Frankfort police somewhat concerned until he finally wandered back to the more familiar and friendly ambiance of the Snake Pit.

Another solon, who wore sunglasses to protect his eyes from sunlight (and others from the sight of his eyes), delighted his friends when he turned up on the floor carrying a quart milk carton from which he sipped frequently. Alas, they discovered that the carton contained two parts of vodka for each part of milk—the better, he said, to soothe the ulcer within.

Whatever its improvements, however, the legislature had not transformed itself into an ethical paradise by the time Chandler set out to rip Henry Carter. In the course of debate, Banjo Bill Cornett of Hindman complained that he had been harassed by lobbyists—"I guess that's what you call them, as ladies are present"—but threatened to shoot anyone who said his vote was for sale. Pat Tanner of Owensboro openly charged on the floor that the administration was attempting to bribe legislators. "The turkey money brought in here for other purposes," he charged, "was being used last night to pass this bill." Turkey, in the lexicon of the legislature, was money spent by special interests to buy votes, and a turkey bill was one for which lobbyists spent unusual amounts.

Incidentally, one of the sturdiest turkeys to fly through the Assembly was proposed repeatedly during the postwar years, when members of successive sessions proposed changes in the laws regulating barbers and beauticians. One year they would introduce a bill outlawing the sale of materials for home permanents, a bill that would have forced women to get their permanents in beauty shops (or shoppes). By the dozens, operators of beauty shops would troop to Frankfort to lobby for this obviously judicious and fair proposal, and the Capital Hotel would ring with the happy sounds of the resulting conferences between legislators and lobbyists. The bill would, of course, eventually be beaten, and at the next session one would be introduced to outlaw beauty shop permanents. Again, the beauticians would flock to the capital to protest this beastly attempt at restraint of trade, and again they and the legislators would enjoy the workings of representative democracy until, again, the bill was beaten.

On one rather famous occasion, Frederic C. "Fritz" Lord, the tall, craggy-featured, distinguished-looking political writer for the *Louisville Times*, and a *Courier-Journal* photographer (whose name has become mercifully lost in the mists of time) were sitting in the lobby of the Capital Hotel when they were approached by two women desiring to discuss the home permanent bill and asking if the two gentlemen were legislators. "Certainly," said Lord, "I am Senator Lord, and this is Representative Smith [or whatever]. Let's step into the bar and talk this over." After a while, both couples retired to the gentlemen's rooms for more direct consultation. Lord and his lady had been ensconced for only a few minutes when the lobbyist burst from the room, barefoot and in her slip, raced down the hall and beat on the photographer's door. "Mary!" she hollered. "If you ain't done it, don't do it! That sonofabitch is from the *Courier-Journal*!"

During the attempt to rip Henry Carter, Representative T. Fowler Combs of Pembroke declared that the ripper bill was only an honest effort to keep the state's money out of the grasp of a drinker. Actually, it was a power grab, and few made any attempt to pretend otherwise. Mrs. Ann Hall of Bypro dished up some of the best oratory of the episode when she compared Chandler and his weak-kneed legislators to the man who had a team of mice that moved a piano up three flights of stairs. "How could they do it?" another man asked him, to which he replied, "I laid the whip to them."

Mrs. Hall went on to charge that "Happy has already had his white biscuits, and now he's come back for the gravy. Having been governor twice and senator once, it ill behooves him now to feed his madness for power on a few little duties stripped from the treasurer." One by one, members of the rebel faction rose to denounce the bill—Paul Huddleston, Pat Tanner, Gil Kingsbury, Harry King Lowman. Charles Williams of Paducah summed up their charges when he declared on the floor, "Henry Carter's only sin was in defending Doris Owens."

But Chandler was still governor; he had power and knew how to use it. It was an embarrassing bill, but it took 12 roll calls and five hours of parliamentary maneuvering before opponents managed to beat it by two votes, 46 to 44. To show the strength that the rebels had accumulated, 28 Democrats and 16 Republicans voted for it; 40 Democrats and 6 Republicans voted against it. This does not mean that Chandler had lost his appeal for the Kentucky voter, despite a record that seemed designed to lose popular support. By the end of 1958, his third year in office, he had, as has been shown, antagonized major segments of his party, contributed to his party's loss of two Senate seats, made a try for the Democratic presidential nomination after having assured the voters he would be governor for four years, fought with members of his own party in the legislature, offended judges of the Court of Appeals, urged enactment of taxes after declaring himself opposed to new taxes, alienated the state's largest city, and managed to insult farmers and women voters. Yet, as later election results were to show, he remained a formidable political power.

While such clashes and controversies were echoing around Frankfort, Bert Combs was quietly floating trial balloons by speaking before civic clubs, teachers' groups, and chambers of commerce, mainly in mountain towns. On March 19, 1958, he solemnly told a reporter in Prestonsburg that he was not ready to say whether he would make another run for the governorship, but this was a smoke screen. He had made up his mind what he wanted to do if conditions were right and was just debating how best to proceed. He knew he couldn't very well move in any direction as long as there was a chance that Earle Clements might get into the race.

"Then Earle came to the Seventh District and stayed with me," he recalled later. "That was along about the last of March, I guess, 1958. We visited several counties, talking to people. I don't know that we ever said it in so many words, but it was understood that he wanted to run, but if it didn't work out, he would be for me. And that was the way we left it. My loyalty to Earle, who had been my good friend, would have kept me from running if he had decided to.

"What really got me into the race was the rebels. During the last legislative session of Chandler's term some of these rebels—Foster Ockerman, John Breckinridge, Hoppy Hopkins—called and asked me to come down to Frankfort and talk to them. They were looking for a candidate to run against Happy's man, who everyone assumed would be Harry Lee [Waterfield]. I met with them and told them I would run if I had Clements' blessing, but that I wouldn't consider it if Earle wanted to run."

After consulting with some of the rebel legislators in Frankfort, Combs met with Clements in Lexington. "He told me he had decided he wouldn't run, and that he would be for me, and that was about it," Combs recalled. "I felt bad about it in a way. It was a traumatic decision for Earle. Actually, one reason that he finally concluded he couldn't run was that he was having some trouble with taxes; there were rumors about it at the time.

"Then we started talking about who would make a good running mate, and Clements suggested Smith Broadbent. I agreed, but told him I thought Smith wanted the top spot, wanted to run for governor, and Earle said we'd have to talk to him. And from then on we knew what we were working for."

The next day, March 29, Combs announced to the press that "I'm sharply interested in the governor's race. We have a job of house-cleaning to do in Frankfort. If someone else can do it better than I can, I'm for him. Otherwise, I'm for Combs."

Though it was 19 months before election time, it was a foregone conclusion in Frankfort that Lieutenant Governor Harry Lee Water-field would run for governor with Chandler's blessing, and it was assumed that he would be a strong candidate. Tall, likable, quick-smiling, conservative in manner, Waterfield had a firm base in Hickman, in far western Kentucky, and had run a good race for governor against Clements in 1947. He had built a good record in the legislature before becoming lieutenant governor and had kept out of most of Chandler's more publicized fights, though he inevitably bore the mark of the man who would support him for the top job.

There were plenty of anti-Chandlerites willing to run. Among those discussed in the press were former Mayor Wilson Wyatt of Louisville, western Kentucky political power Smith Broadbent, Jr., Rumsey B. Taylor of Princeton, Lexington Mayor Shelby Kinkead, state legislator Foster Ockerman of Lexington, and Dr. Adron Doran, president of Morehead State College.

"It was about the first week in April [actually April 9]," Combs recalled later, "and everybody was talking about getting into the race. A few of us met down at Doc Beauchamp's in Russellville. Earle was there, and Doc and Smith Broadbent. Smith wanted to run. I wanted him to run for second spot with me, and he wanted me to run for second place with him. We weren't getting anywhere. It was getting along in the afternoon, and Doc went into the kitchen for a cup of coffee or something, and came puffing back in, said he'd just heard over the radio that Wilson Wyatt had just announced. I was really surprised, because I thought I had an understanding with Wilson. We had talked, and I had told him I wouldn't run if Earle wanted to, and he told me he wouldn't run if I wanted to. At least that was my understanding. I had met the night before with Dick Moloney and Lawrence Wetherby, who were for Wilson, and I had understood from them that neither of us would announce without further consultation. So the announcement took the wind out of our sails. We all went back to the Seelbach [Hotel, in Louisville] and started trying to figure out what we were going to do now."

(Combs did not think, however, that he had been deceived by Wyatt. "I think maybe I was double-talked a little by Moloney," he said later, "but not by Wilson. He was always straight with me. That's one thing that you can say—we never had a cross word." Years later, he and Wyatt joined forces to establish the state's largest law firm. Wyatt, incidentally, had a somewhat different version of the matter. In his autobiography, *Whistle Stops*, he says: "In the course of considering the race, I had a long, friendly meeting with Bert Combs and ended the session in the belief that he was not going to make the race again.")

Combs had to take Wyatt seriously. Intelligent, urbane, and articulate, with a fine speaking voice and a contagious enthusiasm, Wyatt had a lot going for him, including the support of the Louisville newspapers and many of the state's more liberal and reform-minded Democrats. He had made an outstanding record as the youthful mayor of Louisville, partly because of his success in getting his Louisville program passed in the legislature. He had been active in every presidential nominating convention since 1944, had served as housing expediter under President Harry Truman, was personal campaign manager for Adlai Stevenson in his run for the presidency, and was one of the founders of the liberal Americans for Democratic Action. Though he was basically a conservative, with a profitable legal practice based chiefly on corporate accounts, these activities gave political opponents the chance to label Wyatt an ultraliberal or leftist, an image that would prove a handicap in his campaigns for office.

There was a general optimism in the Wyatt camp. He named J.

David Francis of Bowling Green his campaign manager and opened headquarters in Louisville. "We thought we could get enough momentum to cool the Combs people off," said state Senator Richard Moloney of Lexington, one of Wyatt's more prominent advisers. But the Combs backers, while worrying about Wyatt's move, were not about to be scared out of the race. In a deliberate attempt to carry the fight into Wyatt's camp, Combs opened his headquarters in Louisville on June 30 and put Edward "Ned" Breathitt, a highly regarded young state legislator, in charge. Throughout the fall months the imperturbable Clements, who had made public his support of Combs and his opposition to Wyatt, continued to work on uncommitted Democrats who were opposed to Chandler but unhappy at seeing the split in the anti-Chandler ranks.

For his part, Chandler beamed his satisfaction. "The more the merrier!" he told a press conference, and he heaped scorn on Wyatt, whom he dubbed "Ankle Blankets"—a rustic term, or so he said, for spats, implying that Wyatt was a citified dandy who could not represent the good down-to-earth people of Kentucky. Wyatt said that he had never worn spats and challenged Chandler to supply proof, but the irrepressible Chandler simply laughed and repeated the charge. As a matter of fact, Chandler did not invent the term Ankle Blankets. As far as it can be traced, it was apparently the brainchild of Ruby Laffoon, who used it in his gubernatorial race against Louisville's Billy Harrison.

Curiously, Wyatt later concluded that Chandler had done him a favor. "Happy was most helpful to me, though quite unintentionally," he wrote later. "He was rollicking crowds with charges that I wore spats. . . . I was never privileged to see this show, but Happy has always been a great showman, and I am sure I would have been laughing, too, had I been in the crowd. But [in campaigning] I found that Happy had really prepared the way for me. I encountered thousands of people who one by one would respond, 'Well, if it isn't ole Ankle Blankets. I didn't think you'd come to see us.' I grew very comfortable with the . . . nickname. Long after the campaign was over, Harry Davis, a close friend of Happy's, presented me with the fur-lined ankle blankets Happy had waved from the hustings, and I retain them as a treasured memento."

This statement tells a lot about Wyatt's ebullient, positive nature and his unfailing courtesy in the face of provocation. Happy never reciprocated in like vein, nor was Combs able in later years to regard Happy with the tolerance shown by Wyatt.

Waterfield said simply that he didn't care whether he ran against one or both, but it was obvious that a three-man race improved his chances tremendously. (Actually, a fourth man soon entered the contest: Hubert Carpenter, a quixotic Louisvillian who billed himself "the Poor Man's Candidate.")

Most of the candidates for statewide office turned up on August 2 for the picnic and politicking that is held each year at Fancy Farm, a small hamlet in Graves County in far western Kentucky. Traditionally, following lunch on the grounds—which usually consists of such rural staples as barbecue, cornbread, potato salad, fresh vegetables, watermelon, ice cream, and lemonade—the candidates gather on a raised platform and traipse to the microphone one by one to extol their own virtues and belabor their opponents, with whom they have just been sitting. Fancy Farm has seen and heard some fine political performances in the past, but both the Louisville and Lexington papers gave the 1958 show only lukewarm reviews. Wyatt got fair marks for his "statesmanlike" speech, but Combs was judged to have come closest to a firebrand oration. Waterfield got a solid welcome from the western Kentucky crowd, but few people seemed to recognize Carpenter or understand what he was doing there.

The Combs camp was considerably encouraged by their man's performance on the stump. He seemed more confident, more at ease with his audience and more sure of his material than he had been during his previous race. He tore into Chandler and his record, using some ridicule of his own which got a hooting, hollering reception—the kind that campaign managers like to hear. But at day's end the basic problem remained: with both Combs and Wyatt in the race, Waterfield had the advantage and everyone knew it. The knowledge colored the contest as it drifted into fall.

It was a ticklish time. Combs and Wyatt were rivals but not enemies. They had a common enemy—Chandler. They also had, to a considerable extent, a common political philosophy. More frustrating, they had something of a common constituency. Most of the people who were working for Wyatt had been ardently for Combs four years earlier: Rumsey Taylor, Richard Moloney, Barry Bingham, Golladay LaMotte, Ben Adams, Tyler Munford, Thaxter Sims. And there were people in both camps who realized that the two men had to get together sooner or later, preferably sooner; they could not afford to waste time, money, and effort running against each other. And as the campaign heated up, the relatively polite words the two camps were exchanging were sure to become more pointed, creating wounds that would not heal easily. The trouble was that each man wanted the other to run for lieutenant governor. Both saw, or professed to see, signs that the other was weakening. Charges and rumors flew between the two headquarters. Polls were taken, and the results leaked to the press in hope they would nudge the other man into accepting second place.

On November 5, Combs surprised and puzzled people in both his own and opposing camps by filing for governor, four and a half months before the filing date for the primary. The reason, he explained, was to clarify his position so that he could talk to the people every day between then and the election, but no one took this seriously. He could as easily have talked to the voters every day without having filed. His real reason for filing was obvious; he wanted to send a signal to Wyatt that he was not going to get out of the race or accept second spot on a Wyatt ticket. He emphasized the point by filing again on January 6, 1959, to make sure he was in compliance with the law and to demonstrate once more his determination.

On the same day, Combs followed another honored political tradition by making public the platform of principles on which he intended to run, as Wyatt had done two weeks earlier. It was, and still is, something that candidates do, though it means little. Unions expect a pro-labor plank, minority groups demand a minority rights plank, and business groups sometimes look for pro-business sentiments, but the average voter—probably even members of a candidate's campaign organization—cannot at any given time recite two or more planks in the candidate's platform. Were it not for the media (newsmen love to point later to promises implied in the platform that were not carried out), there would probably be no platforms. Which would be just as well.

The purpose of a platform is to make the candidate appear as pure and idealistic as possible without committing him to anything drastic or making him look naive, and Combs's met these requirements. He promised to rid the state of Chandlerism, take full advantage of federal funds available to Kentucky, enact a merit system, protect government against those who would use it to their own evil advantage, promote Kentucky products, improve schools and roads, energize the department of aeronautics, and go all out to attract industry.

This last is a must. No candidate worth a campaign button would go before the electorate without a promise to attract industry; it has been traditional behavior since World War I. Every contender for public office is expected to imply that he has influence and contacts that will bring to the state vast and numerous industrial plants. If the plants later materialize, he will issue bugle-blast announcements claiming credit for the new jobs thus created. If they do not, he will let federal offices report the bad news.

But the time for such shadow-boxing was running short. Wyatt and Combs met in Cincinnati and talked amiably. "We agreed," said Wyatt, "on everything except who should run for governor." It was time to begin serious campaigning. Money had to be raised, and contributors wanted to know which of the men would be the candidate. As long as both stayed in the race, a lot of smart money would either dry up or go to Waterfield. In fact, two prominent regional leaders had warned Clements that unless either Combs or Wyatt withdrew, they would have to "rethink" their position, which meant that they would protect their future by jumping to Waterfield.

"We had a good organization," Bill May recalled later, "good head-quarters. Bob Martin was chairman. John Keck was there, Ruth Murphy. Of course, Earle was running things—Earle couldn't be in something and not run it—but he and Bob Martin got along. Clements, [Louis] Cox, Wetherby, and I were called the Seelbach Foursome. I was supposed to be raising money, and I was working at it, don't get me wrong. I had become emotionally involved in the campaign, which I never had been in the '55 race. And we were having some trouble along that line, no doubt about it. As long as Wyatt and Combs were both in the race, we were going to face trouble."

Something had to give, and quickly. Something did.

During the final weeks of 1958, Clements had a poll made by a national sampling firm, and it showed about what he suspected and feared: the three-way race was going to elect Waterfield. According to the poll, adjusted to include the undecided voters, Waterfield was favored by 44 percent, Combs by 39, and Wyatt by 17. Clements began applying the pressure, showing the poll results to Dick Moloney, who discussed them with Wyatt. Wyatt asked Robert Burke, a prominent Louisville attorney and Democratic activist, to check the findings of the poll. Burke did, and reported that he could find no error in the methods employed. Wyatt discussed the situation with Barry Bingham, and the two reluctantly acknowledged the unpleasant facts. It was time to talk and probably time to act.

"On the night of January 19th I initiated a call to Earle Clements in Washington," Wyatt wrote in his autobiography. "Without asking any questions, he said he would catch the next plane. All sessions with Earle are lengthy; this one especially so. We met just before midnight at the Standiford Airport Motel, and our conversations continued until eight the next morning. There was one way to compel a merger—make an offer that could not be refused. I would be willing to run for lieutenant governor jointly with Combs if the principles on which I had been running would be fully embraced by Combs. I further stipulated that no punitive measures would be taken against leaders who had supported me, but that they would receive equal treatment as support-

ers of the joint team. . . . I agreed that I would work full time in
Frankfort as lieutenant governor . . . in a fruitful way by my handling
of the work of economic development on which I had placed such great
emphasis in my campaign."

Combs was campaigning at Mount Sterling but rushed back to
confer with Wyatt and Clements. Bingham, Moloney, Burke, and
Martin were in an adjoining room during the evening.

"I had gotten a call from Earle at headquarters," Combs recalled
later, "saying that Wilson was prepared to meet with us and that things
looked promising. Earle and Dick Moloney had called a lot of their key
people to be there, wanted them to be satisfied with what happened,
and through the day people kept coming and going, talking, consulting."

"They must have had 50 sessions," says Bill May. "Earle was
playing the statesman, and he was playing it all the way—'Just want to
be of help to my party and my state; help settle this matter between two
fine men'—all that. I was called into the room with Bert, Earle,
Wilson—I think maybe that was all—Dave Francis, who was Wilson's
chairman, and Bob Martin, Bert's chairman, were there, but not in the
room. I told Wilson I had asked to be on the Racing Commission, and
understood I would be, and he said he had no problem with that."

"Actually, there wasn't a lot for me to do once I got there," said
Combs in a typical understatement. It was a very tense occasion;
everyone present was nervous, excited, aware of the importance of the
moment. Combs seemed to feel that since the crisis was apparently
over, there was no benefit in making a big to-do about it.

"Moloney, Burke, Bingham had pretty well convinced Wilson," he
recalled. "I knew, and I think Wilson knew, that we both had some
people who were close to defecting to Waterfield. As soon as he agreed
that we had to merge, there wasn't much to be done. He didn't ask
much; he wanted me to take care of some of his people, such as Dave
Francis, which was no problem, of course, and he wanted me to agree
that there wouldn't be any reprisals against the people on his campaign
staff. Of course, that was easy. We made Dave a co-chairman, sifted the
other people into headquarters. And we agreed to issue a statement of
principles, which we did that night."

The next day at a joint press conference, Combs and Wyatt announced that they had merged their campaigns. Combs would run for
governor, and Wyatt would run as "a full partner," with assurances that
as lieutenant governor he would devote a major part of his time to
industrial promotion.

"That was about it," said Combs. "After the merger, we traveled together for several weeks, to show people that we really were together in the effort, and that it wasn't a shotgun marriage. Then Wilson went out on his own, and so did I. We could cover more ground, reach more people that way."

There was, naturally, disappointment within the Wyatt ranks but a great deal of relief in both camps. Waterfield declared that the merger made no difference to him. Chandler claimed that he had "scared old Ankle-Blankets out of the race" and exulted that it was good to "get the birds in a bunch where they're easier hit," but no one was fooled. It was a new race.

Chandler had more than a casual stake in the outcome. It would be to his advantage, of course, to have a successor of his own choosing in the mansion. It would enhance his political image and future and, equally important, make it almost certain that he would have the Kentucky delegation behind him at the 1960 Democratic national convention, when once more he hoped to make a bid for the White House.

6

Sounds of a Different Drum

So now the race began. Combs and Wyatt waged a tough campaign. So did Waterfield, and he gave notice early on that he was going to be no pushover. His opening at Murray on February 25, 1959, drew an enthusiastic crowd that overflowed the local auditorium. Knowing that Combs and Wyatt were going to tie him to Chandler, Waterfield sought to blunt their attack by tying them to Clements, whom he painted as a scheming dictator, seeking to regain power through his puppet, Combs. He depicted Combs as a man without qualification or experience, spurred on by hatred and resentment over his 1955 defeat. He also had some shots for Wyatt, the "big city candidate" and "tool of the *Courier-Journal*."

Still, it remained a fairly high-level contest. Both Combs and Waterfield were men of dignity and manners; they referred to each other as Judge Combs and Lieutenant Governor Waterfield. But during the last week of April, Chandler announced that he was ready to go out and campaign for Waterfield, assuming that Waterfield wanted his help. Waterfield had little choice in the matter; Chandler was raising money for him, primarily through assessments on state employees. It probably would have been impossible to keep Happy out of the fight, though in light of the returns it appears that Chandler hurt as much as he helped. Where Waterfield needed assistance most—in Louisville and Jefferson County, the populous Third District where Combs and Wyatt were strong—Chandler could be of little use: he was notedly unpopular in Jefferson.

With Chandler's active entry, the campaign took on a somewhat more carnival-like atmosphere. He still referred to Wyatt as "Ankle Blankets" and Combs as "the Little Judge," "an innocent bystander," "this little fella," attempting to make him appear the incompetent tool of Clements and Wetherby, whom he again ridiculed as "Clementine and Wetherbine." But this was familiar stuff, and Combs was no longer the shy, inarticulate mountain lawyer. The ridicule did not seem to fit as well.

The Combs camp got into the act with some ridicule of its own. A sure laugh-getter was what became known as the Crippled Goose, a term that Combs invented. During his second term, Chandler had been charged with shooting a game bird after sundown in the Ballard Wildlife Preserve in western Kentucky, although he protested that he had not been told he was hunting after the legal hour of sundown, which the law forbade. But as such things tend to do, the story grew into an account of how Happy shot a goose on the ground, a goose that had been crippled by another hunter. People speaking for Combs made snide references to Chandler's prowess with firearms, linking it with his failure to serve in either of the world wars. Cartoons showed Chandler clubbing a terrified, wounded goose. Once, during a Waterfield rally, someone loosed a frightened, squawking goose, its wing bandaged and painted red, down the aisle of the hall where he was speaking.

Combs also had what headquarters referred to as his "Castro speech," which was aimed at Chandler rather than Waterfield and usually drew a good laugh from anti-Chandler audiences. At the time of the campaign the state had no merit system to protect state workers; the governor had a constitutional right to hire and fire state employees, and as a result he could usually persuade people on the state payroll to vote for his choice. The governor also could, and usually did, assess state workers a percentage of their pay for a campaign chest, a fact that gave the incumbent an almost insurmountable advantage. Using the votes of thousands of state workers and their families and the slush fund built from their payroll deductions, a governor could often choose his successor.

Chandler, Combs charged, had squeezed millions of dollars from the defenseless workers by a 2 percent assessment on their paychecks, a practice that he, Combs, promised to end with a properly legislated merit system. (Chandler had imposed a merit system of sorts in the final year of his administration by executive order. But, as Combs pointed out, a merit system created by executive order could be canceled by a similar order.) Not wanting to put these funds into a state bank, where they could be traced, Chandler allegedly had cabinet member Vego Barnes (known as Virtuous Vego) deposit the money in a Cuban bank. There, with the revolution, it fell into the hands of Castro, who allegedly pocketed it as the spoils of war. Combs painted a piteous picture of Happy standing on a Florida beach, peering out over the ocean with tears running down his cheeks, crying, "Castro! Castro! Send back my 2 percent!"

This, like the more serious talks, bore the mark of Edward Fretwell Prichard, Jr., the brilliant Frankfort attorney who was working at head-

quarters and trying to rebuild a shattered career. From being something of a boy genius in his native Paris, Prichard had achieved an
enviable reputation in Kentucky and in the national Democratic party.
Entering Princeton at 16, he became a campus celebrity, graduated first
in his class, and created a furor among the faculty when he entered
Harvard Law School, where again he graduated at the top of his class.
He became a clerk to Supreme Court Justice Felix Frankfurter, was
hired as an assistant to Sidney Hillman in the White House, and by the
time he was 24 was a wartime adviser to President Franklin D. Roosevelt.

After the war he had come home to Kentucky and established a
promising law career in Lexington when, in a pointless and arrogant
prank, he helped stuff 233 ballots into 11 Bourbon County ballot boxes
in the 1948 election. He was subsequently tried, found guilty, and sent
to federal prison. Though he was pardoned by President Harry
Truman after serving a few months, the incident blasted his hopes of a
political career, and he was only beginning to regain his equilibrium
and plan a future when Earle Clements recruited him to help in the
Combs 1955 campaign. It was Prichard's first step in establishing
himself as one of the foremost political intellects in the state.

"Prich had worked some in the 1955 campaign," said Combs, "and
we were glad to see him when he came in in '59. I don't know that I ever
talked to him about it. He just wanted to come to headquarters, be a
part of the campaign. He knew he was welcome. I don't know what we
paid him. Not much. Paid his expenses, of course, and enough for
walking-around money.

"Prich hung around headquarters in '55 doing research, writing
speeches, doing P.R. At that time he was almost an outcast. No one
running for office wanted anything to do with him. If he stuck his head
above water they would holler 'jailbird!' He was still battling himself,
disappearing sometimes for three or four days or longer. He just
seemed to want to hole up, hide until he got over his black mood. But
he could turn out a good speech almost any time, and he knew who he
was writing for. In the '59 race, he was very valuable. He worked with
Clements, Bob Martin, Ruth Murphy, June Taylor, Jo Westpheling.
Everybody said he was worth his pay just for keeping Geneva Blue and
Jo Westpheling from coming to blows. Jo and Geneva were co-chairper-
sons for women. Geneva was the cheerleader sort, would sing 'God
Bless America' at meetings. Westpheling was a back-room operator,
and a damned good one."

The venom with which many Democrats, as well as Republicans,
lashed out at Prichard reflected more than a moral revulsion at his

political crime. The fact is that Prichard, an avowed liberal identified with the more liberal elements of the national Democratic party, threatened the conservative hold on the state Democratic party if he should gain influence in the governor's office. The more fundamentalist elements of the party were secretly delighted at his downfall, and were intent on seeing that he did not recover enough to regain power.

Significantly, one of the more vocal critics of Prichard was Chandler, who later, during Combs's effort to call a convention to revise the state constitution, lashed out at Prichard as a jailbird. In tones of scorn, Prichard replied: "It is true that I have served time in the federal reformatory. I have associated with murderers, robbers, rapists and forgers, criminals of all kinds, and let me say, my friends, that every one of them was the moral superior of A.B. Happy Chandler."

Combs was waging what is usually called a vigorous campaign, which meant that he traveled a lot, spoke a lot, huddled with local politicians early in the morning and late at night, ate whatever the local committees put before him, and slept when schedule permitted. It was a grueling regimen, hard on him, hard on his drivers—Dix Winston of Paducah and Johnny Green of Sandy Hook—and hard on his nephew Buddy Combs, who traveled with him to handle arrangements, public address systems, and the like.

He had decided to center his fire on Chandler, though his strategy board at headquarters warned him that if he wanted to beat Waterfield, he would have to fight Waterfield. Combs knew that ordinarily this was proper operating procedure, but in this case he figured that Chandler was an easy target, whereas Waterfield was a pleasant man with a generally good image who had not been too closely identified with Chandler's more unpopular moves. It is also likely that Combs was taking a little revenge. Chandler had ridiculed Combs in their previous encounter in a way that a sensitive man was not likely to forget.

Wyatt, meanwhile, had been obliged to change his tactics radically; before the merger he had been attacking factionalism in the state Democratic party, since Combs and Waterfield represented the two traditional factions, the Clements and Chandler wings of the party. But now he was a standard-bearer for one of those factions, and he had no choice but to join Combs in the attack on the other, though usually he tried to take the high road and emphasize the promises inherent in the platform.

Whether he had, or could have, made any headway with the factionalism issue is questionable. The fact is that Kentuckians have long had a suicidal affection for their factions, which permit them to stay in their old party without paying any attention to its principles.

Perhaps for this reason, Kentucky Democrats fight their internecine primary battles with relish and ferocity, and often it seems that the hotter the primary the better the party showing in the general election. Since the Civil War, the factions have been the natural outgrowth of political and economic forces in a poor state, as well as the political expression of a highly divided state. Kentucky often gives its support to Republican presidential candidates and frequently sends Republicans to the U.S. Senate, at the same time electing a Democratic governor and legislature, demonstrating the fact that the conservative wing of the Democratic party can (and often does) easily accommodate itself in Republican ranks. The Chandler faction, like the Johnson or Cantrill factions before it, appealed emotionally to Democrats and philosophically to Republicans. But the basic pattern of Democratic dominance prevailed throughout the early years of the current century and was intensified when Franklin D. Roosevelt's New Deal cut deeply into Republican strength in the mountains of eastern Kentucky and in Louisville.

Just as the Democratic party—and, indeed, the state's politics in general—was basically southern in structure, so was it southern in nature until well into this century, occasionally liberal in national elections, often agrarian and conservative in state races. Fiscally, it was conservative. Its candidates preached the sanctity of pay-as-you-go financing, opposing bond issues and deficit financing, and denouncing taxes and strong government as instruments of the devil. Thus, though the Democrats did obeisance to the virtue of good roads and good schools, the state was cursed with some of the nation's worst roads and schools because it would not impose enough taxes to modernize them.

In this respect, Happy Chandler was firmly in the tradition of the great southern politicos—a colorful orator with a keen understanding of people's emotions, prejudices, and sense of place, appealing to their love of tradition and fear of change and their resentment of heavy taxation. Chandler boasted of his ability to cut taxes—though he usually raised some as much or more than he cut others—and excoriated those who would plunge the state into debt. As a result, Kentucky had fallen behind the southern and border states that issued bonds with which to modernize roads and universities, thus attracting the industry that Kentucky so badly needed.

Earle Clements made several breaks with this tradition when he instituted his two-cent gasoline tax to finance rural roads, adopted a bond-and-rental technique for financing buildings to house state offices, and managed to raise the state salary limit. But the tradition of southern politics lived on during Chandler's term and was still alive when Bert Combs took to the hustings for the first time. More by instinct than by deliberate design, he was trying to change the pattern. He failed in that first attempt. But in the four years between his first and second tries at the governorship, he had time to study the historic record and its implications, and when he began his second race, he was determined to move the state out of the old southern tradition and into the modern era. Fortunately for his chances, he did not say so; he had learned much about the nature of Kentuckians during his first race for governor, and, as he later said, there is no education in the second kick of a mule.

Rather, he was adopting something of the Chandler technique of personalizing the campaign. Instead of pegging away at the state's needs and his plans for meeting those needs, he devoted much of his effort to an attack on Chandler. It was a negative campaign that he did not particularly like and that Wyatt had frequently criticized before the merger, but it was effective. Furthermore, as long as he stayed on the attack, his opponents were forced to spend a lot of their time answering him and thus found it harder to push him into a corner on such matters as taxes.

And taxes were still a very sore point. The 1958 legislature had voted to put on the ballot a proposal that the state pay a bonus to veterans of the Spanish-American War, World Wars I and II, and the Korean conflict, to be financed by a state sales tax. The referendum did not specify the amount of bonus to be paid or the size of the tax to be levied for its support, and it was thus a doubly ticklish issue for the candidates. Both Combs and Waterfield tried to ignore the whole matter, bonus and tax. It was not on the primary ballot. But it loomed large in the minds of many voters and in press commentary. Congress had opted earlier for the G.I. Bill—which offered veterans training, education, and low-interest loans to help them get started on a civilian career—calling a bonus a poor way to reward the men who had fought for their country, a handout that would soon be frittered away without materially compensating the veteran for the years lost from his career or improving his ability to deal with the future. But Kentucky veterans were hungry for cash, and few voices other than those of some newspaper editorialists were raised against the bonus plan.

It was especially tough for Combs because he was receiving fire on the matter from two sides. Out on the campaign trail, Chandler and Waterfield were baying at his heels, warning the voters that Combs was planning to ruin them with unnecessary taxes. And from his campaign headquarters in the Seelbach, Combs was getting regular and in-

creasingly urgent demands that he come out in flat opposition to the
sales tax.

"The newspapers and the radio were carrying these stories, big
headlines, of Happy and Harry Lee charging that Combs was going to
put all sorts of taxes on people," recalled Ed Prichard. "They were
saying that the bonus was just a trick of his to get the people to vote for a
sales tax. That was silly, of course, since Happy and Harry Lee were in
office when the referendum was voted, and Bert wasn't even in Frankfort. But it was getting a lot of attention, forcing Bert onto the defensive,
and people in headquarters were getting worried. They wanted Bert to
come out and oppose the sales tax. Ruth Murphy and Cattie Lou Miller,
and to an extent Bob Martin, the campaign manager, were getting all
excited.

"Well, they finally got to Clements, convinced him it was a crisis.
Earle had a tendency to see everything as critical anyhow, so they held
a big strategy meeting. Big meeting. Bob Matthews was there, Henry
Ward, Martin, Clements. They were all saying what they should do
about the sales tax, when old Ernest Thompson came loping down the
hall. Ernest had been on the public teat most of his life, half a century, I
guess, sheriff, jailer over in Lexington, whatall. He had been a Clements man until he saw Happy was going to win in '55 and jumped to
Chandler. Got a job on the ABC [Alcoholic Beverage Control Board]—I
think he was commissioner—but then he thought Harry Lee was going
to lose so he hopped over to Combs. (Ernest, said Combs, was like an
old coon dog—he'd hunt with anybody who carried a lantern.) Well,
Earle pointed to him and said, 'Now, here is our good friend Ernest,
who knows more about politics than any of us,' which of course wasn't
true, just knew enough to know how to jump from one slippery log to
another without falling off. . . . Went on like that for a while, and then
said, 'Now, Mr. Thompson, what would you advise in a case like this?'

"Well, Ernest sat there paring his thumbnail with this little pen-
knife—he had a double thumbnail, peculiar-looking thing, and he
would whittle at it. So he sat there whittling at it for a minute, then he
looked up and said in this very important voice, 'Don't let 'em hang it
on ya.' That was it; that was the wisdom of ages—'Don't let 'em hang it
on ya.' But everyone nodded his head and looked thoughtful and said
yes, that was the solution. After a while, of course, someone said,
'Hell, that doesn't make any sense,' and everybody said that's right. So
they still had to decide what to do, so they got on the phone and called
Bert and begged him to disavow the bonus and the tax, or at least the
tax."

This Combs refused to do. Instead, he issued a statement, which he later incorporated into his speeches, saying that he didn't want to impose a sales tax or any other tax but that he wasn't going to disavow it until he saw how people voted on the bonus, that he had heard other governors swear they wouldn't raise taxes and then be embarrassed by the disavowal once they got into office, and that he wasn't going to do it, wasn't going to lie to the people. "It was the best statement made during the campaign," said Ed Prichard. "People credited me with it, but he wrote it himself." Prichard's statement is significant: more and more, Combs was making up his own mind, setting his own policies, issuing his own statements.

It was a hard campaign. Waterfield, a decent, intelligent, sincere man who later amassed a fortune in the insurance business and became a prominent civic leader in Frankfort, ran a good race. He had the usual advantages of an administration candidate: a campaign chest compiled from assessments on the paychecks of state employees, support of at least a majority of state workers, and a ready-made organization in every county. He was an earnest, able speaker with a strong following in the western part of the state (known as the Gibraltar of Democracy). He also had the support of Chandler, though in retrospect he might have done better without it. Frequently, when introducing Harry Lee, Happy would get carried away and usurp the occasion. A campaign crowd drew him as inexorably as swift water draws a spawning fish; it was instinctive. But some observers wondered if his appearances did not make it seem that he, not Waterfield, was the candidate, just as he had previously charged that Combs was no more than a puppet for Clements. And the more Chandler orated, the better target he presented for Combs and the more he invited the charge that Waterfield was only a stooge.

It was not the most intellectual campaign ever waged. An undue amount of time was spent on references to crippled geese, Castro, ankle blankets, and the little judge. During the last week of the race Waterfield's Jefferson County officials, apparently without Waterfield's knowledge, ran an ad in the *Courier-Journal* so scurrilous that the newspaper published an editorial apologizing for having to print it. Briefly, it tied Combs and Wyatt to the *Courier-Journal*, which supported them and for which Wyatt was general counsel; the paper had once had in its employ Carl Braden, a reporter who had been accused of Communist sympathies and who had been convicted of sedition before the state's sedition law was declared unconstitutional by the Supreme Court. Somehow the ad managed in this way to tie Combs and Wyatt to the Communist forces that had killed American men in Korea, concluding: "Remember—it may be you or your son who is called next to make the supreme sacrifice in another Korea." This was undoubtedly the low point in the campaign and probably hurt Waterfield.

In the closing days of the race, both sides made the usual predictions of lopsided victory, all of which proved wrong. On May 27, 559,700 Democrats voted in the primary, a record total, and gave Combs a winning margin of 33,001 votes—292,462 to 259,461—29,624 of which came from Jefferson County, where Combs undoubtedly benefited from the popular dislike of Chandler, the appeal of Wyatt, and the work of the Fourth Street Organization. Outside the county his edge over Waterfield was 3,377 votes. Hardly a landslide. (Incidentally, Bracken County, which had a record extending over half a century of voting with the winner, again picked the winner, casting 1,289 votes for Combs and 1,070 for Waterfield.) Wyatt rolled over his chief opponent, J.B. Wells of Paintsville, by more than 150,000 votes. Republican John M. Robsion, Jr., rode to an expected victory over only token opposition in his race for the GOP gubernatorial nomination, as did Pleas Mobley of Manchester for second spot.

It was in many respects a curious election. A pattern, a persuasive indication of voter attitudes toward competing factions or philosophies, was hard to find. For example, Wendell Butler, a nonaligned candidate for superintendent of public instruction, beat Carlos Oakley, who was slated with Combs. Emerson "Doc" Beauchamp, a strong Combs man, swamped a handful of rivals for commissioner of agriculture, as did pro-Combs Henry Carter in his race for secretary of state. But pro-Chandler Thelma Stovall won over Pearl Runyon, of the Combs slate, for state treasurer.

Furthermore, except for Jefferson County (Louisville), Combs and Waterfield had almost divided the state evenly. Waterfield carried the First, Fourth, Sixth, and Eighth Districts, Combs the Second, Third, Fifth, and Seventh. But, as a Kentucky candidate must to win, Combs carried the cities—Louisville, Bowling Green, Owensboro, Paducah, Covington, Newport, and Ashland. Waterfield carried Henderson, Frankfort, and Lexington. Waterfield had counted on and seemed likely to get an overwhelming vote of support from his home First District; Combs had hoped for the same from the Seventh. Neither got it. Waterfield carried the First by only 6,161 votes; Combs carried the Seventh by 11,721.

The outpouring of Democratic votes for the primary gave the Republicans little room for optimism. Republican Senator Thruston Morton, citing the bitterness of the Combs-Chandler split and acknowledging the importance of Chandler's help to him in his successful race against Earle Clements in 1956, declared that another

Democratic split was possible. Harry Lee Waterfield, however, soon put a damper on such hopes with a generous and courteous statement of concession and congratulations, which he sent to Combs before the vote-counting had been completed. His campaign manager, Frankfort Attorney Joseph Leary, paid a visit to Combs headquarters the day after the election, was warmly welcomed, and set about laying the groundwork for a unified campaign. Chandler was stunned by the defeat, which was, in effect, the second handed him by the voters of Kentucky, though he had not himself been the candidate. Combs had made him the chief issue of the campaign and had won on it, but Chandler would not, could not, admit it. "It looks like the Little Judge blew in on Ankle Blankets' coattails," he said, referring to the heavy vote in Jefferson County. He said he would do "something the others haven't done" and support the nominees, although before he "could be enthusiastic for them, they would have to take back some of the vicious lies the Little Judge told about me." But he refused to send a message to Combs, complaining that he had never received congratulations from Combs in 1955 (Combs disputed this).

Still, Chandler did not see the vote as an indication that things had changed. On the contrary, he issued a straight-faced statement that the outcome of the voting "looks like an overwhelming approval of what we have given the people." This ability to interpret the enemy's victory as a victory for himself tells a lot about the resiliency of the man. He told reporters that he still had a good chance to be the state's favorite son at the approaching presidential nominating convention. And he warned that he might "come back in 1963 and clean them all out—if I'm not busy doing something else. [This was probably a reference to the rumor that Senator Thruston Morton was planning to retire and devote himself to Republican National Committee matters, opening the door to let Chandler resign the governorship and take appointment to the Senate, as he had done before.] The people will be tired of them by then." But a tide was running that Chandler would not be able again to withstand.

Combs ignored the Chandler remarks; to the inner circle of his campaign workers, he appeared more amused than irritated by the governor. As he headed into the general election campaign, Combs remained, to the public and to much of the press, an enigma. In some ways, he seemed the same quiet, reticent man he had always been; in others, he seemed considerably different. As Richard Harwood, political analyst for the *Louisville Times*, wrote late in the campaign: "This year . . . he was a new Combs in terms of style and platform manner. But in terms of basic personality he was still the Combs of 1955. He never lost the reticence and reserve that keep both the public and the people with whom he works at arm's length. If he has ever bared his innermost thoughts to political associates, it is not recorded. If he has any favored confidants, they are unknown. He keeps a tight rein on his emotions. He took his licking in 1955 without a flicker of pain. And he won over Waterfield this year with no more show of emotion."

The campaign of the fall of 1959 was a lackluster affair. John M. Robsion, Jr., was an affable man and able lawyer. The son of a legendary mountain congressman, Robsion had himself served in Congress, compiling a record of consistent support for Republican causes. He was well liked by Republicans and waded into the race with energy. But he was a rather colorless candidate, offering little that was new or unusual to attract the attention of the voter, and as the summer wore away, there were no signs that he or the other GOP candidates were making inroads on the Democrats. To their credit, both Robsion and Combs agreed in the early days of the campaign that racial integration was not an issue between them and not a matter for debate, thus removing a question that could have marred the campaign while injecting some fireworks. Like Chandler, Robsion insisted that Combs had plans to impose a sales tax and promised that he would oppose all tax increases. He warned that Clements would become highway commissioner, were Combs elected, and would have undue influence in state affairs. And he demanded that Combs explain where he would get the money to finance the increased spending for the parks, schools, and roads that he said he would provide.

The redoubtable John Sherman Cooper campaigned vigorously for Robsion. President Truman came to Paducah to urge support for Combs. But the nearest thing to real fireworks was produced when Chandler, on October 23, refused to go to Paducah to welcome Truman. Instead, Chandler, who had promised to support the party nominees "as I always have," unleashed a blistering attack on Combs, Wyatt, and Clements. In a letter to the president, he charged that Wyatt, who had served in the Truman administration, was not a Democrat and had tried to betray Truman by helping found the Americans for Democratic Action, and that Combs and Clements were "bolters." Clements, he said, was "a bolter and liar and always has been," and "Combs is the biggest liar I ever met," adding that "the salvation of the state might well depend on his getting beat."

The venom of this attack on his party's nominees, which officials in the Combs campaign condemned as an open bolt, was an indication of the pain Chandler felt in defeat. It was also evidence of the almost mystical way in which he viewed his political destiny. When Combs and Clements were lukewarm in their support of his gubernatorial campaign in 1955, they were bolters. When he, Chandler, denounced Combs and Clements and called for Combs's defeat, he was a loyal party man.

Truman, whose wartime Senate investigating committee had examined Chandler's wartime dealings with local contractors, did not mention Chandler's blast in his Paducah address. The Democratic state committee, made up almost entirely of Chandler appointees, failed to put any money into the Combs campaign. And Robsion used the Chandler denunciation to warn that a Combs administration would be torn between Democratic factions and devoted to higher taxes.

Robsion might have had a strong issue in the tax charges had the ballot not contained the proposed constitutional amendment authorizing a veterans' bonus and a sales tax to finance it. That pretty well took the teeth out of the charge that Combs was the one planning to impose a sales tax. Neither did the other proposed amendment—to permit sheriffs to succeed themselves—offer either candidate an advantage, since neither had endorsed it and it was believed likely to lose in any case.

So the results of the November 4 voting followed predictions. Combs beat Robsion by 180,093 votes, 516,549 to 336,456, a record for a governor's race in Kentucky and second to the all-time record set in 1932 when Franklin D. Roosevelt swamped Herbert Hoover in their race for the presidency by 185,858 votes. The bonus amendment was approved by 38,039 votes; the sheriff succession amendment lost by 7,008. Robsion beat Combs by 338 votes in his home county of Jefferson, one of the 27 counties he carried (to Combs's 93), while Wyatt in Jefferson was beating Mobley by 11,722. The fact that Combs lost Jefferson County to Robsion, after carrying it so substantially over Waterfield, probably showed Chandler's unpopularity more than Robsion's popularity.

Combs was in no mood to let one county ruffle him. Asked by reporters about his reaction to the Jefferson loss and to Chandler's preelection statement that a Combs defeat would help Kentucky, Combs merely said, "I never argue with my Governor. He may have a point. He's had a lot of good programs."

The jubilation at Combs headquarters was noticeably less than it had been after the primary election, partly because of awareness of the job ahead. Combs and Robsion exchanged cordial messages of congratulations and condolence. Combs began a series of meetings with the leaders of the approaching legislative session and with people he had in mind for his administration. One of the most interesting meetings, however, took place in the Rathskeller of the Seelbach on the morning after the election.

"Clements and I met with a group of engineers who had worked with me on the [Mountain] parkway," recalled Bill May. "I can't claim credit for the idea of the parkway. People for 50 years had been wanting a road from the mountains into Lexington. When I was a boy in Prestonsburg, we didn't know anything about Lexington or Louisville because you couldn't get there. Today you go to Lexington and the shopping centers are full of people from the mountains. The parking lot at Bluegrass Field is crowded with cars of people from the mountains flying out of there.

"But the idea for the parkway belonged to Henry Spalding, up at Hazard. Years before, he had drawn the lines for a highway from the Big Sandy to the Bluegrass, and was always trying to promote it. When Bert began running the second time, in '59, I talked to him about the parkway, and he committed himself to the idea in a rough way. Nothing formal. But I went ahead with plans for it just as if it was going to be built, and at a rally in Prestonsburg, two or three days before the primary, he promised to build it.

"So in August I got with Henry Spalding and persuaded him and Hazlitt and Erdahl, another engineering firm that had had experience here in Kentucky, and together we got three or four firms to gamble that Combs would be elected, and together we started the preliminary work on the parkway, making the maps, surveys, marking the route. It was a big gamble. If Bert hadn't been elected, or if he had changed his mind about the road, we would have been out a lot of money; we'd had a lot of men working a lot of months on those plans. By the time Bert was elected we had the route pinned down. The morning after the election, we all met in the Rathskeller, and we thanked them for their faith, and asked them to keep on working. Which they did. I'd say it saved us about a year when we started building it."

"A lot of the credit for the parkway should also go to B.F. Reed," Combs said later. "He was at that time chairman of the East Kentucky Regional Planning Commission, and a mountains-to-Bluegrass road had always been part of their plan. John Whisman, who was in on the commission, and Reed sold me on the idea, although May and his people went ahead with it."

Combs took a brief vacation. He had been campaigning hard for almost two years and needed the rest. But by the middle of November he was working on a budget, choosing people for his administration, preparing for the critical first session of the legislature. And already, storm clouds were forming. Associated Industries of Kentucky (AIK), a

state industrial lobbying group, had announced with a blast of publicity that it would challenge the constitutionality of the veterans'
bonus and the sales tax to finance it. The suit caused Combs to
announce that he would delay submitting his proposed budget to the
legislature until the others could rule on the constitutionality of the
amendment.

7

The Ducks Line Up

The inauguration of Bert Thomas Combs and Wilson Watkins Wyatt on a cold, cloudy December afternoon was more a demonstration of the raucous, rowdy nature of Kentucky's Democratic party than a display of governmental dignity and pageantry. Frankfort, with its twisting, steep streets, is not an ideal place for a parade, but no inauguration is complete without one, and Combs's was no exception. Democrats, an estimated 40,000 of them—representing a wide range of philosophic persuasions, all parts of the Commonwealth, and varying degrees of sobriety—shivered, shuffled, and shouted their way along the line of march. An open car bearing Combs and Chandler was followed by a similar vehicle carrying Wyatt and Waterfield, protocol demanding that the erstwhile enemies pretend, for a little hour, to be reconciled under the mellowing banner of the party. The charade was to last little longer than the parade.

It is customary for the departing governor to give a valedictory of sorts, expressing the hope that history will treat him gently and wishing his successor well. Happy Chandler was not one to let such an opportunity pass, nor was he content with a mere hail and farewell. Apparently still smarting from the Combs victory, he mounted the inaugural platform as though it were a campaign stump, claimed that he had given Kentucky an administration to light the ages, declared that he had left the state in splendid fiscal condition, with a huge surplus at Combs's disposal, and generally implied that a mistake had been made by the voters. The pro-Combs crowd, angry at having such a sour note played during their victory march, responded in a raucous fashion, and when he warned that "I may just be back" if things did not go to suit him, there was a storm of derision, hoots, and cries of "No! No!" "Go home, Happy!' and other shouts unbefitting the departure of a chief of state. (During the ceremonies, Combs was approached by a worried-looking state trooper who whispered that the police had reports of a man who "says he's going to shoot that sonofabitch." Combs looked at him with a poker face. "Which sonofabitch is he talking about?" he asked.)

But that was the only sour note in the inaugural song. In recognition of the "team victory" of Combs and Wyatt, the latter became the first lieutenant governor to give an inaugural address, a brief but eloquent contrast to Chandler's remarks. "Happy, of course, was seated on the platform," Wyatt wrote later. "I started my remarks by turning toward him and saying, 'Happy, this is a report from Ankle Blankets on the condition of the plowed ground.' He took the ribbing as a compliment and joined in the roar of the crowd." (Apparently, Wilson Wyatt is one of those blessed souls who view the past through rose-tinted glasses. Others who recall that chilly occasion of which he writes will remember that Mr. Chandler responded to Wyatt's remarks with the smile of a man being told a joke on the gallows.) Wyatt then declared that "the secret of a campaign is how to win without proving oneself unworthy of it. By politics we win our victories, by statesmanship we deserve them. There is no greater obligation than that imposed by democracy on those chosen to lead. Only through our best efforts, our best intellect, our best conscience, will we prove equal to our task."

Next, Combs gave the crowd cause for rejoicing when he spoke of the fine victory behind and the bright days ahead. He noted with wry humor that his reading of the figures of the state's treasury condition was somewhat different from that of Chandler (prompting another round of catcalls), but he promised to do, generally, the things he had promised to do during the campaign. Then he and Wyatt placed their hands on the Bible, swore that they had not fought or taken part in a duel, vowed to uphold the laws of state and nation, and were sworn into office—Combs as the forty-sixth governor of the Commonwealth and the first World War II veteran to hold the post. The throng broke up and began preparations for the inaugural ball and the dozens of parties that would consume the night and usher in a new regime. Then it was time for Combs and Wyatt to get down to business.

The first order of business was a press conference. Combs and Wyatt faced a battery of about 75 reporters, but if either man was reluctant or uneasy, it was not noticeable. On the contrary, Allan Trout of the *Courier-Journal* and Richard Harwood of the *Louisville Times* commented the next day on Combs's composure and seeming familiarity with the procedure. There was, noted Harwood, none of the diffident mountain judge about the new governor, who acted as though "he had long been accustomed to the governor's chair. Relaxed and seemingly confident, Combs fielded questions with the ease of an old pro, answering most questions forthrightly, casually admitting when he did not know an answer or had not made up his mind on a matter. Yes, he said, he intended to fire some people, and hire some 'in whom we have faith,' in other words, political allies. He pointed out that legislative action on the sales tax and veterans' bonus would depend on whether the courts upheld the referendum approving the bonus and the enabling tax. He announced a dozen appointments, promised to operate the A.B. Chandler Medical Center at the University of Kentucky according to plan, and said that he had in mind a broad plan of roads, parks, and other things still being designed for the improvement of the economy of eastern Kentucky." In all, Combs got good reviews on his first performance, and seemed rather pleased with it himself.

Combs was determined to do something about Kentucky's constitution—that crippling document written in 1891 when farmers distrusted townspeople and banks and business, businessmen distrusted the farmers, Democrats and Republicans distrusted each other, eastern Kentucky distrusted the Bluegrass and most of the rest of the state, and the Bluegrass resented Louisville, which considered the rest of the state backward. Agricultural western Kentucky and mountainous eastern Kentucky felt left out of government programs, and to an extent their feelings were justified. Eastern Kentucky was still torn by feuds. It is not surprising that a constitution written at such a time was a collection of laws designed to curb the power of Frankfort rather than a blueprint for the efficient functioning of representative government.

And the men who had written the constitution had made sure that it would not be changed suddenly. Two separate legislatures had to approve submitting to the voters a proposal to call a convention to revise the constitution; the following session could make the call. Or the constitution could be amended by popular vote after the amendments were approved and submitted by the Assembly, but only two amendments could be voted on at one time, making amendment a slow process. So suspicious of each other were Kentuckians that these laborious processes seldom succeeded. Voters had refused for 68 years to approve an amendment that would permit sheriffs to succeed themselves; only 19 amendments had been approved; and twice—in 1931 and 1947—voters had turned down proposals for a convention. No matter how dramatically the constitution was shown to handicap government, the people rushed to its defense.

Reform elements within the state had for 20 years been clamoring for a convention, and it had been part of Bert Combs's plans; now he sought a way to hold such a convention within his four-year term. It was the opinion of his lawyers that it would require two separate sessions of the General Assembly to put before the voters a proposal to call a convention. So on December 19 Combs sent out a call for a special session. Since the legislators were not expressing approval or disapproval of a convention but simply agreeing to let the following regular session put the matter to a popular vote, the proposal was quickly approved. It was a minor victory, but it set a positive tone for the approaching regular session.

With that out of the way, Combs turned his attention to a task that is always a complicated and important one for a new governor: finding people for his cabinet, the men who will run the departments of government and whose performance will do much to set the tone of the administration, determine the level of service the people get, and help shape the governor's image. Finding good men for these jobs is not easy. The offices are demanding, pay little, and seldom earn the official much credit. Worse, they are temporary; at the end of four years the officials find themselves looking for jobs. Department heads are always under pressure to hire and fire, to give orders or contracts to the politically faithful. All other things being equal, if all qualifications are roughly the same, there is nothing wrong in choosing a political ally over an outsider or opponent, but any loading of the scales is likely to bring down the media or an investigation. And if a department head stumbles and a scandal erupts, the governor is tarred along with him. As Combs would discover.

Where does a governor find competent men and women willing to take the risks of such temporary employment? A lot of them come from the campaign force; others are recommended by supporters and contributors. Some are young, bright, ambitious, eager for media exposure and reputation; some are veterans who know where bodies are buried. Political savvy is a prime virtue. For example, Combs chose Cattie Lou Miller, who had been secretary to Clements and Wetherby and had worked at Combs headquarters, as executive assistant—not just because she was a loyal Democrat but because she knew Kentucky politics, knew legislative routine, knew which person should be permitted to see the governor and which one should be given an excuse, which phone call was really urgent and which one was a nuisance. Later Combs would appoint her commissioner of public information, the first woman to hold a commissioner's post in Kentucky.

He called on Robert Matthews, a former assistant attorney general from Shelbyville, to be a top assistant; and Wendell Ford, Owensboro insurance man, to be his administrative assistant. William Scent, of Paducah and Louisville, would serve as revenue boss; Dr. Robert

Martin, previous superintendent of public instruction, became finance commissioner; Dr. Arthur Y. Lloyd became adjutant general; Foster Ockerman, Lexington lawyer, was named motor transportation commissioner; and Edward Breathitt, a young Hopkinsville lawyer, legislator, and descendant of a governor and lieutenant governor, was named personnel commissioner. Marshall Qualls accepted the post of conservation commissioner, to be succeeded later by J.O. Matlick, who pioneered in shaping strip-mine control regulations. Frankfort newsman Philip Swift became aeronautics commissioner. Carlos Oakley, a Clements ally, was named welfare commissioner, an appointment that proved controversial. (Oakley had run for superintendent of public instruction and had lost in the primary to Wendell Butler, much to the chagrin of Clements. He had depended on Dr. Robert Martin to line up teachers in support of Oakley; when the returns came in, he turned and said to Martin, "Doctor, your influence, I say, your influence with the school people is onionskin thin.")

As part of his drive to clear the decks before the legislative battle began, Combs issued two executive orders. He abolished the merit system that Chandler had created by executive order, announcing that he would ask the legislature to enact a legislative merit system that could not be abolished or altered by the governor; at the same time he announced that he would aim at reducing the state payroll by 15 percent and asked all department heads to submit plans for the reduction. And he abolished the Highway Advisory Commission that Chandler had created in 1956, a group of politicians whose chief purpose was to decide patronage and to assure that roads were built where they would do the most political good.

There were few tears shed over the demise of either agency. Nor were there many misgivings when Combs canceled four boat-dock leases made by Chandler in the closing days of his administration. There was some question whether he had a legal right to cancel the leases, but, he said, "I thought they were so smelly my action wouldn't be tested in the courts. It wasn't." The leases were not unusual; in fact, it was customary for governors to hand out such plums to allies in the closing days. But Chandler's management of the parks had not been his best performance.

"Happy left the parks in a mess," said Henry Ward, who at the time was general manager of the Louisville Area Chamber of Commerce but had supervised the parks as conservation commissioner under Clements. "He had given out concessions to his political friends for almost everything—beaches, those little paddle boats, docks, ice cream stands. The parks weren't his idea so he wasn't too interested in them, let them slide."

Combs had decided that there should be no private enclaves within the state parks over which the state had little control and from which it got little return. His plan, which he announced on December 29, was to move the parks out of the Department of Conservation into a separate Department of Parks, and to develop them with a special issue of revenue bonds.

Meanwhile, Wilson Wyatt was getting his own troops in line. There was much discussion over whether he should live in the historic mansion on High Street that had been refurbished for the lieutenant governor. Some people considered it an extravagance; indeed, a lot of people thought the lieutenant governor might just as well stay home except when the Assembly was in session and he was required to preside over the Senate. Wyatt had other ideas; he wanted to upgrade the office and image of the lieutenant governor, to be a full-time second-in-command, with substantial duties that would take some of the load off the governor and be of real service to the state. "I suggested to Wilson that for his political image he shouldn't live in the lieutenant governor's mansion," said Combs. "It had acquired a controversial image under Waterfield. But it was Wilson's decision to live there."

Wyatt chose the mansion as a step toward upgrading the office. He had reason for his attitude; he and Combs had run as a team. He had insisted on a partnership status as a provision of the merger and had been assured a free hand in his role as industrial promoter for the state. He had more experience, as an administrator and as a politician, than Combs: he had served as mayor of the state's largest city and as Federal Housing Expediter in Washington. He did not want to be relegated now to ribbon-cutting. The trouble with the lieutenant governor's office as set by the constitution is that it is about as much as the lieutenant governor wants to make it; he can work at it, or he can use it as a handy and well-financed office from which to run for governor. Most do the latter, and the office will never be of much value to the state until it is changed by altering the terms under which it was created.

The mansion may have served for as many social functions during the next four years as the governor's mansion; the Wyatts were more social than the Combses and loved to give parties (though they decided not to keep prison trusties as servants, as had long been the custom at the governor's mansion). Wyatt charged out on a campaign to sell Kentucky to industry, encouraged by the appointment of Bruce Kennedy as commissioner of economic development. But before undertaking active industrial promotion, Wyatt, like Combs, had to turn his attention to the approaching session of the legislature.

A sickly treasury and an outdated constitution were only two of many handicaps facing Combs as he took control. The state was not in good shape; it was regarded as backward by other southern and mid-western states. As fast as Kentucky educated teachers, for example, they left for other states because of the higher pay; fast-growing, prosperous Florida sent recruiters to Kentucky each spring and hired graduates by the hundreds. Kentucky was second only to Arkansas in the number of one-room schools. Fewer than half of its high school graduates went on to college, and it had the highest rate of dropouts in the nation.

A 1958 report by the Automotive Safety Foundation charged that two-thirds of the state's trunkline (federal aid) road mileage was below standards for existing traffic demands; that half of its secondary roads were inadequate for modern industrial traffic; that 20 percent of major city streets were substandard and in need of modernization, and that another 55 percent would soon be substandard because of increasing traffic.

The choice of a commissioner of highways, therefore, became a first priority, and it was here that Combs made a selection that eventually caused him as much grief as any decision he would have to make during his administration. In 1959 the highway department was the largest in state government, had the most employees, spent the most money, and was by all measure the most politically sensitive. City, county, and state political careers rested on the ability to get needed roads and bridges built, and terrific pressure was exerted on the commissioner. The office required a man of integrity, political acumen, and administrative ability, a man with great knowledge of the state and total loyalty to the governor.

Combs's appointment of Earle Clements was therefore by no means illogical, but it disturbed and surprised Kentuckians of all stripes. Some papers openly charged that Clements had demanded the office in return for his support. Others wondered why Clements would take such a job after having been governor and U.S. senator; many concluded that he wanted to use the office to organize the state for his friend Senator Lyndon B. Johnson, who was reportedly running for the Democratic nomination for president.

"We had a meeting over in my office on the farm," recalled Bill May. "I think it was the Sunday after election, but I'm not sure. Bert was there, Earle, I don't think Wilson was, maybe Lawrence. Anyhow, Earle said to Bert, 'If there isn't some reason that would keep you from it, I would like to be your highway commissioner,' and Bert said, 'Well, no, I can't think of any reason I couldn't appoint you.' And that seemed to satisfy everybody."

Combs remembers the incident somewhat differently. "I think Bill confused two different meetings," he said. "What Earle said, as I recall, was something like, 'I think I know of a good highway commissioner for you,' and I said, 'Who would that be?' and he said, 'How about me?' And I said, 'I'll be happy to appoint you. I can't think of a better one. I'm just glad you're willing to take it.' I had already decided to ask him to take the job because he had a great record as a road builder—first as Union County judge, then as governor. Furthermore, Earle and I knew the news media speculation about his influence on my administration would be a sensitive area for both of us, and we both thought that if he became highway commissioner, answerable directly to me, that that would be the best way to handle his role. And, to be frank, it put him in a position where I could sort of keep an eye on him.

"In any event, I asked Earle to take the job. I know a lot of people think he demanded the job as the price of his support, but that isn't so. After all, roads looked like they would be the most important single factor in my administration, and nobody knew more about Kentucky roads than Earle. He was the father of the rural road program. He had gotten the tax passed that created the program. And he was tough enough, had enough stature, that he could handle the pressure. No backroad county judge was going in and buffalo Earle Clements. And he knew how to operate a big department like that. He knew the federal officials involved. He was just a natural for the job."

Whatever the facts, the appointment aroused loud grumbling. The press generally was suspicious; some editorials asked if Clements was stepping down to the commissioner level in order to organize Kentucky for Lyndon Johnson. Others wondered who would be the real governor. The question was not unreasonable; Clements was a powerful and dominating personality, accustomed to giving orders, not taking them. He was a man who liked to run things, not a team player. He set his own course and kept his own counsel. And he had been largely responsible for making Bert Combs governor. There was every real reason to wonder whether Combs could control him, and whether the politicians of the state would turn to Clements if they did not get what they wanted out of Combs.

Further, there was little warmth between Clements and Wilson Wyatt, and the Wyatt wing of the administration was openly suspicious of the big man from Morganfield. Barry Bingham, powerful publisher of the *Courier-Journal* and *Louisville Times*, a friend and ally of Wyatt and a key supporter of the Combs-Wyatt ticket, was flatly opposed to the Clements appointment.

"That's true," Combs said later. "Barry Bingham was very opposed to the appointment. He called and told me so, said he would have to criticize the appointment editorially. I don't know where or when the hostility between the two men started. It went back to a time before Clements ran against Harry Lee Waterfield for governor. Bingham backed Waterfield in that race, but I don't know why."

Suffice it to say, the appointment was suspect. People believed that Combs had named Clements because he couldn't avoid doing so. Earle wanted it, he had a right to ask for it, he asked for it, and he got it. At one of his first press conferences, Combs was asked bluntly if he could "stand up to the man who had helped make you governor."

"If I am not strong enough to keep Earle Clements from taking over, I wouldn't be strong enough to keep somebody else from taking over," Combs said. The answer was not convincing. And as long as Clements was highway commissioner, there were stories of people who, unable to get what they wanted from Combs, would say, "Let's go across the river [to highway department headquarters] and see the man."

But it is unrealistic to expect government to be apolitical. People are elected by people who like them, believe in them, or want something from them, and they must please all three types if they wish to keep on being elected. If the Clements appointment was political, only slightly less political was the naming of Ted Marcum as rural highway commissioner. Marcum, a quiet, flat-eyed, tough mountain man from Clay County, was a cousin of Combs. But he also knew the rural road system of Kentucky, and he knew especially well the beat-up roads of eastern Kentucky. His appointment caused hardly a ripple but would later prove controversial when he complained about having to follow the orders of the highway commissioner who, he felt, had no authority over him.

But if the Clements appointment dripped politics, others were noticeably nonpolitical. Combs rejected the resignation of Safety Commissioner Don Sturgill, one of the earlier Chandler appointees, and asked him to stay on for the time being. Sturgill, a Lexington businessman popular with the press, had guided the state police through four difficult years without major criticism and had managed to attract such able assistants as J.E. "Ted" Bassett, a Lexington horseman who later became commissioner and brought the police to an unprecedented level of efficiency and public acceptance. A tall, tough ex-Marine officer, Bassett insisted on meticulous performance by the troopers, and, in turn, fought in the legislative halls for higher pay, more authority, and better equipment for his "thin gray line." The troopers were devoted to him, and it is doubtful whether the force ever again attained the levels of morale and performance achieved under Bassett (who went on to become president of Keeneland, the famed Bluegrass race course at Lexington).

Politics did have a voice in the selection of the racing commission, a prestigious post always highly desired. Bill May was given the chairmanship, which he had asked for and been promised during the campaign. Millard Cox of Louisville was given another seat, as were Merle Robertson, Louisville banker; Leslie Combs, Lexington horseman and owner of the famed Spendthrift Farm of Fayette County; and Frankfort attorney Louis Cox, a longtime personal friend of Bert Combs. John Dugan, of Louisville, another Democratic stalwart, was named secretary of the commission.

The Kentucky Education Association, meanwhile, was demanding a $50 million increase in the school budget, though Combs reminded them that schools were already getting 63 cents of every general-fund dollar. What the school people did not know was that they were about to get more money than they had ever expected, and that Combs would make more improvement in schools than had any administration in history.

One headache facing a new governor is the constitutional provision limiting the General Assembly to one 60-day session every two years, and ordering it to convene a few weeks after the governor is elected. The fact that the legislature is in session so little of the time puts the major portion of governmental power in the hands of the governor, who is in office all the time, and the quality of the legislative session depends to a considerable degree on the program the governor puts before it. Yet he is required to face the first session of his term, and to propose to it a program of new laws and a budget that will control state spending for the next two years, only a few weeks after he takes office. The creation of interim committees with powers to investigate, hold hearings, and prepare legislative proposals has increased somewhat the power of the legislature, but the substantial share of the power still resides with the governor.

The days before the legislature convenes are tense for people around the governor. Before the session opens, there is a meeting of the legislators at which new members are briefed and leaders are chosen for both houses. The governor has a vital interest in the proceedings and keeps a close eye on what goes on. He is usually on the program and tells the legislators in general what he is going to recommend to them. The legislators have a fair idea, from the tenor of the campaign, what the governor is going to propose, and there is typically a great deal of after-hours discussion of possible legislative action.

The governor needs to know how the legislative winds are blow-ing, because if he is going to be successful, he must have the understanding and support of the legislature. If his party, and particularly his wing or faction of the party, has a majority in the Assembly, an incoming governor can usually control things during the early going; he has enough power, in his control of the budget and the administrative departments, to keep in line even some members who would not otherwise be for him. Legislators who are going to submit controversial bills of their own, or who want projects and appointments for their home districts, are not likely to buck the governor until they have to.

But no governor likes to use all of his ammunition early. That is why he wants his House and Senate leaders to be strong, politically knowledgeable, personally loyal, and competent in parliamentary maneuvering—just as he wants his own people in the chairmanships of the various committees that shape, approve, or block bills.

New Year's Eve was cold but dry. The Wyatts said farewell to 1959 with a large and very festive party, the Combses with a somewhat smaller one. It had been a momentous year, but both men knew that the new year would be crucial. Combs was in his office by eight o'clock on the first day of 1960, "getting my ducks in line" for the legislative session. Two days later the legislators began moving into town, and on January 4 both parties elected officers for the session. There were no surprises. Democrats outnumbered Republicans 80 to 20 in the House; as expected, Harry King Lowman was elected speaker, and Thomas L. Ray of Fairdale, majority leader. In the Senate, Alvin Kidwell was elected president pro tem, and James C. Ware was chosen floor leader. These selections did not solve all the personnel problems Combs faced.

"One of the most sensitive problems I had to deal with before the session was Dick Moloney," Combs recalled later. "Moloney wanted to be House speaker or majority leader, but I was already pretty well committed to Harry King Lowman for speaker and to Tom Ray for majority leader. Moloney may have been the most able man in the legislature. But Harry King was a good speaker. Very sound. Knew every twist and turn of procedure and understood the political process. Moloney always thought like a political boss, though he was a good public servant. He always wanted to come to me through Earle. He was hurt, I know. I don't think he ever got over being passed up for majority leader." (Prior to 1980 the Democratic governors handpicked legislative leadership; since then, with the declaration of legislative independence, their influence is less noticeable and infrequently applied.)

On January 5, Combs appeared before the customary joint session to set the legislative wheels in motion.

"I had two big issues to put before the legislature before the budget was introduced," said Combs, "the constitutional convention and the $100,000,000 bond issue. I had to have that bond issue. Just had to have it. If we didn't get it, we weren't going to build the roads we had in the works. Now, part of the money that I wanted for parks was in revenue bonds, and we could issue them without approval of the voters. But that big bond issue for roads was critical. A lot of it was to be used to match federal funds. The interstate highway program was just getting started well, and it would have ground to a halt in Kentucky without the 9 to 1 money we got from the federal government. As it turned out, with the bond issue money we finished our interstate system much sooner than most of the surrounding states, including Tennessee and Virginia." (Some critics said that completing the interstate network ahead of schedule was of no great importance, but as Combs pointed out, it would have been a major matter had Kentucky lagged behind neighboring states and been a highway bottleneck.)

Although it did not sound like it, Combs's address to the Assembly was a historic one. It did not set the legislators on fire; they sat quietly throughout his speech, applauding only at the beginning and end. But afterward their comments, and those of reporters, showed a realization of the importance of the address. Combs had announced that the legislature had a moral obligation to pay veterans a bonus, since the voters had approved one, and to levy a sales tax to finance it. He proposed more home rule for cities, a merit system for state employees, a law to protect state workers from assessments for political purposes, agricultural research, and new emphasis on conservation. He proposed an authority to oversee building for schools, a separate parks department, new truck taxes, new laws to control oil and gas production, and "more adequate provision for higher education, mental health, transportation, and services to senior citizens and dependent children." But he added that until the courts ruled on the validity of the referendum that had approved the veterans' bonus and supporting sales tax, some of his tax proposals would have to wait.

The address was, in brief, a general outline. Combs was telling the legislators what he was going to tell them. The real meat and potatoes of his program were not put on the table until he presented his budget message on February 16. And in the meantime his sales tax and bonus bills sparked the beginning of a fight between Combs and Chandlerites that would continue throughout the session. Senator Ed Richmond of Owensboro threatened a new "rebel" group against Combs if other tax cuts were not made to offset the sales tax. Richmond, along with Senator Rex Logan of Smith's Grove (and, after the 1961 senatorial elections, Senator Casper "Cap" Gardner, also of Owensboro), led these attacks. But Combs had the votes; he was in a strong position on both tax and bonus.

Richmond, Gardner, and Logan, however, were to be the core of a tough and vocal opposition. Logan, especially, would continue to be a problem, attacking Combs-Wyatt programs on the Senate floor and at one point launching such a venomous attack on Wyatt that some senators considered offering a proposal to censure him.

"Rex was a very erratic guy, to put it kindly," said Combs. "He just didn't seem able to be moderate. He was for me at first, but I think he turned against me when I wouldn't make him patronage man for Warren County. He just wasn't the type for it. It would have hurt me, and it would have destroyed him. He just didn't have the temperament for it."

It was an open secret that Combs would ask for a 3 percent sales tax, and opposition to both bonus and tax proposals came immediately. Private interests, most represented by the state chamber of commerce, did not oppose the sales tax but insisted that it be balanced by cuts in existing taxes, especially the personal and corporate income taxes. No one wanted to vote against the bonus, but sporadic efforts were made in the House to limit the supporting sales tax to 1 or 2 percent. Other efforts, especially by legislators from eastern Kentucky, sought to make the bonus more generous than the $500 maximum payment proposed by Combs. Some wanted the bonus paid only to veterans living in Kentucky; others protested that Kentuckians who had moved to another state deserved payment also.

Organized labor, which opposed the sales tax in its entirety, demanded that food, at least, be exempted. Railroads asked the legislature to recognize the peculiar nature of their operations by exempting materials to repair and build rail equipment, and diesel fuel for locomotives. The thoroughbred industry insisted that horse sales be excluded lest the industry move to another state. The coal companies urged that machinery and materials used to produce coal, oil, gas, and other minerals be exempted as manufacturing equipment. Farm lobbyists wanted to exempt things the farmer bought that were necessary for farm production. Chambers of commerce sought exemptions for raw materials used in manufacturing. And so on.

"Everybody who has testified on it says it is a good bill," said Combs a week after the bill was introduced. "But then they suggest just one little bitty amendment. If we accepted even half of the amendments, we wouldn't have any bill at all."

8

Tax Money Makes the Mare Go

A.B. Chandler did not wait for the Combs administration to get under-way to begin denouncing it. In this, he was typical of the factional divisions that have made Kentucky politics so harmful. After presiden-tial primaries, a losing candidate who attacked his party's nominee would be considered an apostate or worse. Indeed, candidates losing the race for the presidency traditionally temper their criticism of the winner and his programs, even if he is of the opposing party, at least until another campaign arrives. But Chandler attacked Combs even before the new governor took office, and once the Combs program was announced, it became the object of Chandler's ridicule and abuse.

It was inevitable now that Chandler should get into the act. It had to be painful for him to see so much going on in Frankfort while he was forced to sit and watch. It was especially galling to see his enemies ready to put into motion his old bugbear, the sales tax. He announced that he was still opposed to it, and that the bonus could be paid without the tax. "They've made their first serious mistake," said Chandler. "They've betrayed the people, just like I said they would. The people approved only enough tax to pay for the bonus, and that wouldn't be 1 per cent. But Combs will put the rest on because he has always wanted a sales tax, you understand. I tried to warn the people of this."

Combs stuck to his guns. He knew that, as critics were charging, a 3 percent sales tax would yield far more than was needed to pay the proposed bonus, but he wanted the excess for the programs he was getting ready to propose to the legislature in his budget message. He knew he had to keep the bonus small and the exemptions few.

Two days after his address, Combs asked the legislature to approve a 43-mile, four-lane, limited-access $30,000,000 toll road from Win-chester to Campton, the first stage of the 150-mile East Kentucky Turnpike that Henry Spalding and Bill May had envisioned. It would have been a shock had the project not been approved, for the first phase of it was already well underway, and Combs had committed the state to considerable expenditure on it. Fortunately, only a few offered any opposition; eastern Kentucky had historically been neglected in the matter of roads, and the Assembly recognized the need.

The Eastern Kentucky Turnpike (or Mountain Parkway, as it became known) was unusual. Before its creation, a toll road—such as the Kentucky Turnpike from Louisville to Elizabethtown—had to show that it would be used by a certain amount of traffic before it could justify a bond issue to finance its construction or improvement. The Mountain Parkway couldn't begin to qualify for bond assistance on a traffic-count basis.

"That was one of the inequities that eastern Kentucky suffered, as both Wilson and I had pointed out to federal road officials," said Combs. "You couldn't get federal money unless a road carried a lot of traffic, but in east Kentucky there weren't any roads to carry a lot of traffic, so there wasn't a lot of traffic. We couldn't get roads without traffic, and we couldn't have any traffic until we got roads.

"So we built the Mountain Parkway on the theory that it would generate enough traffic to justify its cost. And, of course, it did, and the formula became part of the Appalachian Regional Commission concept of generative aid to depressed or backward areas."

Combs had other political skirmishes. He had long thought that the state needed a separate circuit court in Franklin County to handle the numerous cases coming before state governmental agencies, and now he asked that such a court be created. This removed Franklin from the circuit of the highly respected Judge William Ardery of Paris, whose friends (and others who used the move as an excuse to attack Combs) charged that the new-court bill was intended as a ripper. But the state Judicial Council, on December 11, 1959, had recommended the new circuit, and Combs carried the day on its recommendation.

Combs employed Felix Joyner, a government technician who had served in the administration of Earle Clements, as a consultant on government reorganization, a significant act, since it kept Joyner, who would become one of the most valuable officials in his administration, in Frankfort. Mark Frische, another young "brain truster," was named to help Joyner with the reorganization plan.

In keeping with his pledge to practice strict economy, Combs bought a medium-priced Buick as his official car instead of the customary Cadillac limousine. That was probably a mistake. No one seemed impressed by the economy, and there was some criticism, especially when it was revealed that he had bought the car from a Prestonsburg supporter, Ed Music, though he got it at cost. The governor, said the critics, should maintain some dignity of office; a cheap car made the office seem cheap. Later, still stubbornly refusing to indulge in the luxury of the traditional Cadillac, Combs would buy a Chrysler Imperial. Again, the economy impressed no one.

There was grumbling in the press when it was revealed that Mrs. Troy Savage, sister of Mrs. Combs, had been hired as housekeeper of the governor's mansion. Actually, the hiring of Mrs. Savage was nepotism, plain and simple, and Combs admitted as much. But she was in reality less housekeeper than companion to Mrs. Combs, who was never completely at ease in the mansion and was frequently homesick. Mrs. Combs was not the first governor's wife to view life in the mansion with something less than affection. Before its most recent renovation at the direction of Phyllis Brown, wife of Governor John Y. Brown, Jr., the mansion was not a particularly comfortable or convenient residence, or a very handy place in which to entertain personal friends. The basement is occupied by a rather extensive command post for the Kentucky State Police troopers who guard the mansion and its occupants, and drive and guard the governor when he is away from the mansion. The beautiful first floor is designed for formal entertaining but hardly for informal family life, and the governor's family spends most of its time in the second floor residential quarters—which were not, until recently, particularly attractive or comfortable.

Mrs. Combs, an unpretentious woman from Knott County, viewed the mansion as stuffy and demanding. In Prestonsburg, she had had just about what she wanted in life—a handsome, successful, respected husband who was home much of the time; a comfortable, attractive house; her children around her, and plenty of neighbors and friends. She didn't have her husband's ambition, his habit of looking far down the road. Formal entertaining and large crowds, such as those that swarmed over the mansion at Derby time, unnerved her. It is doubtful that she was ever really happy after she left Floyd County.

The cities handed Combs a couple of additional hot potatoes. Louisville wanted authority to impose an occupational tax; unions and taxpayer groups were hotly opposed. Rural forces and suburban representatives were also opposed to bills giving cities home rule, putting a five-cent limit on parking meters, making it easier for cities to merge or annex, exempting city water companies from regulation by the Public Service Commission, and allowing cities to garnishee wages to collect delinquent taxes. Nearly all of these powers are enjoyed by cities in other states, but the inability of Kentucky cities to manage their own affairs reflects the anti-city bias of the framers of the 1891 constitution, and the refusal of rural legislators to give up a mechanism for forcing urban support of rural measures in the Assembly.

There was a measure of irony in Combs's experience with his proposal for a merit system that would protect state workers from political firing and payroll assessment. It was a plan every official, employee, and student of government could be expected to applaud. But no sooner had he introduced his bill than the Legislative Research Commission complained that it was a branch of the legislature, and putting its employees under the system would make them answerable to the executive branch; the Department of Safety protested that the state police required classification and standards not applicable to other employees; the Personnel Board argued that it should have jurisdiction over enforcement. LRC employees and state police were eventually exempted from regulations covering other employees, and the House finally passed the bill, 86 to 7, on February 24; the Senate 26 to 6, on March 6.

Combs encountered a similar problem with his efforts to create a unified program of child welfare services. Former Governor Lawrence Wetherby had created a Youth Authority, which had included nearly all of the functions Combs wanted to see coordinated by a single agency, but the Authority had been shattered by an executive order from Chandler. Now there was disagreement among child welfare forces as to whether the governor should take children's services out of the Department of Economic Security and put them in the Department of Welfare with children's institutions; take the institutions out of Welfare and put them in Economic Security; or take children's services out of Economic Security, take the institutions out of Welfare, and make a new, separate department of government. Combs chose the third plan.

Disagreement over the bonus erupted as soon as House Bill 85 was introduced on January 20. It specified a bonus to all veterans of the Spanish-American War, World War I, World War II, and the Korean War who had lived in Kentucky for at least six months before going into service, who had served for at least 90 days, and who were living in Kentucky on November 3, 1959, the day the bonus proposal was approved by state voters. Veterans who had served only in the continental U.S. were to get a maximum of $300, based on $9 per month of service; those who had gone overseas were to get a maximum of $500, based on $15 a month for overseas duty.

No one seemed happy with the bill. Eastern Kentucky representatives demanded more money and wanted the bonus paid to men who had gone into service from Kentucky and then moved away—reflecting the fact that thousands of eastern Kentuckians had left for jobs in the North as soon as the war ended. Veterans' organizations demanded that the residency requirements be dropped, opposed the 3 percent sales tax, and asked that all tax receipts be earmarked to pay the bonus. Republican members of the legislature offered their own bill, calling for flat payments of $300 and $500.

Eventually, Combs agreed that heirs or dependents would get the bonus if the veteran had died, that a majority of the members of the review board set up to handle appeals would be veterans, and that Adjutant General A.Y. Lloyd, who was to administer payment of the bonus, would be instructed to interpret generously sections of the bonus law dealing with residence and service. Even so, Republicans in the House boycotted the measure when it came to a vote on February 10, apparently in the belief that the law would eventually prove unpopular. The bill passed easily, however: 78 to 0 in the House, 24 to 13 in the Senate.

Combs also signed a bill calling for a referendum on a constitutional convention, and announced that it would be tried immediately in the courts to see whether its first passage in a special session was constitutional, or whether the constitution required passage of a referendum proposal only by regular sessions.

Wyatt was personally pleased when the legislature repealed the income surtax, enacted under Chandler, which he had criticized during his separate campaign and promised to repeal. This effected a 36 percent reduction in the personal income tax and took about 140,000 low-income people off the tax rolls. Whether this was a wise move can be debated. Kentucky needed every penny, and once a tax is repealed it is hard to get it back.

Combs signed another bill raising the marriage age for females from 14 to 16, and asked the legislature for $4,500,000 to start a health care program for welfare recipients, one of the first of its kind in the nation. He created a board of transportation to check on use of state cars and halt reported abuses. And he proposed a flat 50-cent fee for parking at the state fairgrounds and exposition center in Louisville, a fee the fair board had wanted for some time but had been afraid to impose.

State parks posed other problems. Kentucky had built a good basic system of 10 major and 16 smaller parks and shrines, most of the land having been given to the state. But the parks had never been regarded as a major state function. With the exception of aging lodges at Natural Bridge, Cumberland Falls, and Pine Mountain, and some housing at Kentucky Dam Village—left by the Tennessee Valley Authority when it had finished building Kentucky Dam—facilities in the parks provided little lure to vacationers or tourists.

Combs had plans to change all that. After the legislature approved his proposal for a separate department of parks, he named Edward Fox, once business manager at Kentucky Dam Village and assistant director of parks under Henry, to launch the parks expansion program. Combs envisioned a chain of expanded parks offering people in every part of the state a vacation spot near home, and serving as the heart of a drive to build a tourist industry. With $10,000,000 from the proposed bond issue and another $10,000,000 in revenue bonds, he proposed to build modern lodges and cottages, golf courses, tennis courts, swimming pools, boat docks and marinas, playgrounds, gift shops, riding stables, museums, and amphitheaters, at the same time preserving the nature trails, preserves, and camping areas for nature lovers. He didn't see the new parks as money-makers but hoped that they would draw so many people that motels, stores, boat docks, and other tourist facilities would spring up around the parks to accommodate the overflow. In this he was disappointed. Tourist development near the parks never met expectations, partly because tourism in Kentucky tends to be seasonal, and privately owned tourist facilities can seldom operate profitably on a single-season basis. Furthermore, all state parks are in dry territory where alcoholic beverages, demanded by tourists, cannot be sold.

But in general, the parks themselves were an outstanding success, not only bringing modern vacation accommodations close to every Kentuckian but producing millions of dollars every year from out-of-state visitors. Tourism is Kentucky's third largest industry, bringing in more than $3 billion a year from 15,000,000 travelers, of whom approximately 9,000,000, or 60 percent, are from out of state and 40 percent are Kentuckians traveling or vacationing within the state. State parks account for 1,041,000 overnight visitations—with out-of-staters accounting for 53 percent of the visitations—and take in $28,000,000 a year. Before the Combs administration was over, out-of-state visitations to the parks more than doubled over the preceding four years. Eventually, tourist use became so widespread that Kentuckians complained that they could not get reservations in their favorite parks during vacation months, and there was agitation in the legislature for a limit on out-of-state visitors or a system under which Kentuckians would get favored treatment. Nothing came of it.

But the major attention in the early weeks of the session was centered on the budget bill Combs was preparing. Kentuckians had not had time to judge either Combs or his program before Happy Chandler, on February 13, decided that he had seen enough to satisfy him and loosed a blast at the entire Combs program. "Combs has lost the support of the people after two months in office," he declared, adding that the sales tax was "a fraud against my people." (Happy had a penchant for claiming the population of Kentucky as his own, regardless of their expressed sentiments regarding that ownership.) The harangue showed that Chandler still believed—like the girl in the song—that if he wished long enough, wishing would make it so.

The fact was that Combs was getting pretty much what he wanted out of the Assembly. Both his strength and his methods were dramatically demonstrated on the morning of the bonus bill vote in the House, when he breakfasted with House members at the mansion. The bonus bill was, he knew, the severest test he faced; if the lawmakers approved the bonus, they had to approve the sales tax to support it, and it was the sales tax that held the key to Combs's program. But Combs did not mention the bonus bill at the breakfast. The next day, when the Senate was to vote on it, Combs left Frankfort to make a speech. There was a great deal of speculation about Combs's ways of dealing with legislators, but he has insisted that he chose leaders on whose honesty and intelligence he knew he could depend, maintained a close and constant contact with them, and kept a close head count of votes.

"They knew what I wanted them to do," he said later. "I didn't have to spell it out for them. They knew they would have to call on me for things they wanted for their constituents, and they knew I could remember their voting records. I had also pretty well sold them on the idea that the people had given me—and them, too—a mandate to improve state government and the state, and a lot of them sincerely agreed, people like Kidwell, Ware, Mitch Denham. These were not just ordinary politicians. They really wanted to improve things."

Other administration business had been cleaned up before the budget was introduced. The bill establishing the Business Development Corporation of Kentucky, to promote new industry and help existing business, whipped through the legislature without a negative vote. House Bill 273, establishing the Kentucky Public School Authority—principally an agency to help local school districts finance school construction—passed with only two opposing Senate votes. Such legislation was prelude. The legislators knew that the real work would come with the budget. It was the main topic of discussion in the lobby of the Capital Hotel. Lawmakers met in tense little groups along the corridors of the capitol building to discuss it. Lights burned late into the night in the governor's office, as the all-important document was shaped and sharpened.

On the morning of February 17, 1960, Combs rose early, ate his usual quiet breakfast in the family quarters on the second floor of the mansion (he seldom ate breakfast in the formal dining room on the first floor unless he had company), and walked quickly from the mansion to the capitol. He showed no signs of nervousness as he entered the elevator shortly after ten o'clock and rode to the third floor, where the lawmakers awaited his address. He knew he was going to shake the state as he stood before the joint session in the House chamber.

His speech was a blockbuster. It proposed a 3 percent sales tax, with exemptions only for car sales and such farm items as the machinery, fuels, and equipment used in producing crops, which could logically be considered manufacturing machinery. And it called for greatly increased spending for almost every state service, especially for education. Combs described his $1,024,025,723 biennial budget, the first billion-dollar budget in Kentucky's history, as a means of "lifting Kentucky from her old depressing place at the bottom of the ladder."

Actually, Combs's budget offered few innovations or new departures for the state. Rather, it raised the level of state services and support for its institutions to the point where the resulting structure appeared to be new. The Kentucky Education Association had been readying its weapons for an assault on the legislature, where it planned to demand an increase of almost 50 percent in school funds; suddenly, here was the governor asking $271,130,530 for public education for the 1960-62 biennium, $102,714,630—62 percent—more than was being spent for the current biennium! Furthermore, almost half of the massive increment was earmarked for increases in teachers' salaries.

Another $25,000,000 increase was tagged for transportation and new school buildings. State colleges would get $5,325,000 for new buildings; the University of Kentucky and its A.B. Chandler Medical Center, an additional $10,522,000. The latter brought loud grumbling from the Combs Democrats in the legislature because of the tongue-lashing Chandler had given the sales tax that would make such an appropriation possible, and the leadership in both houses proposed changing the name of the school to the University of Kentucky Medical Center. Combs resisted the temptation, but the name galled him. "Chandler had obligated the state for the medical school, but he hadn't given it much money," he said in 1984. "He blasted the sales tax that produced the money for the school, but was perfectly willing to take credit for the school it built and put his name on it when we dedicated it." (In 1973 Chandler told his son Ben, as an example of the efficiency of his administration, "They didn't want us to build the medical center, you understand, and said we couldn't pay for it. Well, we built it and we paid for it.")

Additional funds for education included $5,614,000 to raise bene-

At seventeen, Bert Combs got his first real job, as clerk for attorney Murray L. Brown (foreground) in his Manchester law offices. Combs does not appear to be overjoyed with his prospects. Courtesy of Bert T. Combs.

Below, Bert Combs takes to the campaign trail in 1955, running against Happy Chandler in the Democratic gubernatorial primary. Earnest, honest, sincere, he was no match for the flamboyant Chandler. Royaltone Studio, Russellville.

Again a candidate for governor, a more seasoned Combs campaigns in 1959. Here, he and running mate Wilson Wyatt hit the porches in the days before television.

Some of the foolishness expected of candidates in a farm state.

President Harry S. Truman came to Paducah to endorse Combs and Wyatt. Governor Chandler, smarting over the primary defeat of his candidate, Harry Lee Waterfield, refused to welcome the president.

Below, Combs, Wyatt, and their wives and campaign workers savor victory on election night 1959 in Louisville. Kentucky Department of Public Information.

The victors,
November 1959.

Governor Combs entertains some of his younger supporters in his office.
Kentucky Department of Public Information.

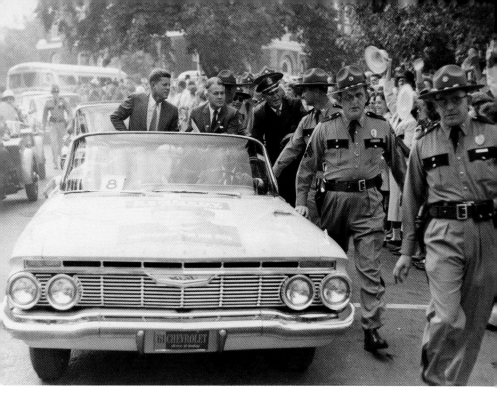

Above, Combs rides with presidential candidate John F. Kennedy, campaigning in Lexington in 1960. Photo by Lou Fain. Below, he accompanies Vice President Lyndon Johnson and Robert Martin, president of Eastern Kentucky University. Johnson was in Kentucky to attend the dedication of new buildings at EKU. Photo by Daniel Webster.

Three small-town boys who left their marks on Kentucky: Governor
Bert Combs, Colonel Harland Sanders of Kentucky Fried Chicken fame,
and Edward T. "Ned" Breathitt, who succeeded Combs in the
governorship. Kentucky Department of Public Information.

Combs jokes with
Democratic war-
horse Emerson
"Doc" Beauchamp
in Beauchamp's
Highway Depart-
ment office in
1961.
Royaltone Studio,
Russellville.

William H. "Bill" May, an old mountain boy and Combs stalwart, did all right for himself in the Bluegrass.
Below, Governor Combs delivers the State of the Commonwealth address to a joint session of the legislature on January 1, 1962.

Governor Combs
—the man in the
white raincoat—
on the Capitol
grounds in
January 1960.

Former Governor Combs stands before his beloved floral clock, for which
the state garden clubs honored him, on May 6, 1966.

fits for retired teachers from $750 to $1,200 a year, $3,140,000 more for free textbooks, and $2,000,000 more for vocational education.

For roads, Kentucky's other sickly service, the budget asked a record $139,825,000, plus $30,000,000 in bonds that had not then been sold, and proposed another $90,000,000 bond issue to finish up the interstate highway program. Roads, of course, are financed not from the general fund but from the highway fund, into which road-user taxes are funneled, but in this instance they would also get the additional bond money.

Combs went on to announce that work had begun on the mountain toll road, and added that another toll road was planned for western Kentucky and possibly a third for the central area. Record sums were also provided for new construction in the state parks (which would also be included in the planned bond issue), and Combs asked that parks be taken out of Conservation and given their own departmental status.

The budget carried record appropriations for almost every aspect of government: dormitories for every state college and the University of Kentucky, new beds for Central State Mental Hospital, more money for crippled children, general welfare payments, public safety, economic development and industrial promotion. It proposed an agricultural research center and new farm facilities at the university, new airports. Before the governor's opponents in the Assembly could regain their balance, HB300, containing the heart of his program, was introduced in the House by Majority Leader Thomas Ray.

Combs's "first 100 days" had begun, and they would leave their mark on the state.

9

The Calm Revolutionaries

Even before Combs delivered his budget message, reporter Richard Harwood had warned, in the *Louisville Times*, that a "calm revolution" was brewing.

"The first 100 days of the new administration in Frankfort may be an epochal period in the modern governmental history of Kentucky," he wrote. "There is a whisper of revolution in the wind—revolution in the political structure of the state, revolution in the public service at Frankfort, revolution in the status of Kentucky's cities, revolution in basic relationships between the state government and the people in critical areas of life."

And, as in most times of revolution, there was an undercurrent of excitement around the capital, a feeling that great things were about to happen, things talked about for years but always out of reach; that there was going to be new school money; that teachers and professors were going to be paid as much as their counterparts in other states; that the colleges were going to get money for modernization and expansion; that new roads and parks were going to be built; and that state agencies dealing with dependent children, the poor, and the mentally retarded were finally going to get money that would let them modernize.

Press reaction to the Combs budget proposals was generally good, although some pro-Chandler editors complained that the budget was extravagant and proved Chandler's contention that only a small part of the sales tax revenue would be used for the bonus. On this point they were correct: Combs had planned to use the major share of the tax for his program—and even that, he knew, would not be enough.

Despite its size and complexity, the budget bill glided through the House 96 to 0, and the Senate 35 to 0. After the session ended, Happy Chandler inveighed against Combs's reckless spending, his bloated budget, and the cruel burden of his sales tax. But when it came time to vote, the Chandlerites, like the Republicans, had fallen into line. Combs signed the bill on March 10, and the stage was set. He had been given the state's first billion-dollar budget.

On the surface, the first months of the Combs administration were hectic, with a flood of bills in the legislature, new appointments announced almost daily, and a steady drumbeat of political charges and countercharges echoing in the press. But the administration, as well as its program, was taking shape in rather calm fashion. Dr. Robert Martin resigned as commissioner of finance to become president of Eastern Kentucky State College; he was succeeded by Robert Matthews, who was later succeeded by Felix Joyner. Wendell Ford stepped up to be top assistant, and Fontaine Banks, a blunt, fireplug ex-Marine moved into the executive offices to become liaison man with local officials and politicians. It was a relatively young group, able to work the long hours required during the early phase of an administration.

In his dealings with the legislature, Combs had from the beginning adopted a policy of walking and talking softly. "Whereas Chandler hugged and flattered, thundered and threatened in order to get the votes, Combs leaves the legislature to the legislative leaders," wrote Richard Harwood. "If he uses any force, it isn't evident."

At the same time, Combs kept in close and constant touch.

"Almost every morning during the session," he explained later, "the party leadership would come down to my office before the houses convened, and we would talk about what should be done that day. We would take checks to see where we stood on votes, who we could count on, where we might be in trouble. We pretty well knew where we stood. They'd tell me if they were getting any special pressure, and I'd do the same if I thought it was important.

"Each of them had his own grapevine, of course, and when they left the office each grapevine would begin to work, so that every member who was with us knew right away what was going to happen that day, which bills would be brought up, what to expect. We had such a majority that there was seldom much doubt about things, about votes. Leonard Hislope or Rex Logan would get up and make windy speeches, but they got nowhere. If we didn't feel fairly sure we had the votes, we wouldn't bring a bill up. We'd work on it.

"I relied on Harry King Lowman, Tom Ray, Dick Moloney in the House, and on Wilson [Wyatt], Kidwell, and Jim Ware in the Senate. Several times during the session I would have the Democrats over for breakfast, and if they had complaints or questions we would bring them up and work it out. I had the Republicans over once or twice, too. I always tried to remain on friendly terms with the opposition, and a lot of them were actually personal friends. We understood that we were just after different things.

"Reporters talked constantly about arm-twisting. It didn't happen. There just wasn't any. The press never did believe that, I think, but it was a fact. It just wasn't necessary. Once or twice during the whole session I had to call a man in and remind him that we had done things for him or were going to help him, and that we expected his help in return. But we usually knew if there was something back home that made things difficult for him, and we tried to take that into consideration.

"People would come in and ask for things—a road, a bridge, some little thing here or there, usually something perfectly legal and ethical. If it wasn't, they would usually try to go through someone else. But when they asked for something, they more or less knew, acknowledged, that they owed us support in return. In politics you don't have to spell things out; you shouldn't have to say, 'If you don't vote for my bill, you'll get no road.' They know that.

"Of course, this unspoken understanding of how things work doesn't always work out the way you intend. Henry Ward was always a great one for being Mr. Clean. He always made a big show of refusing to play politics; made a lot of politicians mad that way. I remember once when he was highway commissioner, he called in Bill Cooley, one of Bill Leonard's boys, an old hand in the Highway Department. Got him on the carpet. Said to him, 'Cooley,' you know, bellowing at him like Ward did, 'I'm told you've been hauling campaign literature in a state vehicle. What about it?' And Cooley said, 'Yeah, I guess I've hauled a ton.' Ward bellowed at him, 'Who told you to do that?' And Cooley said, 'Why, nobody, Commissioner. I knowed the time had come. I know what I'm supposed to do.'"

An example of this mutual understanding came when Combs vetoed a bill to raise legislators' expense allowances from $10 to $25 a day. "I'm opposed to any public official increasing his own compensation," he explained. But he showed no upset when, the next day, both houses overrode his veto. He had told his people that he would have to veto; they understood that and didn't resent it when he did. He, in turn, knew that his people were going to override his veto, and they understood that he would not be offended if they did.

His veto of the milk bill was another matter. That highly controversial measure would have set a minimum price that could be charged for milk. While consumer groups saw it as a means of squelching competition, the milk industry generally favored it, as did most retailers, who saw it as a means of ending price cutting and bringing some order to the milk trade. Combs was attacked angrily for the veto. He was also attacked by Jefferson County officials for vetoing a bill that would have let Louisville and Jefferson County collect all taxes, state and local, on the installment plan. Louisville Mayor William Cowger accused Combs of "blocking an effort to make the payment of taxes easier for the small taxpayer," but Combs retorted that localities had no business collecting state taxes (actually, he had no intention of letting state tax revenues get out of state hands).

While the budget and the sales tax were undoubtedly the most important issues facing what was probably the most important legislative session of the century, they were not the only critical ones. The practice of strip mining was becoming the subject of major controversy, and the fight echoed in the Assembly. Strip (or surface) mining had been practiced in Kentucky for half a century, but only since 1950 had it become a major industry—and a major villain to the environmentalists of the state. In strip mining, earth and rock are removed from the surface of the coal seam and the coal is then scooped out, without the need to sink a shaft to reach the coal. This avoids the danger of having men underground, but the damage to the earth, unless the disturbed rock and topsoil are restored to their original site, is enormous, especially in the mountains.

And it was in the mountains of eastern Kentucky that the real battle over strip mining erupted. Several big companies had been stripping for several years on the fairly flat or rolling land of western Kentucky, where restoring the terrain was relatively simple. It was another matter on the hillsides of eastern Kentucky, where the disturbed earth slid or was washed down the steep slopes to clog and pollute streams, cover roads, and ruin homes and farmland. The huge gashes left on hillsides, as well as the muddy spoilbanks below, were an aesthetic affront as well as an ecological threat. People were beginning to insist that the strip miners be forced to repair their damage to the land.

The environmentalists and other anti-strip-mine forces formed around Harry Caudill, a tall, drawling young lawyer-author from Whitesburg who would soon achieve fame with his book *Night Comes to the Cumberlands*, a furious indictment of mining, especially strip mining, and the ravages done by mining to his native hills. Caudill was championing a bill to require coal operators to repair some of their damage. It was, actually, a rather mild proposal that promised to be hard to enforce, and the penalties it carried were light compared to the damages being done and the money being made by the industry. But coal operators saw it for what it was, the first step of many, the camel's nose under the tent, and they moved to block it.

This put Combs in a ticklish spot. Through his fight against Chandler and his efforts for roads, schools, parks, and reforms in general, he had acquired something of a "Man on a White Horse" image, enjoying the support of an admiring corps of do-gooders and editors. Aside from enjoying the role, Combs recognized its political value. At the same time he had to keep in mind that the base of his political strength lay in eastern Kentucky, where coal put money into the pockets of thousands. And he was a personal friend of many of the coal operators directly concerned with the control legislation.

Combs did not exactly bite the bullet on the strip mine bill; indeed, he hardly nibbled it. He did not oppose the original bill, but neither did he defend it when the coal lobby began to move. The Assembly finally passed a bill that was at least an improvement over the existing weak control regulations. Harry Caudill was pleased, though later, when he saw the law in operation, he condemned it as "damn near worthless" and said he regretted his part in its passage. The usually supportive *Courier-Journal* sneered editorially that "Governor Combs . . . knuckled under to the strip mine lobby with all the bold courage of emasculated hummingbirds." Combs replied blandly, "I relied on Harry Caudill. He helped write it."

Caudill was more pleased with his role in an investigation of state education by the House Investigating Committee on Education, of which he was a member. Years later he said, "I am proud of what we did, prouder, I think, than of any other thing I had part of." On March 10, 1960, while the Senate was considering a bill to create a continuing commission on public education, the investigating committee released a report that was scathing in its criticism of practically every aspect of state education and the educational hierarchy. The committee report declared that much of the education budget would be wasted if reforms were not made in a system "riddled with politics, waste and incompetency." It went on to charge school officials with "greed and inefficiency, nepotism, political selection of teachers who were hired, fired and transferred according to their support of the local superintendents, misuse of school buildings and vehicles, and the granting of contracts to political favorites."

The report questioned the fitness of teachers and administrative educators to educate the children of Kentucky. The hand was the hand of the investigating committee, but the indignant voice was the voice of Harry Caudill denouncing "self-serving paragons of mediocrity who can twist to their ungodly advantage the best laws ever written" and including in its condemnation "professional educators in the Department of Education, the 212 school superintendents, the ruling clique of the Kentucky Education Association and the presidents and deans of the state's colleges."

The report came too late in the session to spur any real reforms or long-range probe of school spending, nor did it seem to influence the

Senate, though the Assembly appropriated funds with which to run the committee on public education for two years. Actually, the legislature, like Kentuckians in general, has never known how to go about improving the state school system. The legislators have sensed, vaguely, that there is something basically wrong in funneling more and more money to the same educators who got the state into its mess in the first place, but they have never been able to decide on an alternative. The system of local school boards and powerful county school superintendents has been shown to be unprogressive, mired in politics, and often corrupt. County school superintendents are—almost have to be—politicians first and educators second, if at all. They work to elect a school board whose members will elect them; loyalty, not fitness, is the first virtue. Frequently, especially in small and rural counties, the school system is the largest employer, the largest purchaser, and the largest contractor in the county; naturally, the superintendent is politically powerful—and active. Teachers are often given the day off on election day so they can work the polls. Those who do not vote properly often find themselves out of a job or in unwanted schools. Suppliers and contractors are also chosen for their politics as well as their products, and it is not rare to find the superintendent or members of the school board owning or having interest in firms that do business with the county schools.

The system of local control was instituted in the nineteenth century, not to assure quality education but to make sure that the schools did not teach dangerous or suspicious doctrines, and to see that they did not cost too much and thus force local officials to raise taxes. The system has perpetuated provincialism. School boards have been more concerned with observing local mores than with exploring new areas of thought or methods of education; more interested in athletics than academics, since winning teams tend to keep taxpayers happy without frightening fundamentalist citizens. Boards and superintendents are seldom equipped to decide optimum school hours, course requirements, grading methods, promotion and graduation standards, or selection of teaching materials, textbooks, and library books. Until ways are found to bring informed judgments to bear on these decisions, and to make standards and requirements uniform throughout the state, Kentucky is going to continue to waste huge amounts of money on its schools.

Combs had an illustrative experience with the school lobby toward the end of the 1960 session. As the final weeks of the session approached, he found himself a hero with the school people. He had given them more money than they had ever dreamed of getting.

Teachers' salaries had been markedly increased, new classrooms built, new buses ordered. A community college system had been launched, new classroom and dormitory buildings raised on every college campus. Everyone was ecstatic.

But then Combs, at the behest of some of the legislators who had issued the school report, backed a bill that would have prohibited athletic contests on nights before classes or examinations, so that students could be alert to study. You would have thought he had advocated free sex and compulsory Communism. Coaches, principals, superintendents, parents, and students all rose up to denounce him. The idea of putting studies before basketball games was un-American, un-Kentuckian, probably un-Christian. Combs backed down. Within two years, the same people were moaning for more money for the poor kiddies of Kentucky.

The investigating committee's work did serve Combs a warning that he was up against more than a historic lack of money in his drive to upgrade Kentucky schools. And it would be recalled vividly a few months later when a major scandal erupted in the schools of Carter County, one of the horrible examples of a politically run school system cited in the report.

As a matter of fact, the legislature, like the state it represented, was not exactly a hotbed of liberalism. After a torment of bad oratory, it passed a conflict-of-interest bill aimed at improving the ethics of the legislators. When it tackled a bill to reduce the work of firemen in cities of the second class from 60 to 56 hours, it ran into a tidal wave of tears, as officials from Lexington moaned that such a move would bankrupt their city. (It didn't.) When Combs proposed a modest workers' compensation bill to increase benefits to disabled workers, which meant increasing employers' contributions to the account financing the benefits, Associated Industries of Kentucky and the state chamber of commerce screamed as though they were having their tonsils removed through their ears. Like the bill to establish a prevailing wage for state construction projects, it barely squeaked through.

Combs had easier going with a group of what might be called reform measures, including one requiring voting machines in every county by 1963. On the other hand, the legislators passed a truck-weight bill increasing maximum truck weights so much that Combs refused to sign it, letting it become law without his signature. And in the closing days of the session it approved a proposal for submitting to the voters a bond issue including $10,000,000 for the new parks program, a $7,500,000 omnibus tax bill, and $2,035,000 for the "Little Reconstruction Finance Corporation" industrial lending agency, which had been saved when the court of appeals reversed Judge W.B. Ardery's ruling that the agency was unconstitutional.

The conduct of the Frankfort press corps during Combs's first session was curious. Although most of the predominantly liberal corps liked Combs and were enthusiastic about his program, a number of reporters made a habit of prophesying doom for him. When the House rules committee took over in the first week of March, deciding which bills would go to the floor for consideration, there was a great sighing among reporters that the governor's program was in trouble. Every windbag speech on the floor, every mumble of discontent, every criticism of an administration bill was automatically ominous. Combs was "in trouble." "A possible revolt" was brewing. His "control was challenged." Any time-consuming speech by Rex Logan or Cap Gardner created "chaos." Readers must have imagined the poor governor slinking out of Frankfort in despair and defeat. Actually, he was confident, fairly relaxed, and in good shape in his legislative dealings. Most of his big bills had already been passed, and few of the rest were in real difficulty. The bill to permit Jefferson County to impose an occupational tax gave him some temporary trouble, mainly because eastern Kentucky legislators were resentful of Louisville for voting against the veterans' bonus. But Combs gave it a quiet nudge, and it squeaked through the Senate on a day when 22 bills were passed in less than four hours.

In the final rush, the Assembly also approved measures creating a turnpike authority empowered to issue bonds for toll road construction, banning billboards within 600 feet of the new interstate highways, and adding two professors to the University of Kentucky's board of trustees. It authorized a state employees' merit system free from control by the governor, and it made several changes in tax laws. In all, the legislature enacted more than 300 bills into law, more than 200 of which were signed by Combs. He vetoed only 18, the remainder becoming law without his signature.

But a nagging little issue was beginning to attract increasing attention in the press, and though it did not directly concern Combs or his new administration or reflect unfavorably on him personally, he knew it was the kind of nasty political spat that might easily escalate into a major scandal. And eventually it did. During the last week of February 1960 the *Courier-Journal* published a story describing a squabble in Carter County between county school superintendent Heman McGuire and a group of citizens who charged that McGuire had exceeded his authority in handling school personnel and had mismanaged school funds The citizens wanted McGuire out. McGuire refused to quit, and he was supported by members of the county board of education, most of whom had been elected with his help.

The Carter County situation was one of those that had prompted the blast at school politics contained in the report of the investigating committee. But when the legislature did nothing about the report, McGuire and the Carter County board relaxed, assuming that the worst was over. It wasn't. The press took up where the committee left off, and it soon became apparent that it was on the trail of an interesting character in Mr. McGuire. A professional educator who had come up through the slippery ranks of school politics, Heman McGuire could play a county school system the way a country man can play a banjo. He rewarded those who supported him with purchases, contracts, or jobs. School board members who opposed him were not reelected. Teachers who questioned his orders found themselves in remote and difficult schools, while those who did as they were told and asked no embarrassing questions got good assignments. When the teachers were given a holiday on election day so that they could work at the polls, they did not have to ask for whom they were working. Heman told them.

The situation did not stop at the county line. McGuire was nominally a Republican, possibly because Carter was a Republican county, but he was not averse to using his political influence on behalf of Democratic candidates for state office. For example, he was a friend to Wendell Butler, the Democratic state superintendent of public instruction. Butler had once sold him school supplies. Under Kentucky's constitution, the superintendent, who heads the Department of Education, is an elected official, a requirement that has produced superintendents whose education did not extend to a knowledge of good English or an appreciation of ethics but whose political instincts were impeccable.

In 1947, when he was president of the Kentucky Education Association, McGuire made no effort to hide his use of his office to help political candidates. Or to hurt them. Of Carter County's Earl Bellew (who was running for state representative), McGuire said, "Certainly he should be for me because I have taken care of his wife in one of the best school positions in the county." Other statements were similar: "I saw he and Charlie Johnson [this from the county's top educator] talking. . . . Now, just a few years ago Charlie Johnson and his wife were in bad financial condition. . . . I gave him and his wife both schools." "An indictment was approved by the Carter County grand jury against him . . . the case was coming up for trial. I got the prosecution stopped against him." "The Catholics are trying to get control of the public schools in Kentucky . . . there will be a move in the legislature to permit Negroes to go to school with white children . . . I am against that . . . I am against allowing communism from Russia being taught in our schools."

When the citizens of Carter County finally rebelled in the winter of 1959–60 and charged McGuire with embezzlement, tax evasion, irregularities in handling school funds, and unethical personnel policies, Wendell Butler refused to remove him, investigate the charges, or even call for an audit of county school finances, declaring that in America people are innocent until proven guilty and that he would not impose state authority over local control until the courts had found McGuire guilty.

It took more than two years for the wheels of bureaucracy and justice to grind Heman McGuire from office. In the meantime McGuire was proving an embarrassment to Combs. People thought Combs had the power to remove McGuire from office and wondered why he didn't. But thanks to the constitution, the governor has no authority to remove a county superintendent; neither could he order Wendell Butler, head of the state's school system, to remove McGuire. About the best he could do was to call on McGuire to resign, which he did. McGuire, of course, had no intention of resigning and said so. He had a good thing going; he was indisputably the political power in his county, had friends in both parties, and made about as much in salary as did the superintendent of Jefferson County schools.

Combs called Attorney General John Breckinridge and suggested that he go to Carter County and take a look at the schools. "While you're there," he said, "you might want to count school buses." Breckinridge did just that and found that the county had fewer school buses than it had paid for and fewer than were listed on its inventory. In other words, somebody had gotten money to buy buses and hadn't bought buses, or had paid for buses the county didn't get. That, actually, was the error that led to McGuire's downfall.

On May 25, Attorney General Breckinridge told Combs that while the governor could not oust McGuire, he had the power to order the state auditor to audit the Carter schools. Combs sent State Auditor Joe Schneider to make the audit, but Schneider had hardly started when Roy Hammond, chairman of the Carter County Citizens League for Good Government, wrote him a letter saying that people figured a state audit would be a whitewash. This angered Combs, who said, in effect, "All right. You asked for an audit, and we were giving you one. If you don't want it, we won't do it." There was no sense spending state funds for the audit, he said, if the outcome was going to be suspect.

Hammond quickly recanted; a committee called on Combs to ask that the audit be resumed; and Schneider returned to work, announcing that an outside firm would assist. He found pretty much what the citizens group had charged: that McGuire had used school funds for personal purposes; that he had charged the county for school buses which, if purchased, were never delivered; and that he had used his office to punish those who did not support him politically.

Combs asked the state board of education to investigate these charges. The board agreed and named Judge James Stites of Louisville, a highly respected former chief justice of the Court of Appeals, to head the investigation. Stites's findings implicated not only McGuire but four members of his county board. The state board removed the four members, and new members were named who tossed McGuire out. The case was not settled until the fall of 1961. Then, in March 1963, McGuire was found guilty of evading payment of U.S. income taxes, fined $5,000, and sentenced to a year and a day in prison. He was also ordered to repay to the Carter County school system some $36,000 in misappropriated funds.

Combs came out of the episode in pretty good shape. Heman McGuire was out, and Combs seemed to be the man who had foiled the villain. Yet the legal and constitutional weaknesses that had let McGuire operate for so long were still on the books. It was still possible for a Heman McGuire to get control of a county school system and use it for his own power and profit. The superintendent of public instruction could still refuse to remove a McGuire, and still had so much power that he could defy the governor's reform efforts. The 1891 constitution was still a millstone around the neck of Kentucky.

But while the Carter County mess was becoming an irritant, a far more serious scandal was brewing within the Combs administration, and it would prove hurtful. During the final days of the legislative session, however, Combs wanted only to bring it to a successful close, and this, everyone but Chandler and a few of his followers conceded, he did. He not only got from the legislature practically every measure he asked for but enjoyed the overwhelming support of his party throughout. Whereas Chandler as governor had managed to pass bills only with Republican help in both houses, Combs almost invariably had more than 80 percent of the Democrats with him. James Ware sponsored 51 bills in the Senate, losing three. Tom Ray sponsored 68 bills in the House; none that came to a vote was defeated.

On February 25, Richard Harwood reported that "in the legislative session of 1958 Gov. A.B. Chandler got 80 percent of Republican votes as against only 40 percent of the Democratic votes. His program was in

constant trouble. In the crucial tests thus far, House and Senate Democrats have cast 81 percent of their votes for the Combs program. As a
result, Combs's batting average with the Assembly thus far is 1,000."

But early in March 1960 the Department of Highways had reportedly contracted to lease 34 used dump trucks from an associate of
Thurston Cooke, the Louisville automobile dealer who had served as
finance chairman for the Combs-Wyatt campaign. Before this "truck
deal" was finished, it would cast suspicion on the administration and
cause a rift between Combs and Earle Clements that would never be
totally healed.

10

Of Trucks, Clocks, and Varmints

As the legislators packed to go home, Combs was hailed by the press as a master politician, a man in cool control of his office. The *Louisville Times* called him "a Kentucky Truman, surprisingly tough when necessary, courageous, humorous, willing to take responsibility, and with a firm grasp of the historic and political realities of the governorship." This view was not, of course, unanimous. Happy Chandler announced that Kentuckians were ready to revolt against the sales tax and declared that the Combs administration had a "bad moral tone." A spokesman for the Associated Industries of Kentucky called Combs a "labor lobbyist."

The truth was, however, that neither the Chandler faction nor the Republican party had offered an alternative program or countered any of Combs's major bills with substantial substitutes. Kentucky factions still battled over power, not programs.

But Combs had little time to savor his victory. On March 27 he signed the bill taking Franklin Circuit Court from Judge W.B. Ardery's jurisdiction, with a new judge and commonwealth's attorney to be named on September 1 to serve until the November 1961 elections. The new court made some sense, since so many important cases concerning state agencies originate in Franklin County, where Frankfort is located. But Bill Ardery was popular, and the action, which was interpreted by many of his friends as a move to strip him of influence, was not forgotten for years.

There were kind words from business leaders when it was announced on April 4, 1960, that the state had cut payrolls by 7 percent. (Some newsmen said it was only 5 percent, but it is hard to tell at any given moment how many peple are on the payroll. At all times there are hundreds, even thousands of employees applying, quitting, or being hired.) "Cutting the fat" out of government is a hallowed tradition; all governors do it. Even those who load the payrolls with friends, relatives, and drones who can be depended on to vote correctly invariably rustle up some figures to show that they are squeezing the taxpayer's dollar. Yet somehow the state payroll always seems to be bigger than before. Anyhow, the objective is not to get fewer people on the payrolls but to get fewer drones and more competent workers, but this bit of common sense seldom appeals to the voter.

For the moment, Combs's chief objective was to save the sales tax from groups that wanted to slash it. This, he knew, would not be easy; the best way to defend the tax would be to show people what they would get in return. But parks, schools, and improved services could not be produced overnight. He needed time. And he needed some way to persuade the people to approve a convention to rewrite the state constitution.

On April 10, Combs made what many people—including a lot of his own—considered a mistake by taking $50,000 from his contingency fund to build a floral clock on the lawn of the capitol building. He had seen one in Edinburgh, Scotland, and thought a similar one would be a colorful addition to the capitol grounds. It sounded unusual, to put it kindly—a large, raised concrete clock face on the slanted surface of which flowers would be planted seasonally and large hands would tell the time, the whole thing to be surrounded by a reflecting pool. Critics protested "littering the dignified lawn" of the capitol. Happy Chandler chortled that "instead of the time being 11 o'clock, in Kentucky it is two petunias past a jimson weed."

But time proved the critics wrong. The "flower clock" became one of the most talked-about and popular tourist attractions in the state and the most visited spot in Frankfort. The cost was more than covered by the coins people tossed into the reflecting pool.

But stories about a "truck deal" appearing in the Louisville and Lexington newspapers were beginning to worry Combs. They appeared to involve Earle Clements and his official dealings with Louisville Ford dealer Thurston Cooke, and Combs knew that the press would blame him for any wrongdoing involving Clements, for whose appointment he had already been widely criticized. And from the first story, reported in the *Courier-Journal* by Kyle Vance, it was obvious that there was something very unusual about the agreement under which 34 dump trucks were leased from the Louisville Equipment Rental Company for Highway Department work.

Whether the "truck deal" was as bad as it was painted at the time is a matter for debate. Earle Clements protested as long as he lived that it was a bargain for the state (although he also said at one point that he had been prepared to cancel it). In essence, it was an effort, hallowed in political tradition, to throw some business to a friend. Thurston Cooke was a heavy-set, jovial Ford dealer from Louisville whose personal charities and company slogan—"Thurston Cooke Is the Place to Look"—were widely known. He was respected as a leader in the Baptist church and had served as finance chairman for the Combs-Wyatt campaign. Later, he encountered financial troubles when he was forced to reclaim a number of heavy-duty trucks whose new owners could not meet their payments. He leased the used trucks to Lloyd Harris, a Kentuckian operating at the time in Alabama, but Harris, basically a small-time operator, found that he could not efficiently operate a fleet of 50 trucks and asked Cooke to help him get rid of most of them.

Cooke called "someone in the Highway Department," and a few weeks later the department leased 34 of these heavy-duty, tandem-axle trucks from the Louisville Equipment Rental Company. Who or what was the Louisville Equipment Rental Company? asked the press. Good question, but no one seemed to have an answer. It appeared to be a firm based in a vacant building next door to Cooke's Ford agency on Louisville's Frankfort Avenue. Officially, it was operated by E.R. Van Meter, a Louisville contractor and alleged associate of Cooke, and Robert Grubbs, Cooke's attorney.

Harris had sent 15 of the trucks from Alabama—ten to the Highway Department and five to Louisville Equipment for repairs—when Kyle Vance published his story questioning the lease arrangement. The state had never before leased such equipment, he pointed out. Some Highway Department employees complained that the beds of the big trucks were too high to be loaded with existing department equipment. Furthermore, reported Vance, it would cost more to lease the trucks than to buy them outright for their "bluebook" or used-truck value.

Newspapers began asking embarrassing questions. What was this lease business? Who was Harris? Why was the Highway Department going to Alabama to buy secondhand trucks for what new trucks would cost in Kentucky? Who owned Louisville Equipment Rental Company? Were the trucks in poor repair? Director of Purchasing Harry Klapeke and others claimed that one advantage of the big trucks was that they could hold far more than the smaller trucks then being used by the department. But Vance charged that if they were loaded to capacity, they would violate state load limits; and if they were loaded only to the legal load limit, they would hold no more than smaller, cheaper trucks. Was Clements involved, editorials asked? Was Combs protecting Clements by failing to investigate or cancel the deal?

As a matter of fact, Combs didn't know the answers to most of these questions. The whole thing had mushroomed into a front-page scandal while he was involved with the legislature. But the press expects the governor to learn and reveal the facts once suspicious circumstances are exposed, and it appeared that Combs was failing to act in order to protect his old friend and mentor. Or was he part of the thing?

On April 12, Combs asked Clements about the lease arrangement, reminding him that the newspaper stories were beginning to hurt. Clements assured him that everything was legal, ethical, and beneficial to the state. Combs, though worried, decided to wait and see whether additional facts being revealed in the press would clear up the confusion and quiet suspicions. They didn't; on the contrary, press criticism grew louder. On April 15, Combs asked Clements for a full report on the lease contract, a request that angered Clements, who viewed it as a slur on his integrity. His report next day made no mention of Thurston Cooke, but by that time stories were beginning to appear in the press about Lloyd Harris and his ties to Cooke.

Combs began his own investigation. He and Dr. Robert Martin met with Clements to discuss the matter, but Clements repeated that the deal was a good arrangement for the state and blamed criticism on the press, which had opposed his appointment to begin with. Significantly, Martin, a great friend and admirer of Clements, disagreed and urged Clements to find out what was going on and get it cleaned up. What Clements did not say was that Cooke was in deep financial trouble because of his failure to sell the trucks and needed time to raise enough money to head off collapse. Had this been made public, it is conceivable that Combs might have been able to mollify public opinion and give Cooke time, for until then Cooke had tried only to extricate himself from a bad business deal.

But the press and political foes were demanding to know why Combs did not act. Actually, Combs was not sure, then or later, that he had the authority to go over the head of the commissioner of highways in the matter of equipment. But on April 19 he did, canceling the deal.

That did not end the matter. Clements took Combs's action not only as a personal affront but as an act of ingratitude. He felt that his integrity had been impugned. On the day after the contract was canceled, he addressed the chamber of commerce in Louisville and later held a news conference at which he defended every aspect of the truck lease, insisting that it saved the state money, that no trucks in ill repair would ever have been accepted, that the trucks under lease were not too big to be loaded with state equipment, and that they would not have had to carry illegal loads in order to justify their cost. And he did not resign his post as highway commissioner, as some had expected. Not then. But a noticeable coolness began to develop between him and Combs.

Friends later speculated that Combs might have done better to persuade Clements to cancel the deal rather than do it himself. They were probably right; that might have avoided a clash that hurt the state as well as Combs. But persuading Clements to back down when he felt his honor was involved was no easy matter. He was a proud and stubborn man.

"I never knew Cooke very well," Combs said later. "Actually, Wyatt knew him better than I did. But he was Earle's man—partly, of course, because he had raised money for us in the campaign. None of us thought he would do anything unethical, being one of the top Baptists in the state. He had a fine reputation. But, you know, the real reason Earle got into the deal was because of Prich [Edward Prichard]. I don't think anyone knew that at the time. I doubt that many people know it now. Earle and Prich were always very close. Prich's attachment to Earle began when he came home from Washington and backed Clements against Waterfield for governor, though Phil Ardery, Prich's law partner, was for Waterfield. Cooke had put Prich on a retainer as counsel for the company, no doubt at Earle's request. Prich was still having his troubles and needed the money. That was the biggest reason Earle didn't want to hurt Cooke, that and the fact that Cooke rated a lot of respect."

In retrospect, the episode seems hardly worth the uproar. As Combs pointed out, the state had spent and lost no money; it had accepted no questionable merchandise; and no unethical conduct had been proven. But the aroma of suspicion clung to the entire transaction long after it had left the front pages; reminders of it surfaced again the following year when Thurston Cooke was found guilty of financial juggling, which he undertook to save his auto empire when the truck deal fell through. It was, in all, a rather tragic affair—for Cooke, a kind, friendly, generous man who was undone by bad luck; for Clements; and in the end for Combs, who, though he had committed no wrong, saw a shadow fall across his previously clean image. This was in the old tradition. The reputations of more Kentucky governors have been damaged by the conduct of their appointees than by their own misdeeds.

The truck deal was a setback, though at the time more annoying than critical. So was the rift between Combs and Clements. Some political writers declared that the inexperienced Combs and Wyatt could not have managed the political maneuvering of the legislative session so successfully had it not been for the advice of the canny Clements. But this was not the case. The presence of Clements in the administration no doubt helped to keep some legislators cooperative, but Combs seldom asked him for advice. And Clements, to his credit, seldom offered it.

His support gave the administration the benefit of great expertise in a critical department of government, and a great political intellect that could be called upon. But there was also a negative aspect to his presence in the office: as long as he was in the Highway Department there would be doubts in the minds of some about who was actually running the administration. The image of an inexperienced governor operating under the influence of the wily, powerful politician who had done much to create him did not help Combs or allow him the stature that his handling of the legislature had merited. The fact that Combs had not fired Clements did nothing for his image; on the other hand, the fact that he had canceled a contract so stoutly defended by Clements did give him the appearance of a strong and capable leader.

And for the fight ahead Combs needed a favorable image. His first legislative session had been a great success. It had given him the program he wanted and the money to carry it out. Many observers, including some of his own officials, thought he would rest easy for a while, content to see the construction of roads, parks, schools, and hospitals; the impact of better pay for teachers; and the increased help to the elderly, the sick, the mentally ill.

But Combs wanted more. Far more. It took a while for people to realize that what he had in mind was a complete, fundamental restructuring of the nature, shape, and quality of state government. The sales tax had been a crucial first step; it had given the state money with which to operate a modern government on a level of service similar to that of other states. But Combs knew that Kentucky government would never be a truly modern operation as long as it was shackled by the constitution of 1891. The constitution simply had to be revised.

A comparison of Kentucky's constitution and that of the United States does not flatter Kentucky. Indeed, it is remarkable that the Kentuckians of 1891, given the example of the U.S. Constitution, could have written such a wordy, rambling monument to suspicion and distrust. The aims of the two documents were as different as the mood of the times in which they were written, and thereby may hang the whole unfortunate story.

Kentucky in 1891 was a state still divided by emotions and interests echoing from the Civil War, divisions of white against black, farmers against townspeople, small farmers against big planters, agrarians against urbanites, Bluegrass against Ohio River cities, pro-Union Republicans against Democrats still burdened with southern memories, central Kentucky against the L&N Railroad, and small towns against each other in competition for railroads.

The framers of the U.S. Constitution designed it not only to install liberty but to forestall tyranny. The danger of government, they realized, even one in which power rests with the people, is that it constantly risks giving people the power to destroy the liberties that permit them to govern. In brief, it is the people, through government, who threaten government by the people. So government must be curbed, but not so much that it is not free to provide for the people the rights to life, liberty, and the pursuit of happiness, which entail national security and individual welfare. James Madison saw the danger of powerful people working through the agencies of government against the democratic foundations of government. And so he proposed a system wherein the branches were made powerful enough to endure but not so powerful that they could not be checked by one another.

Kentucky went about it more or less in the reverse. It protected the rights and liberties of the people simply by giving government too little power to threaten those rights and liberties. Instead of empowering government to act and limiting its power through checks and balances, it made government weak through constitutional curbs. The legislature could meet only once every two years, and then for only 60 days. It could amend the constitution to give itself more power only through a laborious process that could not be accomplished during the lifetime of any legislature. It could not resort to other than pay-as-you-go financing to fuel progress. Governors could not succeed themselves and could therefore bring to fruition during their terms only short-range programs. They did not have control over their own administrations, since many of the most important officers serving during their terms were elected and outside their influence or control. The judiciary was a hodgepodge of political and appointive posts that assured only that judges would be subject to the caprice of politics. Government could pay employees only limited salaries, geared to the time at which the constitution was written and quickly outmoded by changing economics.

The state constitution curtailed the operating efficiency of towns and cities by giving them power to act in many critical instances only with approval of the legislature (infrequently in session) and the concurrence of the governor. Sheriffs could not succeed themselves, though other county officials could. The government could not incur debt of more than $500,000. And so on. The checks, in brief, were embodied in the constitution, which was designed to curb rather than guide the operation of government.

The state could not, Combs realized, operate freely and efficiently until these curbs were relaxed and the constitution was revised to provide a general statement of principles and guidelines, as did the federal charter. He was hoping that the success of his program and its apparent popularity would persuade the voters to take the next step, just as it would encourage political leaders to lend themselves to a vote-getting cause. Most of all, he saw it as an integral part of a program to give Kentucky a modern framework of government that would reassure the people of Kentucky and involve them in the mood, the enthusiasm of a new day.

Charter revision was the major item but not the only one Combs was trying to sell to the Kentucky voter that summer. He wanted approval of the proposed bond issue for building roads and parks. He wanted a new, intermediate court to lighten the load of the Court of Appeals. He hoped to convince the people that the improvements made possible by the sales tax were worth the cost, and persuade them to resist those politicians calling for repeal or reduction of the tax.

Combs also wanted to do something about the chronically weak economy of eastern Kentucky. It was a disheartening problem. Nothing undertaken by state or federal government had seemed to get to the heart of the nagging weakness that plagued the eastern and southeastern areas of the state. By the time of the Civil War, the hill counties were already a cultural and economic backwater, falling steadily behind the Bluegrass in schools, roads, public services, industrial investment, personal income. The violence that tore and divided families during the war, the feuds that divided and crippled its communities later, served to keep eastern Kentucky mired in its isolation and poverty, regarded by the rest of the state and country as backward, violent, and ignorant. The mountains were Republican, and when the Republicans fell into disfavor with the Goebel episode, the mountains lost stature and influence in Frankfort. Furthermore, more than any other section of the state, eastern Kentucky became the province of outside corporations who profited from the mountains' coal, oil, gas, silica, and timber but cared little for the welfare of the people, plowed little of their gain back into the counties, and bought and corrupted city and county governments to prevent them from enacting a tax system that would let the mountain people share in the wealth of their land.

The East Kentucky Turnpike would be the first modern highway reaching the eastern third of the state. No section would benefit more by the new spending for schools and the establishment of community colleges. The new parks and small lakes were calculated to attract tourists. New or improved airports at Paintsville, Hazard, Pikeville, Middlesboro, and London would help tie those areas closer to the rest of the state. But these measures, Combs knew, would not be enough. The region needed new industrial investment and new jobs to enable it to break away from its dependence on coal, with its boom-and-bust cycles and resulting unemployment.

His concern with the Appalachian region of the state led Combs to appoint John Whisman, slender, studious executive director of the Eastern Kentucky Regional Planning Commission, to represent Kentucky at a meeting of representatives from six Appalachian states who would urge the establishment by Congress of a regional authority to seek cures for Appalachia's old ills. Both Combs and Wyatt believed that the area's troubles could not be relieved without federal funds and federal power. At graduation ceremonies at Whitesburg High School that spring, Wyatt called for changing the formulas under which road, dam, and work projects qualified for federal assistance so as to give an advantage to depressed mountain areas.

In late April, Combs announced with obvious pleasure that the state had been given a $754,000 grant by the Kellogg Foundation, to be spent—along with matching state funds—to seek solutions to the economic puzzle of eastern Kentucky. Combs called it a "breakthrough in the psychology of gloom" of the 30-county region and chose Dr. Frank J. Welch, dean of the University of Kentucky College of Agriculture and former director of the Tennessee Valley Authority, to head the study. Combs then met with Governor Millard Tawes of Maryland, and the two of them hatched the idea for an organization to focus federal attention on the Appalachian region. On May 20, he attended a meeting of six Appalachian governors in Annapolis, Maryland, out of which came the Appalachian Governors' Conference, the forerunner of the Appalachian Regional Commission. Combs served as chairman of the conference for its first two years and, with the help of Seventh District Congressman Carl Perkins, urged Congress and President John F. Kennedy to establish a permanent agency designed to meet Appalachia's specific needs. The Appalachian Regional Commission was part of Kennedy's program to help Appalachia, though it was enacted into law after his death.

At a national governors' conference at Glacier Park the following month, Combs told the meeting that a special federal policy was needed for road funding in such depressed areas as eastern Kentucky, along the lines of his financing of the Mountain Parkway. This "imaginative use of the bonding power" to provide financing for roads that would generate traffic needed to justify their cost seemed an obvious alternative to the traditional, and deadening, formula of providing money on the basis of existing traffic counts. The federal officials gave Combs's proposals a cool reception. The course of bureaucracy quickly becomes a rut.

There are always social functions that a governor must attend or preside over—the Governor's Derby Breakfast, for example. The Derby Breakfast was an old Kentucky custom, usually featuring country ham, eggs, grits, beaten biscuits, and various fruits and preserves, all served with and after traditional mint juleps properly offered up in silver goblets. Actually a sort of early luncheon for late-rising Derby guests who had been partying the night before, the Derby Breakfast ordinarily began some time before noon and ended in time for the guests to get to Churchill Downs for most of the afternoon's races and the climactic Derby itself. It didn't hurt the social or political status of public officials, politicians, horsemen, and other citizens to be asked to bring their guests to the governor's house for a drink and some food before the race; beginning with Happy Chandler's first term, the Governor's Derby Breakfast had become an increasingly popular event.

Combs decided, in what may have been intended as a Jacksonian gesture, to add a lot of old friends and just plain people to the guest list; he made preparations for 250 guests at the mansion. More than that showed up. People who were not supposed to bring guests, family, friends, or kinfolk brought guests, families, friends, and kinfolk. State troopers on guard duty complained, "You can't stir 'em with a stick." People wandered around the mansion as if on a sightseeing tour; security was impossible. Combs decided that the next breakfast would be held on the lawn, and in succeeding years what had been a small, rather elite gathering became a mob scene, with thousands of Kentuckians from all corners of the state standing in line from around eight o'clock in the morning until past noon, to file past and shake the hand of the governor and move on into huge tents filled with food-laden tables, bands, and hard-working politicians. From an elegant social occasion, the Governor's Derby Breakfast became a popular gathering. It lost something in elegance.

Combs also initiated the custom of having a state employees' picnic; naturally, he was expected to attend, take part in various activities, judge contests, and eat all manner of food. In addition, he journeyed to Hopkins County to hear a plea for state help in controlling salt marsh mosquitoes—apparently breeding in old strip-mine pits filled with water—which were becoming so thick that cattle could not graze in pastures and farmers could not work in the fields. He sched-

uled a conference on the problems of aging, to which 4,000 persons
were invited, and presided over the opening session.

Combs also launched a "Keep Kentucky Beautiful" campaign
which, at first glance, looked a lot like every other governor's clean-up
campaign. He saw it as something more. The state put on a big
publicity drive, its symbol a youngster called Daniel Broom—pat-
terned, of course, after the old scout but equipped with a broom
instead of the historic long rifle. Though it seemed rather routine at the
time, and certainly less important than Combs's more substantial
beautification projects, it was the forerunner of Ladybird (Mrs. Lyndon
B.) Johnson's "Keep America Beautiful" campaign. It brought Combs
praise from state garden and conservation clubs, but it yielded substantial results only when backed up with laws to get junked cars off
the road and screens around roadside junkyards.

"We had contests all over the state," recalled Combs, "between
regions and counties, giving awards to those thinking up and carrying
out the best ideas. Connie Quinn developed the program and made it
work. We gave plaques to county judges and Jaycees. I remember
when we gave a plaque to this one old judge, and he got his words
mixed up and said, 'I don't appreciate this great honor, but I want you
to know I deserve it from the bottom of my heart.' "

On August 14, Combs observed his forty-ninth birthday, and
shortly thereafter organized another of Kentucky's colorful (if that is
the word) eating occasions. This was in the state tradition, for Kentuckians are prone to strange feasts. In eastern Kentucky they have a
Poke Sallet Festival, at which is featured a salad made of the young
shoots and leaves of the poke bush (the only parts of the weed that can
be safely eaten, since the mature leaves and berries are poisonous).
There is also in the mountains a day given to eating—or pretending to
eat and thus leading naive outsiders to eat—ramps, which are a wild
and vicious offshoot of the onion family. In other parts of the state
people make great to-do over various types of fish, pork, and barbecue,
all of which are likely to induce stomach distress, and in Fulton they
observe a Banana Festival featuring a banana pudding so huge that
citizens who have misplaced small children or dogs immediately become uneasy about the pudding's contents.

Combs originated the Varmint Supper. (Some say this questionable
practice was first observed during the administration of Governor
Lawrence Wetherby, but it first came to public attention, at least,
because of Combs.) "Varmint" is a rural corruption of the word
"vermin," which provides an idea of the menu, one that was never
given the Good Housekeeping Seal of Approval or hailed by the

gourmets of America. Possum, raccoon, squirrel, groundhog, and even—some say—snake were served up and supposedly eaten by the gathering of friends, political cronies, hunting companions, government officials, and an occasional newsman—all of whom, it is safe to assume, had been given enough to drink so that they could pretend to enjoy the fare. As a matter of fact, the groaning board also groaned with quail, dove, rabbit, duck, goose, venison, and more customary game, along with a good variety of vegetables, breads, and desserts. But it was the varmints that earned for the supper its reputation. The varmint tradition was carried on for years after the Combs era— because of the fellowship, it may be assumed.

11

The Shackles of Tradition

It is curious to note how the "Three C's" of Kentucky—Chandler, Clements, and Combs—dominated the politics of the postwar period, and how frequently they seemed to share the stage. Possibly because he was following a Chandler administration that had left considerable political debris in its wake, Combs seemed to encounter the shadow of Chandler at every turn. For example, in the fall of 1960 he raised another small dust storm by stopping payments to the architectural firm of Meriwether, Marye and Associates, which was supervising the construction of the University of Kentucky medical center, after a state audit indicated that the state had overpaid the firm by more than half a million dollars. His action raised an immediate political outcry, since Meriwether and Marye had not only been employed during the Chandler administration but had designed Chandler's new home, only recently completed in Versailles.

"I don't see what that has to do with the medical center," said Chandler. "They are just trying to smear me. But I'm used to that. As far as my house is concerned, I can assure you that it was built with my own money, and I'll be glad to show you the records on that."

However, H.G. Wittenberg, a Louisville contractor who was then chairman of the state fair board, told reporters that he had supervised construction of the house for Chandler and had not been paid for his services. And State Auditor Joe Schneider said that the state had first contracted, during the Chandler administration, with Meriwether and Marye for a fee based on the medical center's cost of construction but had then changed it to a fee based on estimated cost of construction, which resulted in the alleged overpayments of $520,265. Hugh Meriwether, head of the firm, said the charges were "a mass of lies and innuendo" aimed at him because he was a friend of Chandler's and had served as best man at Happy's wedding. He said he would meet with Combs and explain the situation.

"He did," said Combs. "He just didn't explain it to my satisfaction. We changed the contract."

Another, even darker storm was brewing. Like a hurricane that is born as a ripple of air over the mountains of Africa and slowly grows to dangerous proportions as it swirls its way across the Atlantic, a wordy battle had erupted between officials of the city of Newport and Campbell County and a group of ministers who charged that city and county officials were not enforcing the vice laws. On May 25 the ministers visited Combs and for 90 minutes complained that prostitution, gambling, illegal liquor operations, and violence were being ignored by the police, sheriff, and judges of Newport and Campbell County, and asked the governor's help.

Nothing does less to brighten and lighten a governor's day than a complaining visit from reform or purity groups. These worthies invariably want the governor to do something that will earn him the gratitude of the moral element (which will forget it before the next election) and the hostility of much of the political and economic structure of the town (which will remember).

Newport was a town with a juicy reputation, not unusual for a small town located across a river from a metropolis. Situated on the Ohio River just opposite Cincinnati, it lured the more adventurous after-hour customers to its night spots, many of which offered girls and gambling as well as liquor and music. The fact that the law was not enthusiastically enforced in Newport was hardly news. It had long been a good-time town, with a strip of gambling and striptease joints where visiting firemen could always find a girl or a game. But exactly what the ministers wanted Combs to do about it—or what he had the power to do—was not clear. It was Combs's belief that he could remove the local officials only if a hearing found them guilty of misfeasance or neglect of duty. No such hearings had been held; in fact, there were no formal charges against the officials and no concrete evidence against them other than the testimony of the ministers. He could not send the state police into Newport, as the ministers asked, since the law stipulated that the state police could assume jurisdiction within a city only if asked to do so by city officials. But he promised the ministers he would do what he could.

They left feeling that they had found an ally. Combs called Attorney General John Breckinridge to see what could be done. Like the squabble in Carter County between Heman McGuire and the citizens' committee, the Newport mess was not something Combs would have chosen. He had other, more important, statewide concerns. But there was no avoiding these situations once they had been brought into the open. There is nothing newspapers love more than a vice exposé, and the Louisville, Lexington, and Cincinnati papers jumped on the plaints of the ministers like hounds loosed on a fox trail. Reporters swarmed into Newport and happily loaded their expense accounts to prove that vice was, indeed, rampant. Girls stripped down to nothing. Booze could be had at all hours. There were places where gambling went on and prostitutes sold themselves for the money of evil and lustful men, while enforcement officials turned their backs and, it was alleged, profited from their lack of vigilance.

The reporters tore themselves away from Newport long enough to go home and expose the shocking conditions. The decent element of Kentucky quivered with shock and indignation. What, the papers thundered, was the state going to do about it? The answer, it soon became apparent, was—for the time being—very little. Combs had other things to do.

Among his more pressing concerns was the approaching 1960 National Democratic Convention in Los Angeles. It was certainly no secret that Earle Clements had been working tirelessly to line up support for his longtime ally, Senator Lyndon Johnson of Texas, and hoped to deliver Kentucky's 17 votes toward Johnson's nomination for president. This posed a problem: Wyatt and Combs had run on a platform that promised to abolish the unit rule, which gave all the state's votes to the candidate having the majority of delegates. Many members of the State Central Committee concurred, and at the preconvention meeting of the committee it was agreed that there would be no unit vote. But Combs had promised Clements to back his support of Johnson; once in Los Angeles, Combs passed the word that, while every delegate had a right to vote for his choice, he was for Johnson. He also made it plain that he was putting no pressure on anyone. He told the delegates to notify his assistant, Wendell Ford, how they wanted to be recorded so that the delegation could be announced, but added that he did not even want to know what the individual votes were.

"Earl had asked me early on to be for Johnson," Combs recalled, "and I said fine. I couldn't see any reason why not. We didn't know who would be running, and Johnson was a good liberal, an F.D.R. man and a southerner, so I made the commitment. Then when the Johnson-Kennedy contest began, Johnson called me, since I had control of the delegation, and I told him yes, I have promised Earle and you can depend on it. But I told him we had a problem, that Wyatt and I had been against the unit rule and couldn't back out on it. I told him there would be four or five Kennedy and Stevenson votes, and that he could count on 27 or 28 of the delegates—each had half a vote. Wilson was for Stevenson, of course, made a seconding speech for him. Happy was one of the solid votes for Kennedy in the delegation. He was a friend and admirer of old Joe Kennedy, Jack's daddy. I couldn't control him, and didn't want to. Anyhow, that's the way it went, and that kept everybody reasonably happy. We had a caucus, but that was just a formality. We just had half votes. We split all the votes into halves, so that more people could be recognized.

"After Kennedy was nominated, we decided to go for Stu Symington for vice-president because we didn't think Johnson would take it. Most people didn't. He surprised a lot of people, including Sam Rayburn and Bobby Kennedy, when he did. He accepted over their protests. Earle didn't think he would take it, and we got caught off balance when he did.

"But the one thing Earle was maddest about wasn't Johnson or Kennedy. The convention people had put us in this fleabag hotel. A real one. Clements and some of the others got there early and the man assigned them their rooms, and when Earle saw his, he called the manager and demanded a better one. He said, 'There must be some mistake. I'm Senator Clements. I'm sure I'm supposed to have another room.' And the manager said, 'Yeah, you're right. You're in the wrong room. That's the governor's room. You'll have to move.' And he put him in a smaller room. An even worse one. It griped hell out of Earle."

Wyatt had worked hard for Adlai Stevenson, as had John Breckinridge. Dick Moloney of Lexington was for John F. Kennedy, as were Chandler and several Jefferson Countians. Kennedy won on the first ballot. After Kennedy's nomination, Bill May led the move for Stuart Symington for vice-president, and Johnson won. As May said later, "We didn't cash a ticket." Back home in Frankfort there was a general feeling among some Democrats that "we spent our time feeding hay to a dead horse."

"I didn't agree with that," said Combs. "I still don't. I was genuinely for Johnson. I knew him personally and didn't know Kennedy. I thought it would be good for the country to have a president from the South. If we had wanted to be expedient, we could have switched to Kennedy after we arrived in Los Angeles. But the one thing our conduct there proved is that once a Kentuckian gives his word he stands hitched. We didn't strike out. We came home with a friendly vice-president. The press, especially Harwood, ridiculed our performance, but by objective standards we did all right."

But the convention did little to strengthen the party, especially the Combs wing, which needed all its strength for the fall senatorial campaign in which it was backing former Governor Keen Johnson to run against the formidable Republican Senator John Sherman Cooper. John Y. Brown, former state legislator and congressman and unsuccessful candidate for governor, had also entered the primary race, and in a switch of historic proportions Happy Chandler was backing him. Keen Johnson had been Chandler's lieutenant governor, and had named Happy to the Senate, whereas John Y. Brown and Chandler had long been political enemies. It was Chandler who had gotten J.C.W. Beckham into the Senate race that Brown had hoped to win against M.M. Logan and had thus cost Brown his chance. Brown had always been an advocate of the sales tax that Chandler so hotly opposed, and he had once accused Chandler of double-crossing him in his effort to win the governorship. Factionalism made strange bedfellows.

But even had Keen Johnson been supported by a united party, he would have had an uphill fight. A strong Republican tide was running nationally, and John Cooper had always been a strong candidate.

"We knew Keen didn't have a chance," said Combs. "He knew it. He just ran because we needed someone to make a race, a respectable race, against Cooper. We really didn't do much for him. Keen was sick during most of the campaign."

Whether the convention weakened further the Combs-Clements relationship, as some have charged, is questionable. Relations between the two men continued to be proper, though both seemed to realize that a change was about due. A temporary embarrassment arose on August 17, when the Civil Service Commission announced in Washington that it was investigating whether Clements, as highway commissioner, had been in violation of the federal Hatch Act forbidding those on federal payrolls or handling federal funds from taking part in federal elections. (The investigation was later dropped.) But that was not the important factor. Clements and Combs had already been talking, and Clements had told him that he wanted to resign and join Lyndon Johnson's campaign. "In fact," said Combs, "Johnson himself had called me to talk about it. Now, it's true that a tension, a coldness, had developed between us. But Johnson's nomination gave us, you might say, an out, an excuse. So Earle came to me and said he wanted to go to Washington to work for Johnson, and we went so far as to talk about a successor. I asked him how about Henry Ward, and he said that was fine. So Henry came over and we talked, and then we had a little luncheon for Clements. I forget whether Ward was there, but it was understood that he would be the man. There was agreement. And there was nothing sudden about Earle's resignation."

On August 18 Combs called a press conference and announced that he had talked with Clements in Washington the night before, and that Clements had decided it was time for his resignation and thought the announcement should be made in Frankfort. The resignation, said Combs, would become effective September 1.

Clements' departure was something of a milestone in state politics. It marked the beginning of the end of the Clements wing of the state Democratic party and the coming of age of the Combs wing. Furthermore, it was something of a tragedy. Earle Clements was a man of sensitive pride and great ego; he was also an innovative, hard-working, and progressive governor. But despite the provocation his conduct posed, he viewed Combs's action in canceling the truck deal as not only disloyalty but a rebuke, and Earle Clements was not a man to take lightly a public rebuke. He hid beneath his calm, courtly, almost cold demeanor a fiery temper that he often kept barely in check.

I had experienced his anger myself during his tenure as governor. I was walking down the capitol corridor beside the Senate chamber one day during the legislative session of 1948, shortly before the legislature was scheduled to reconvene following lunch. I fell into step with Governor Clements and, at the suggestion of Senator Richard Moloney, asked him why he had erased from the House orders of the day a bill that would have removed REA co-ops from the jurisdiction of the Public Service Commission. Earle had his arm around my shoulder in friendly fashion and had just addressed me as "Podnuh." But in a second he stiffened with anger, his face flushed, and the veins in his temples stood out as if he were being choked. Grabbing me by the lapels, he almost lifted me off the floor and slammed me against the wall of the corridor. "You sonofabitch!" he growled, and with each phrase banged me against the wall—"You've been—trying—to gut me—ever since—last—November"—in a demonstration of rhythm the artistry of which I did not fully appreciate at the moment.

I wanted to protest that the accusation was false, as indeed it was, but was too occupied to coin witticisms appropriate to the occasion. Fortunately for me, Attorney General Jo Ferguson and a state trooper were standing a few feet away. The poor trooper seemed more horrified than I, not being eager to lay hands on the governor nor yet eager to see him demolish a member of the press. Ferguson was more decisive.

"Governor!" he shouted, "Governor!" and jumped between us, to my intense relief. Without another word, Clements whirled and stalked away. He did not speak to me for several years. I continued to write about him, of course, and years later, when he was running for the Senate, I encountered him in Madisonville, where he was working Main Street. To my surprise, he greeted me warmly and introduced me to a man whose identity I have forgotten, saying, "This is a friend of mine, a fine writer. I say, a fine writer. I once did him an injustice, I'm afraid, but he has never held it against me."

That, I think, was the most complete apology Earle could muster, and I appreciated it. After that we became friendly again; I enjoyed some good talks with him and two pleasant visits to his home in Morganfield before he became angry once more at the newspaper (not without cause, I fear) and included me in his resentment. I had not been part of the incident that aroused his anger, but I had called editorially for his resignation as highway commissioner during the episode of the truck deal, and I understood why he resented that. Our differences were healed only shortly before his death. I regret those periods of hostility. They were my loss.

After his resignation his temper erupted in a cold fury and during the ensuing 20 years became legendary, as Clements seized, shook, cursed, or struck opponents, former friends, or even people with whom he was having a casual discussion. He became so bitter toward Combs that he made an alliance with Happy Chandler—who had ridiculed and reviled him and opposed almost everything Clements had tried to do—and opposed candidates associated with Combs, the man with whom he had been so pleasantly and productively associated for so long.

This was painful for Clements' friends, most of whom were also Combs supporters. Historically, the factionalism dividing the dominant Democratic party has bred a bitter brand of politics, for the winning faction usually gains control of the state, and some losing Democrats have found it easier to make common cause with Republicans than with the winning faction. During his years in office, Combs remained on fairly good terms with most Republican legislators. It was the followers of Happy Chandler who proved to be the bitter foes.

In the final five years of his life Clements mellowed considerably and patched up his disagreements with practically all of his old enemies, but he never entirely forgave Combs. In 1984, only a few months before his death, a dinner was given in Clements' honor at Louisville's Seelbach Hotel, the headquarters of so many of his great old political campaigns. He spoke courteously to Combs, who had insisted on attending, but did not mention him in his remarks. Chandler was not present at the dinner.

But painful as it was, the departure of Clements could not be allowed to disrupt the operation of state government. Combs and Clements had already agreed on Henry Ward as a successor, partly because of his broad experience. He had served five terms as a state legislator, had been a candidate for lieutenant governor, had served on the staff of Earle Clements in Washington when Clements was in the Senate, and was general manager of the Louisville Area Chamber of Commerce when Combs asked him to be highway commissioner. He had a reputation for integrity, and enjoyed a sound rapport with the press. Equally important, he had the confidence and support of Clements. And he brought into the Highway Department such expert aides as Robert Bell, who had served previously with Ward in the Department of Conservation and as assistant to Lieutenant Governor Wyatt. (Bell was to become one of those men who, like Felix Joyner, would be almost indispensable to state government; he would serve as commissioner of parks and of revenue before a change in party control removed him from Frankfort.)

"I went to see Earle and talked to him, and he urged me to do it," Ward explained later. "I wanted to be certain that he wouldn't object. I was very fond of Earle. He had been good for Kentucky. I learned a lot from him."

There was no single program more important to Kentucky or to the success of the Combs administration than the massive highway building program that encompassed interstate highways, turnpikes, two- and four-lane federal roads and thousands of miles of new or improved state roads. With Ward in charge, Combs could feel safe in turning his attention to other concerns: the approaching November elections, the referendum on the proposed constitutional convention, and the $100,000,000 bond issue.

Aside from the primary responsibilities of a governor, though, there are dozens of little ceremonial duties he is expected to perform. One that Combs was obliged to face was the Governor's Tour, the value of which is not subjected to speculation by generous people. The tour, sponsored by the state chamber of commerce, took the governor, together with administration figures who had nothing pressing to do and business and civic leaders from Louisville and Lexington, on a bus tour of a dozen or so smaller towns. These tours had at least the virtue of making the small-town officials and business people feel that they had not been forgotten by Frankfort and helped them realize that the officials and business people of bigger towns had problems much the same as theirs. Often businessmen in one town would board the bus and travel with the entourage for a few hours or for a day or two. There was usually a good deal of drinking, loud talk, and hackneyed jokes, rather like an outing of overripe collegians.

One of the most enthusiastic of the tourists was Colonel Harland Sanders of Corbin, who would later achieve fame and fortune as the founder of the Kentucky Fried Chicken empire. The tour invariably stopped at the Colonel's roadside restaurant on U.S. 25 just north of Corbin for a lunch of fried chicken, mashed potatoes with gravy, rolls, salad, and at least a dozen side dishes. Although Sanders scorned whiskey and insisted that he was and had always been a teetotaler, the touring dignitaries were always treated to a series of mint juleps or just plain bourbon before the traditional Kentucky feed. Whenever possible, the Colonel seized the opportunity to say a few (or more than a few) words. He was never noted for shyness.

Combs endured these jaunts and tried mightily to be one of the fellows, but to accompanying newsmen it seemed that his heart was never in it. He was by nature a rather thoughtful man with a quiet humor; he loved small poker games or gatherings of political friends but found the boisterous atmosphere of the bus boring after a few hours.

More to his liking was his practice of "taking government to the people," a tactic he developed for finding out what people were saying, what they were interested in, or what they wanted of government. Beginning with a trip to Mayfield, Combs set up a temporary governor's office in 33 Kentucky towns during his term in office. It proved a popular practice.

It also proved strenuous. He could not simply drive into town, set up shop in the courthouse or city hall for a few hours, talk to a few people, and then leave. The visit of the governor is and was an event for the average small town. Notices appeared in the local newspaper; radio stations announced the occasion; officials and civic leaders, even if of the opposing party, had to be on hand to greet him. There were pictures to be made, speeches to be given. It was a rare day when the governor and his party were not dragged off to a civic club luncheon. Sometimes he had a hard time getting to hear the plain citizens he had come to see and listen to.

This meant 14-hour days for a large staff. Most of the advance work fell to Ed Easterly, the former head of the Associated Press in Louisville who was Combs's press secretary, and his assistant, Christa Finley. Administrative assistant Wendell Ford—later, Ed Fossett—usually went with Combs to see that he was briefed and to act as liaison with the locals. Dix Winston or Fontaine Banks kept track of patronage questions. Sometimes Cattie Lou Miller, later commissioner of public information, would go along or send someone from her office, as would Bruce Kennedy or Jim Nutter from the Department of Economic Development. There was nearly always someone from the Highway Department or its local office.

But Combs was convinced that the project was worthwhile. More people, he found, were interested in roads and jobs than in anything else, but hundreds came simply to see the state's chief executive. It was their chance to shake hands with the governor, and they often brought the children along. Occasionally, a few would stand in line to complain about the sales tax or failure to get a relative into a state hospital, but more came just to say they thought he was doing a good job (or a poor one). Easterly learned early to take stacks of photographs along, and Combs invariably did a brisk business in autographed copies.

During the first week of September, Combs surprised most people by naming Republican Henry W. Meigs judge of the newly created Franklin Circuit Court. A New York native and University of Kentucky law graduate of 1949, Meigs had married Sally Willis, daughter of a judge and former governor, Simeon Willis. (It was ironic that Willis was the man Combs had defeated for appellate judge in his first political race.) Friends of Judge W.B. Ardery and the Chandler wing of the party had expected Combs to appoint someone from his own political group and were prepared to denounce the appointment. The selection of Meigs, who went on to a distinguished career, killed the criticism before it could sprout. Combs also calmed some minor grumbling before it could develop by naming an 11-member Human Rights Commission—the first such created in a southern state—with Canon Robert W. Estill, Rector of Lexington's Christ Church Episcopal, as chairman.

Throughout the summer of 1960, however, Combs had been getting reports of discontent with the veterans' bonus program. Relatives of veterans who had moved out of state to find jobs after World War II felt that these veterans were still Kentuckians and as deserving as those who had been fortunate enough to find jobs at home. Combs had to admit to a certain logic in their complaints. He knew, furthermore, that if the resentment grew it could endanger Democratic chances in the approaching fall elections, as well as the chances for winning the referendum on constitutional revision. During the first week of September, Combs issued a call for a special session of the Assembly to consider expanding the bonus. It was something that had to be done. The special session convened on September 19. Combs asked the legislators to extend bonus payments to Kentuckians who had lived in the state when they enlisted but had since left, and to appropriate $925,000 to match $2,800,000 in federal money for an expanded program of medical care for the aged. With little oratory, the legislators approved both measures and, on September 24, adjourned.

In retrospect, Combs probably made an error in omitting out-of-state veterans from his initial act. Paying them did not make a serious dent in sales tax revenues, and leaving them out had created a lot of ill will toward Combs even among eastern Kentuckians who were greatly helped by his programs. By October 1963 a total of $126,573,196 had been paid to 400,219 veterans and their beneficiaries, an average payment of $316.26. Of this, approximately $36,000,000 was paid to 100,000 out-of-state veterans.

Combs then turned his attention to the constitutional revision referendum scheduled to appear on the 1960 ballot. From all signs, the issue was in good shape. As soon as the legislature had approved the referendum in the spring, Combs had gone to work to build the broadest possible organization to support the call. To the Constitution Revision Committee, authorized by the legislature, he named Thomas Ballantine of Louisville, Dr. Rufus Atwood of Frankfort, Earl Bellew of Olive Hill, Dr. Herman Donovan of Lexington, Parker Duncan of Bowling Green, Robert Ruberg of Covington, and Judge James Stites of Louisville, with Attorney General John B. Breckinridge as an ex officio member. Ed Jackson of Louisville was elected executive director by the committee; Patton G. Wheeler was chosen research director, and Carl Chelf, research analyst.

Throughout the summer months of 1960 an impressive array of speakers had crisscrossed the state urging voter approval. Dean W.L. Matthews of the University of Kentucky Law School threw his prestige behind the proposal. John Y. Brown endorsed it, as did Keen Johnson and Republican leader Louie B. Nunn. So did the Joint Alumni Council, representing UK and the four regional colleges. The great majority of state newspapers, including the Lexington and Louisville dailies, campaigned editorially for it. Sam Ezelle, AFL-CIO spokesman, spoke for it. So did Philip Ardery, counsel for the rural electric cooperatives; J.E. Reeves, political science professor from the University of Kentucky; and representatives of the University of Louisville. On August 26 the Bipartisan Committee for Constitutional Improvement, under the leadership of co-chairmen Edward Breathitt and Jefferson County Judge Marlow Cook, opened headquarters in Louisville.

Combs himself made more than 30 speeches for revision, aided by the brilliant, moody Ed Prichard, who wrote speeches on all aspects of the matter though he had privately expressed to Combs his reservations. (He would have preferred, he said, to have presented the voters with a revised constitution and had them vote on it, rather than ask them to approve a convention where unnamed delegates would make unspecified revisions.) Wyatt, too, was a frequent speaker and was heavily counted on to help carry the all-important Louisville and Jefferson County vote. Earle Clements gave the proposal his approval.

Curiously, there was relatively little organized or even vocal opposition. Happy Chandler, as expected, came out against revision, in part probably because Combs was for it. Besides, he had nothing to gain by supporting it; if it passed, it was Combs's victory. If it should fail, he might as well take advantage of Combs's loss. Allied with Chandler in opposition was the aging, colorful and courtly Edward C. O'Rear of Frankfort (who was described by friends as "resenting everything from the outcome of the Civil War to the advent of the twentieth century") and a few Republican legislators such as Harlan County's Senator Nick Johnson. O'Rear attacked revision on constitutional and legalistic grounds; Chandler tore into it with his usual free-swinging oratory, calling it a "fraud against my people" and insisting that once the delegates gathered to revise the charter, nothing could keep them from junking the whole thing and bringing chaos to the Commonwealth. Late in the summer a Committee of 1,000 with Paris newspaperman J.M. Alverson serving as chairman, was formed to spearhead the opposition, but aside from Chandler and O'Rear it seemed to have little muscle behind it.

Yet a strange feeling of uncertainty and concern hung over the campaign. The feeling among audiences didn't seem quite right. All the right people were making all the right statements and expressing the right sentiments, but there was little apparent enthusiasm behind the drive for a convention. Late in October, Ned Breathitt, who had been hard on the speaking trail, reported to a meeting chaired by Combs that "I get a very bad feeling here in Frankfort. Something needs to be done." As a result of the meeting, "Truth Squads" were sent out to follow speakers for the Committee of 1,000 and correct their misstatements. But the existence of the squads was an indication that the committee was having some effect.

Actually, the approaching election day did not look very promising for the Democrats. John F. Kennedy was encountering strong opposition because of his Catholicism. From the beginning, polls showed Keen Johnson trailing John Sherman Cooper, and the only poll conducted on the chances of constitutional revision showed the convention just squeaking by. Combs threw himself into the final week of campaigning tirelessly, knowing how much modernization of the old 1891 constitution meant to the state and to his efforts to leave a modern governmental structure as his mark on Kentucky history. On the eve of the voting he was worried but believed that the convention would win.

It didn't.

Indeed, the November 1960 elections were a debacle for Kentucky Democrats. John Kennedy, while squeaking into office, lost the state to Richard Nixon by 80,752 votes, shrinking to almost zero any influence Kentucky might have had in Washington. Keen Johnson lost decisively to John Cooper. Out of 667,278 votes cast, constitution revision lost by 17,724. Perhaps the worst aspect of the loss was the vote of Jefferson

County. The Combs forces had expected to carry Jefferson for revision
by a minimum of 20,000 votes and hoped for a margin of 40,000. They
lost by a margin of 10,000.

It was a shock to the Combs group and to the more liberal wing of
the Democratic party as well: revision had carried handily in Republican precincts of eastern Louisville while losing in traditionally Democratic ones. Chandler, of course, exulted that the people, given a
chance, had repudiated Combs and all his works, but it was not that
simple. The same precincts that voted against revision voted strongly
for the highway and parks bond issues that also appeared on the ballot
and were backed by Combs.

Combs took the blame on himself.

"We should have won it," he said years later. "We could have won it
if we had been together on it. But Earle wasn't for it. He said he was, but
he never gave it the support he could have. He was still highway
commissioner when the battle began, and he thought it would hurt
chances for the bond issue, which included all that money for roads,
and after he got out as commissioner, he didn't do anything. And he
thought it would hurt Kennedy and Johnson. He thought that Kennedy could carry Kentucky with the right climate, but I doubt that he
could have.

"And Prich was against it, although he wrote and talked for it. He
thought it would be better to write a revision and submit it to the
people. They finally did that, in Breathitt's term, and the people beat it
in every county.

"And Miss Lennie [McLaughlin, Secretary of the Louisville Democratic organization] and McKay Reed [Democratic chairman] set
Louisville against it. Wilson was supposed to see them about it, and I
guess he thought he had it arranged, but they were never for it. They
passed the word against it. I should have gone to see them myself. That
was my fault."

But there were others than Combs at fault. Many people, including
political writers and editorialists, expressed shock and puzzlement
that Louisville and Jefferson County had voted against revision, but
the reason was quite simple. Revision didn't win because Democratic
leaders didn't want it to win. McKay Reed and Lennie McLaughlin
never passed the word to precinct workers to support it, and the rank
and file, knowing that silence was negative, passed the word against it.
Reed and McLaughlin and other Democratic leaders had no real stake
in revision; they were content with what they had, didn't know what
revision would do to their operation of the county machine, and saw no
reason to take chances. Furthermore, they didn't want to give too

much encouragement to the young liberal Democrats who were in favor of revision and who might use a victory to gain influence within the Fourth Street Organization.

Actually, it was the closest the state ever came to approving a revision of its antiquated charter, but it was still a loss. And the loss hurt. After his "revolutionary" legislative session, Combs had taken a series of beatings. The truck deal was not his fault, and he had moved to stop it at considerable cost to himself and his political strength, but it was a blot on the record of his administration. The Heman McGuire scandal in Carter County was surely not his fault, since he had no authority to remove McGuire or clean up the mess in the schools, but it had erupted during his term. The same applied to the vice scandal in Newport and Campbell County. And now his favorite cause, constitutional revision, had been turned down by the people, largely through the defection of Democrats.

The man who had seemed invulnerable a few months earlier now looked vulnerable indeed. Rumors started circulating that Combs would resign as governor to take a federal judgeship. Others said he would quit to run against Republican Thruston Morton for the U.S. Senate. Wyatt had already said, privately, that he planned to run against Morton in 1962, but now there was political speculation that Combs would resign and turn over the governorship to Wyatt, opening the way for Wyatt to run for governor in 1963. Chandler, already planning his return to the state house, crowed about his victory over the Little Judge and declared that he would like nothing better than a chance to run against "Ankle Blankets."

It was a gloomy way in which to approach a new year. Yet not everything was negative. On December 20, Frankfort correspondent Allan Trout wrote in the *Courier-Journal* that "the Combs-Wyatt administration is something new for Kentucky in that it is actually modern, not in the narrow sense of governmental techniques, but in that it is dedicated to the task of making Kentucky a modern state, the equal of its sister states in the social, cultural and economic areas by which the excellence of a state is measured." It was some solace. Combs felt that he had lost a battle but not a war, and at a meeting held in the House of Representatives in Frankfort, a Constitution Revision Study Committee was formed amid vows that the fight would go on. It did, but it never managed to revise the constitution.

Outsiders have never been able to understand the refusal of Kentucky to get rid of this handicap to modern government. The fact is that few Kentuckians know much about the state constitution (newspaper surveys have shown that many confuse it with the U.S. Constitution and feel a patriotic urge to defend it), and because of its length and complexity, few care to study it. But Combs saw in the close vote indications that the voters, given enough information and leadership, might yet be ready to change the charter. Perhaps in a more enlightened age, it will happen.

On December 17, Combs announced a program almost as dear to him as charter revision and roads: a parks program to cost between $10,000,000 and $20,000,000. It would include five new parks—at Rough River, Buckhorn Lake, Greenbo Lake, Falmouth Lake, and Big Bone Lick—and Kentucky would join with Virginia in the creation of their first interstate park at Breaks of the Sandy, near Elkhorn City in Pike County. Pine Mountain, Jenny Wiley, and Lake Cumberland were to be greatly expanded. Natural Bridge facilities were to be rebuilt. In all, there would be eight new lodges, cottages would be added at nine parks, and 16 new picnic shelters would give every park picnic facilities. Nine parks would get boat docks, 11 would get golf courses, and 15 would be given bridle paths and either riding stables or access to stables.

In addition, approach roads and roads within the parks would be improved. Swimming pools, tennis courts, basketball courts, game rooms, and playgrounds would be built along with the lodges. Grocery stores would be added to accommodate campers, fishermen, and visitors staying in cottages with kitchens. Snack bars would cater to day visitors.

"We are in the tourist business in earnest," said Combs, though it was his plan to draw tourists not only to the parks but to the recreational facilities he hoped that private investors would build around the edges of the parks. He planned to keep rentals and charges in the parks reasonable enough so that all Kentuckians could use and enjoy them but not so low that private facilities nearby could not compete. And, as much as anything else, he saw the parks as sources of jobs and places of healthful recreation for people living nearby, places where families could come and have a good time for little or no money. Though the lodges and other income-producers might make money, Combs never visualized the parks system as a money-maker but as a public service that would, by making the state a tourist haven, help its economy.

As he began his second year in office, Combs could take considerable satisfaction in what had been accomplished. He had taken some hard licks, and at a party for state workers he joked, "I got a cake today, which shows I have at least one supporter left." Actually, he was better off than he appeared to be, and the pendulum of public opinion would soon begin swinging back. At a small gathering following the party, he ticked off what he thought were "some little steps we've taken":

Improvements in the schools.

The huge highway program.

The sales tax and a 40 percent cut in income taxes.

The parks program and the establishment of the Department of Parks.

The merit system and the abolition of assessment of state employees.

The Department of Child Welfare.

Reform of election laws, with voting machines required.

Conflict-of-interest laws.

Taking government to the people.

Expanded programs in health, agriculture, and conservation.

Programs to help depressed areas.

New industrial investment and expansion of existing industry.
(Wyatt had announced that Kentucky's economy had expanded by $8,000,000 a day during the second quarter.)

Of course, one of the big ones, constitutional revision, had gotten away. Combs tried to view it philosophically, and prepared for a new year.

12

Win Some, Lose Some

A conventional man on the surface, Bert Combs seemed at times to take an adverse pleasure in being unconventional in his attitude toward the legislature, patronage, the state payroll. Sometimes it appeared that he was purposely encouraging an image, creating a character. At a "taking government to the people" day in Louisville, he heard that some boys were having an air rifle contest nearby; leaving his official party straggling behind, he strode over to the gathering of boys and borrowed an air rifle from one of them. "I used to be a pretty good shot with one of these," he told the bemused youth, and proceeded to plunk eight out of ten shots in the bullseye. "That's really the governor?" asked the boy. "He's pretty good." Combs sighed and went back to the office where a line of people awaited him.

As is often the case with governors, a mystique of sorts began to spring up around Combs. People repeated and enlarged on his remarks if they contained a scintilla of humor, as though they were monuments of wit. His nicknames for members of his inner circle—Field McChesney became "Field Mouse"; Felix Joyner, for some reason, was "Yogi"; Ed Prichard, "Philosopher"—were seen as the work of a creative genius. Assistants imitated his accent, exaggerating his mountain twang; his most mundane remarks, repeated with proper accent and gestures, became examples of insightful folk wisdom. He became known as the "Gray Fox," and his graying hair and white raincoat became trademarks. Like Wyatt, he was on the go a great part of the time, wetting the palms of staffers by insisting on flying into and out of postage-stamp hillside airports at any hour of day or night and in any kind of weather in his twin-engine Beechcraft.

Combs began 1961, however, in a very traditional way by announcing that he and Wyatt had set a goal of 50 new industries for 1961. Promising industrial growth has long been as customary for politicians as praising Kentucky women and horses. Henry Clay promised to lure business to Kentucky when he was campaigning for the U.S. Senate in the 1820s. Combs and Wyatt had been more specific than most in vowing to bring in job-producing plants, and Wyatt had been devoting to the task almost every moment not consumed by legislative and ceremonial duties. But this goal was rather lofty (where they got the figure of 50 industries is anyone's guess).

Just how successful was their drive for new business, new plants, new jobs is uncertain. State economies depend on, are tied to, the national economy. When the country is in a recession, the state feels it, and in 1961 the country was in a recession. Capital spending was down. A slumping market hit hard those things that Kentucky produced—coal, whiskey, tobacco. Mechanization of coal mines had cost the state 48,000 jobs since World War II. The Louisville area alone had lost 21,000 jobs in government offices and installations. The gradual disappearance of the small family farm had taken 8,000 jobs a year. These were factors over which the state had little influence.

In some respects Kentucky had done better than the nation as a whole. Between 1946 and 1960 the number of factory workers grew by 14 percent nationally, while Kentucky gained 30 percent. During the Clements administration, 1947 to 1951, the state's industrial labor force grew by 8.6 percent and nonfarm employment by 14.2 percent. During the Wetherby years, factory jobs increased 20 percent and nonfarm employment 11 percent. In Chandler's term, 1955 to 1959, factory jobs rose only 1.8 percent and nonfarm jobs only 3.6 percent, but it would be unfair to blame Chandler for this; the recession that took 14,000 nonfarm jobs from Kentucky played a role.

That there was a Kentucky rebound in 1960 is beyond dispute, though the end of the year still found 124,000 people without jobs and a quarter of a million living on surplus food distributed by the federal government. In 1960 new industrial investment, actual or planned, amounted to $376,000,000. New investment in factories alone amounted to $164,000,000, compared with less than $50,000,000 in 1959. Wyatt reported 10,000 new industrial jobs in 1960, which created another 10,000 jobs in construction. At this rate, not only was Kentucky ahead of the nation, but its rate of investment and job growth were running at a record rate. How much of this could be attributed to the Combs-Wyatt program and how much would have come about in any case is, again, a matter for conjecture. State administrations traditionally take credit for economic gains and blame the national economy for economic slippage.

Since the matter of the constitution was sticking in his craw, Combs named 28 people to a group to recommend reforms in the state constitution. He knew it was the one historic step he needed and had so far failed to take, and he wanted desperately to do something about it before he left office.

But the first weeks of the new year of 1961 were given over to low-key, low-profile matters. The Court of Appeals made the governor's life a little easier by approving, four to three, the legislative act of the special session giving the bonus to both resident and out-of-state veterans. He got further good news when Bowling Green attorney Paul Huddleston, who had filed suit on behalf of two Warren County doctors charging that the bonus itself was unconstitutional, had dropped the suit. It had not worried Combs, but it was good to have it out of the way.

Then on February 26, Combs realized an old ambition when he broke ground for the long-awaited East Kentucky Turnpike. The first section of 44 miles would extend from Interstate 64 at Winchester to Campton. One branch would then run from Campton to Salyersville and on to Prestonsburg, while the southern branch would extend from Campton through Hazard and on to Whitesburg. It was a gratifying day for Combs and for backers of the road.

As a matter of fact, Combs was feeling pretty good about things during the first months of 1961. He had taken a beating in the fall elections; the loss of the constitutional revision referendum had hurt; and he knew that his image had been damaged, too. Some predicted that in the upcoming primaries he might lose control of the legislature to candidates backed by Chandler and Clements. Chandler was already claiming victory and preparing to run for governor in 1963, declaring that the people had "caught up with the Little Judge." But Combs had a feeling that things were not that bad. Everywhere he went, people seemed friendly. His programs were being well received. If political writers bemoaned his fortunes, editorialists praised his actions.

He decided that it might be advisable to have a responsible pollster, such as Lou Harris, come to Kentucky and take the public pulse. But before he could take any comfort from the poll, here came the Newport ministers again, asking him to remove eight public officials in Newport and Campbell County. When they had asked him, the year before, to help them kick out the officials, Combs had told them he would need more solid information than they had given him. Now they gave him more than he had asked for. In a 31-page affidavit, the ministers charged that Circuit Judge Ray Murphy, County Judge A.J. Jolly, Sheriff Norbert Roll, Newport Mayor Ralph Mussman, Newport Police Chief George Gugel, Newport Detective Leroy Fredericks, County Police Chief Harry Stuart, and Detective Gordon Reed had allowed gambling, prostitution, and illegal liquor sales to flourish in the town and county.

Combs and Attorney General John Breckinridge were trying to figure out how to get a handle on the Newport situation when Combs was again called to testify before a legislative investigating committee about the truck deal. There wasn't much that he could add to what was already known. He admitted that he had told Clements that they were obliged to do something for Thurston Cooke if it could be done properly. He could recall meeting Cooke on two occasions but said the purchase of trucks had not been discussed. He felt later that he had told the truth and been less than convincing.

Then, suddenly, mass demonstrations erupted in Louisville, resulting in the arrest of 177 blacks demanding admission to stores and restaurants. Owners protested that they would be put out of business if they let blacks in. Mayor Bruce Hoblitzell declared that his integration committee was working to gain admission for the blacks but that he had to proceed cautiously; actually, he was stalling. Restaurant owners seriously believed that if they let blacks in, whites would stay out, and they were putting heavy pressure on City Hall. A committee of blacks came to Frankfort to ask Combs for help, and Combs didn't make anyone very happy by announcing that he and the state's Human Rights Commission were taking a wait-and-see stand on the Louisville protests. Kentucky actually didn't know what to do about the civil rights movement. It had always been wishy-washy on the black question; it had been unable to make up its mind about slavery. Now it was having a hard time deciding how to view protesting blacks.

To top things off, Combs and Senator John Cooper, in an effort to get economic help for depressed eastern Kentucky counties, asked President Kennedy to send four cabinet members to the mountains to see for themselves the depressed conditions of the area. They didn't get much encouragement. Combs then asked the Tennessee Valley Authority to build its projected new steam plant in Kentucky—if possible, in eastern Kentucky. TVA officials announced that they would build it on the Clinch River in Tennessee. A group of Campbell County businessmen announced that they were forming a Committee of 500 to combat vice in Newport, and again asked Combs to investigate the lack of law enforcement in the county.

Suddenly it seemed that everything was coming unglued. Combs began to worry about the legislative elections coming up in May. Chandler was talking loudly of his intention to "take it away from them," and Combs knew that he could not afford to have a Chandler-controlled legislature dealing with the sales tax, budget, school, and road legislation. There were nine seats that Combs wanted to win in the Senate, 32 in the House, but newspapers were warning of "rumblings of discontent" among Democrats and "signs and sounds of revolt against the sales tax" that threatened Combs's hold on the legislature. Ordinarily, the more liberal newspapers of the state deplored the power of the governor over the legislature and called for changes giving the lawmakers more independence. They were singing a different tune now, realizing that a Chandler-controlled legislature could jeopardize the progress made by the 1960 session.

A governor's influence over legislative races is always a matter of question. Usually there is less popular interest in legislative races than in races for governor, Congress, or the presidency, and if a governor's local people—his patronage man, highway people and other state workers, and friendly local officials—get out a reasonably good vote, the governor can carry it for legislators friendly to him. At the same time, lack of popular interest and a resulting small vote can be dangerous; a well-organized opposition making a strong effort can turn out enough votes to give the governor a setback.

It is in such situations that the time-honored drama of politics shows its efficiency. According to the traditional scenario, a local official (county judge, patronage man, magistrate) is visited by the leaders of a county community who are in need of a road, a bridge, a playground for the school. The judge or magistrate tells them (usually in all honesty) that though he wants desperately to help them and knows the reality of their need, he does not have the money. They insist that something be done. He finally says he will go to Frankfort and see the highway commissioner. The commissioner tells him that his road (bridge, etc.) is not budgeted, that money is tight, and that he will just have to wait.

The judge goes home and reports to his constituents, who reiterate the emergency nature of their need. The judge then bravely announces that he will take the final step: like a Daniel approaching the lions' den, he says he will go see the governor. He returns to Frankfort and finally gets to see the governor, who is deeply touched by his situation, though he obviously cannot go over the head of his commissioner and promise money that is not available. But, he says in tones dripping crisis, he knows that the judge has been a good friend, the kind that can be counted on in the approaching elections. He will see what can be done.

The judge goes home. The next day the governor calls to tell him that he has performed a near miracle: he has taken enough money from various other projects to finance the judge's needed road. The judge calls in the road-needing citizens and tells them that he has performed a miracle, gone right to the top for them, and, sure enough, the governor himself is going to get them the road. The people are beholden to the judge. The judge is beholden to the governor. The party is strengthened in the community involved, and the governor can count on a little help on election day.

Combs was not above using this well-established procedure. He began to call his people across the state, checking on the critical races, seeing where he could afford to promise a road or a bridge, making sure that any available jobs were being used to produce the desired results. Putting on the screws, but gently. Actually, Combs preferred to work directly with the legislators, but he had to elect the legislators first.

"You hear a lot about how governors pour money into these legislative races," Combs said later, "but there's not much to it. You can't. There are too many. I tried to help people that were with me and were in a tight race. I'd go in and speak for them, and of course we'd see that what could be done was done. There's not an awful lot you can do within the law nowadays."

And first, there was Newport to deal with. Tension there was growing. The Committee of 500 had drafted George Ratterman, a former professional footballer living in Fort Thomas, to run for Campbell County sheriff. Ratterman, immediately dubbed "second stringer" by the opposition because he had played backup quarterback to the famed Otto Graham of the Cleveland Browns, promised to clean up vice if elected. His opponent was G.W. "Hoot" Gibson, Alcoholic Beverage Control agent under Chandler. When asked by reporters about the reform movement, Gibson said he had not heard of any reform movement. Asked if he favored a cleanup of vice and gambling, Gibson recoiled as if he had been confronted by a rattlesnake with wings. "Vice?" he cried. "Where? I haven't seen any!"

Combs sent special Alcoholic Beverage Control agents into Newport on April 21. They cited six bars for liquor law violations. This didn't satisfy the Committee of 500. But the committeemen shortly had a problem of their own, and this time it rubbed off on the Combs administration—in a rather ludicrous way. George Ratterman, their White Knight for sheriff, was found in an apartment over Newport's Tropicana nightclub (the apartment belonged to Tito Carinci, manager of the club) in what is usually referred to as a compromising situation with a young lady billed as April Flowers. Ms. Flowers was a striptease dancer in the Tropicana. Actually, as she later explained, her name was Juanita Jean Hodges; she had taken the name of April Flowers to advance her stage career, such as it was. As to what she was doing in a bedroom with Ratterman, well, she said, that was a long story, and involved.

Ratterman claimed that he had been framed; so did Ms. Hodges (aka April Flowers), who said she had been asked by Carinci to cut short her strip act and go up to his apartment. There, to her shock and amazement, she found the unconscious Ratterman on a bed, and while she was trying to rouse him, four men broke in and carried him to the police station. Ms. Flowers said that as the men, who identified themselves as police officers, bore the befuddled Ratterman away, one of them winked at her—indicating, she surmised, that he assumed she was a party to the event. She insisted that she was not. Eventually, the courts agreed that Ratterman had been framed, and the forces of evil were foiled again, though both Ratterman and the forces of reform were left looking rather silly. They and the public did gain, however, at least one chuckle from the affair when, at a hearing in Lexington, Ms. Flowers flourished a Kentucky Colonel's commission which, she revealed, had been signed by Wilson Wyatt as acting governor.

Embarrassing.

Instead of laughing it off, as he might well have done, the rather straitlaced Wyatt appeared more shocked and amazed than Ms. Flowers, nee Hodges. He had no idea how this had come about, he insisted, and instituted a full investigation to find out. Kentucky Colonel commissions, which cost nothing, involve no obligation, and look nice framed on the office wall, are highly prized, and the average governor hands out dozens, if not hundreds. The commissions are supposedly given to people who have rendered valuable services to the state, but in actual practice anyone with influence in the governor's office can usually get a commission for someone he wants to impress or to whom he owes a favor. How did Ms. Flowers happen to get one? Simple: someone had asked a secretary in the office of Secretary of State Henry Carter to get a commission for one Juanita Jean Hodges, who had—the applicant testified—performed admirable and valuable services for the state (and who is to say she had not?). Ms. Flowers said her benefactor was a Lexington judge who was a good and great friend, but some in state government blamed Henry Carter himself, an aficionado of the dance who had been seen in the Tropicana on at least one occasion watching Ms. Flowers reveal all. In any event, Carter approved the commission and sent it on to the governor's office to be signed; the governor happened to be out of town; and Wyatt, as acting governor, signed the nefarious document.

Assistants to Wyatt said that Carter, who was not a Wyatt enthusiast, had planned the whole thing to embarrass the lieutenant governor. The secretary was also known to take a drink upon occasion, and upon such occasion to develop a pixieish sense of humor. In any event, someone had sneaked one past, and Our Lady of the Flowers became, so far as is recorded, the first Kentucky Colonel to wear a G-string. Wyatt immediately ordered that she be stripped, this time of her commission, but it was not clear that he had this power, since only a governor or acting governor giveth a commission and only a governor or acting governor taketh it away, and by this time Wyatt was neither governor nor acting governor. As newspaper headlines declared, justice bumped and ground its majestic course, but Ms. Flowers had her commission, the public had a good laugh, and the reform forces had a temporary embarrassment.

This did nothing, of course, to clean up the situation in Newport, and before Combs could give it his full attention, there was the matter of the May primary elections in which legislators would be chosen. He approached these with more confidence than some thought justified, partly because the Harris Poll he had authorized showed that he was more popular than political writers thought. At the same time, he realized that he had a lot riding on the vote, which would be something of a referendum on his first year in office and especially on the vital sales tax.

At the end of the primary election day, Happy Chandler declared from Versailles, "If I were in Combs' shoes, I'd be nervous at this stage of the game. When he gets the noses counted, he may find he's like Little Bo Peep, he's lost his sheep." But when the votes were counted, the voters had confounded the experts by giving Combs a smashing victory. In nine key Senate races, Combs forces won seven. Chandlerites had won two, but one of those two had assured Combs of his cooperation on key issues.

In 32 key House races, Combs men won 25, Chandlerites seven. In no section of the state was there any indication of a revolt against the sales tax. In northern Kentucky, where anti-tax feeling was supposed to have been strong, the pro-tax delegation made a clean sweep. Frank Bassett of Hopkinsville, Chandler's majority floor leader in the 1958 Senate, was badly beaten by Combs-backed John M. Dixon. In Louisville, longtime Chandlerite Leo Lucas was soundly beaten by Michael Ascolese, a Combs supporter. Combs men fared well, in fact, in all urban areas, where anti–sales tax sentiment was supposed to be strong. Spencer Cobb of Nicholasville not ony beat longtime Chandler ally Sam Sternberg but outpolled him in Chandler's home town of Versailles.

Overnight, Combs evolved from political sad sack to popular hero and political genius, a veritable mountain phoenix, risen from the ashes of failure to soar on the wings of victory. Suddenly the Combs program was seen to be a thing of brilliance. Political writers decided that the fall election, in which he had not been directly involved, had been misleading.

As it probably had been. John Cooper, approaching the status of an institution, would have had trouble beating Keen Johnson only had the Democratic candidate for president, John F. Kennedy, run a very strong race in Kentucky. He had not. Just as Kentucky Democrats had voted for Republican Herbert Hoover in 1928 over Catholic Democrat Al Smith, so did they bolt this time to the Protestant Republican Richard Nixon. And while Combs's constitutional convention had lost, it was by the narrowest possible margin; it might well have carried had a few Democratic leaders not quietly gutted it.

So now Combs could turn his attention back to Newport and other details of government. Shortly before the primary, he had broken again with tradition by establishing a formula for distributing rural-road money. Historically, money for secondary roads had been divided among the counties by the rural highway commissioner partly on the basis of need, partly by the rule of political convenience. The commissioner's home county usually did well. So did most of the counties where the voting went correctly, where administration officials lived, or where political wheels needed grease. It was accepted practice. But now, Combs decreed, after dividing a fifth of the road funds equally among the 120 counties, a fifth would be distributed on the basis of rural population, a fifth on the basis of rural road mileage, and two fifths on the basis of rural area.

There were, apparently, few repercussions, though it was a historic move. It marked, for all practical purposes, the disappearance of the last vestiges of the old bipartisan commission that divided road funds according to personal choice and political need. Politics had not been removed from the department; it is doubtful that that will ever happen. Nor was the internal arrangement of the department completely efficient. Rural Highway Commissioner Ted Marcum had stubbornly maintained that he was legally independent of Highway Commissioner Henry Ward, a policy which, had it stood, would have made coordination of highway systems difficult if not impossible. But more important, sociological changes were taking place that would soon alter the position of the Highway Department as the state's largest department, with the largest payroll, the largest budget, and the greatest political influence. Welfare agencies were reaching deeper into the social economy of Kentucky as federal laws extended aid of various kinds to more and more people, and the regrouped and renamed Department of Human Resources would gradually become the state's largest agency.

But in June, Combs got some gloomy news to balance the rosy. State revenues for the fiscal year were $3,000,000 less than anticipated, $211,000,000 instead of $214,000,000, and the state was obliged to cancel $1,495,000 in building contracts, including repairs on the capitol and other state buildings.

Combs set in motion machinery to bring some resolution to the Newport issue, naming John L. Davis—former Kentucky Bar Association president from Lexington—as special commissioner to conduct ouster hearings against four Newport and Campbell County officials charged with failure to enforce the laws. Attorney General John Breckinridge was directed to conduct the prosecution. Davis announced that the hearings would be held in Frankfort and gave the defendants 20 days to prepare their defense.

It was the beginning of the end for the good times in Newport. Charges that George Ratterman's civil rights had been violated in the April Flowers case brought federal Attorney General Robert Kennedy and his Department of Justice into the case and sent federal agents swarming through Newport. When a former prostitute told of payoffs to officials, Circuit Judge Ray Murphy (one of those so tagged) quickly called for a special grand jury. But just as the Ratterman case enabled Kennedy to move in, so did the payoff charges open the door for Attorney General Breckinridge, who got Murphy to step down and replaced him with tough Judge Ed Hill.

In the end, Combs barred Police Chief George Gugel and Chief of Detectives Leroy Fredericks from office for four years. Sheriff Norbert Roll resigned and left town. Combs later removed County Police Chief Harry Stuart. The ministers and businessmen were jubilant, and for the time, at least, Newport was nothing more than a rather unexceptional river town across the Ohio from Cincinnati. April Flowers, commission and all, wiggled off into the purple dusk of history.

So far, Combs had a perfect average. He had gotten Heman McGuire removed from his office as superintendent of Carter County schools. He had slain the dragon of vice in Newport. He had blunted criticism, for the time being at least, of his role in the truck deal. He had turned back the Chandlerites and had come through an election with a comfortable majority in both houses of the next legislature. He had also promised to try to bring peace in the Louisville racial trouble, and on July 8 he presided over the opening of the Governor's Conference on Human Rights, which went on record in favor of a law outlawing discrimination by race, religion, or national origin. The sales tax was yielding about what had been projected. The Eastern Kentucky Turnpike was under construction, bonds for a Western Kentucky Turnpike had been sold, and bonus applications were being processed at the rate of 1,400 a day.

Federal park officials were discussing the possibility of a large national park in the land lying between Kentucky Lake and Lake Barkley, which was just beginning to fill. The 170,000-acre strip reaching from near the Ohio River south into Tennessee had formerly been known as the Land between the Rivers, a region famed for the production of moonshine whiskey, said to be among the nation's finest. The area would eventually be made into a national recreation area called Land between the Lakes, under control of the Tennessee Valley Authority, and become an outstanding tourist attraction.

In July, Combs accepted 640 acres of scenic mountain land in Harlan County for Raven Rock State Park, named for a great granite outcropping at the summit of a ridge. (The name would later be changed to Kingdom Come State Park, after the valley lying to the west and featured in the famous novel by John Fox, Jr., *The Little Shepherd of Kingdom Come*.) The park was a nice counterpart to the Little Shepherd Trail, a spectacular road stretching along the Pine Mountain ridgetop from Harlan into Letcher County—most of it blacktopped but some fairly rough—offering some of the finest scenery in the state and containing nearly every species of mountain tree, shrub, and flower. The development of the trail was of particular satisfaction to Wilson Wyatt, who had promoted it almost from the day of his inauguration. A few days later Combs broke ground for a new lodge at General Butler State Park near Carrollton. And put out a beehive on the grounds of the governor's mansion. As far as is known, that was a first.

In Kentucky there is, of course, no vacation from politics. The summer of 1961 had hardly begun when the rumor went around that Clements was studying a comeback and had an eye on the Senate race for which Wyatt was preparing. Harry Lee Waterfield, it was said, was also a possible candidate—raising the question of which man Happy Chandler, who was about to launch his campaign for the governorship in 1963, would support.

There was also talk that Combs might jump into the race; the Harris Poll of March had indicated that he could beat Senator Thruston Morton and possibly anyone else on the horizon. He could not succeed himself under constitutional restrictions, and it did not seem reasonable that a man with so much political muscle would choose not to use it. Combs scotched the rumors by announcing that he was supporting

Wyatt and predicted that Wyatt would win easily. He also stated that he had made no choice for governor. (Actually, he was leaning toward Ned Breathitt but had earlier said that a governor should not try to dictate the choice of his successor. He would change his mind on that.) John Breckinridge responded that he was going to run for governor regardless of whom Combs supported. State Treasurer Thelma Stovall, one of the few surviving Chandlerites in state government, announced that she would accept the new merit system but only under protest. She also threatened to file suit to have it declared unconstitutional. She didn't.

The economic situation in eastern Kentucky, meanwhile, refused to improve. Despite work beginning on roads, parks, dams, schools, and airports, unemployment in the distressed 37-county region exceeded 20 percent in some places. Approximately 150,000 people in the region were eating government-distributed surplus foods. Combs created a new office to handle federal area development programs with John Whisman, his authority on Appalachia (himself a mountain native) as its director, in order to bring the region under President Kennedy's new redevelopment program, which could mean as much as $394,000,000 for the mountains.

In the months immediately after sales tax revenues started rolling in, it had seemed, as Finance Commissioner Robert Matthews said, that "we had more money than we knew what to do with." This feeling didn't last long. As the summer of 1961 burned itself out, it became apparent that the new programs enacted in 1960 were stretching the treasury. Budget studies showed that it would take $236,000,000 to run the state in 1962-63, and $246,000,000 for 1963-64—about $13,000,000 more than anticipated income. Combs had to ask for a 5 percent cut in all agency requests for the upcoming legislature.

In steamy September weather, Combs made surprise visits to five state parks "to see them in normal operation." The visits were not always totally satisfying. At one park he sat in a beautifully decorated dining room overlooking a cool lake surrounded by dense forest, while soft music filled the air-conditioned room. Then a waitress arrived to take his order. Combs shook his head. "You spend a million dollars to build a dining room with a great view," he said wearily. "You put in expensive carpets. You air-condition it. You pay experts to come and decorate it. You train cooks and cashiers, you pipe in music, you fix good food. Then here comes a waitress with a toothpick in her mouth and says 'Whut kin I getcha?' Blows the whole thing. Might as well be in a greasy spoon."

His experience was somewhat similar to that of Henry Ward who, while commissioner of conservation (in charge of parks) asked for pancakes for breakfast one morning in the dining room at Kentucky Dam Village. He was told the dining room didn't serve them. Ward, not a patient man, blew up. He called for the manager and told him in unmistakably clear language that the dining room would start immediately to serve pancakes. The manager promised that he would. And did. A few months later Ward was once more at the park and again ordered pancakes, only to be told by the waitress that they didn't have any. "We served them for a while, but we don't anymore," she said. Ward demanded to see the manager. Again the poor manager, called on the carpet, said yes, they had served pancakes for a while. "But they were so popular," he said, "it was just hard to keep the ingredients in stock, so we just removed them from the menu." Ward didn't know whether to laugh or cry. Looking at the man, he shook his head and said, "Oh, hell!"

But there were always little political battles to fight. For example, on September 15, Mrs. Joyce Weddington of Prestonsburg filed suit in Franklin Circuit Court asking that the state be forced to honor leases that would permit her to drill for oil and gas in both Carter Caves and Natural Bridge state parks. Mrs. Weddington's husband, Joe, was a business associate of Happy Chandler's; the leases, issued in the closing days of the Chandler administration, would have permitted drillers to mar large sections of park land. It took a court battle to block them. They were typical of a handful of such leases issued by Chandler and canceled by Combs, probably without legal authority, in the early days of his administration. The day after the Weddington suit was filed, Heman McGuire introduced Chandler at a Carter County gathering, praising him as having "the courage to tell the *Courier-Journal* to go to hell." Happy then defended the oil and gas leases in state parks, explaining that he had advertised for bids as the law required, and that his friends had made the highest bid—$350!

Politics seemed to rear its head at every possible juncture, even on a project so apparently nonpolitical as the Eastern Kentucky Turnpike. When Combs and Wyatt toured eastern counties during the first week of October to investigate the need for more road improvement, Hazard banker and regional Republican power Dewey Daniel called the turnpike "the best thing that has happened to us in our lifetime," adding that "everybody should get down on his knees and thank God for Bert Combs." But Democrat Happy Chandler declared in Frankfort, "That road, that toll road Bertie gave them, it wasn't needed. It starts nowhere and goes nowhere. If you get on you can't get back off, and if you get off you can't get back on. It won't pay for itself, mark my words.

[Actually, its bonds were retired and tolls were removed in 1985, paid off ahead of schedule.] I could have done just as well by straightening out the roads we had." Chandler used the same words to ridicule the Kentucky Turnpike, now part of Interstate 65.

Throughout the fall, Combs and various members of his cabinet were busy breaking ground, dedicating things, announcing contracts. In one day—in nine and a half hours—he and Wyatt dedicated nine airports (at Cynthiana, Olive Hill, Harlan, Campbellsville, Elizabethtown, Greenville, Elkton, Murray, and Fulton). He and Ward attended the beginning of work on the Western Kentucky Turnpike and on November 1 opened the stretch of Interstate 64 between Louisville's Outer Loop and Kentucky 55 near Shelbyville. He and Wyatt opened the annual Shakertown Fall Festival, praising the restoration as a boost for historical preservation and for the tourist industry.

On December 17, 1961, an appointment was announced that gladdened the Christmas season for Wilson Wyatt. In his efforts to sell Kentucky to technological and other sophisticated industry, he had long been intrigued by the experience of North Carolina, where the existence of the "Research Triangle" had reportedly persuaded many industries to locate. This research complex consisted of the facilities of the University of North Carolina, Duke University, and North Carolina State University, all located within a few miles of each other and offering technical firms a variety of talents and installations not usually available close at hand.

Wyatt foresaw such an installation in Kentucky as part of a drive to let the state catch up with others in job-producing plants. He fought for and won funds to convert grounds of Spindletop farm, on Ironworks Pike just north of Lexington, into headquarters for such a research center. And he regarded it a feather in Kentucky's cap when he announced that Beardsley Graham, the former manager of Lockheed Aircraft Corporation's missile and space program, had been employed as president of the Spindletop Research Corporation. Graham took over at the beginning of 1962 and at once set about designing a building to house the research facilities. In the next two years he had put together the core of a first-rate research plant. In the end, unfortunately, Graham experienced frequent clashes with members of the administration. The research center was never used as fully as Wyatt had hoped. Demands for its services were not as great as he had foreseen, and subsequent legislatures were hesitant to appropriate the money that would have let it grow and function as planned.

But the real task at hand for Combs was to prepare for the coming session of the legislature. It was bound to be rough. The second session of any governor's term poses problems, if only because he often has trouble controlling or even influencing the legislature. The average governor has fewer members of his own party or faction in the Assembly in the second session. He has already committed himself to a program during the first session and cannot woo or bully lawmakers with threats or promises to give or withhold such plums as roads, bridges, buildings, regional offices, vocational schools, and so on. Members with ambitions of their own are more likely to oppose the governor or lead rebellions with an eye on the cameras and headlines. Happy Chandler, for example, faced an outright rebellion during his second session and had to scramble for Republican votes in order to pass any kind of program.

Combs appeared to be in better shape than most and was confident that he would be able to organize both houses, but he felt he could not afford to risk unnecessary fights. He was going to have to ask the Assembly for a budget even larger than his record budget of 1960. He was going to have to present the legislators with the involved and far-reaching plan for the reorganization of state government proposed by the commission headed by Felix Joyner.

The plan was significant. It proposed the creation of three departments out of what had been rather minor divisions of state government but whose functions were becoming increasingly varied and important. For example, a health and welfare agency would deal with child welfare, economic security, handicapped children, health, mental health, tuberculosis control, and mental retardation. A natural resources agency would encompass conservation, mines and minerals (and the increasingly important surface-mining control), fish and wildlife resources, and parks. A business and professional agency would oversee the departments of alcoholic beverage control, banking, insurance, motor transportation, occupations and professions, and the Public Service Commission. Only a few major departments would be left independent, a proposal bound to stir objections inside the bureaucracy as well as within a legislature accustomed to doing business with existing agencies.

But educational matters promised to be the thorniest the governor would face. In a sense, this was ironic. Combs had done more for education than any governor in history. He had given more money for teaching, created more community colleges, built more school and college buildings. Yet now he was facing the prospect of an all-out attack by the professional educators, the superintendents, school board members, college presidents, and—first and foremost—the superintendent of public instruction.

Combs's relationship with Wendell Butler had been extensive and uneven. In 1955, when Combs ran against Chandler, Robert Martin ran on his ticket for superintendent of public instruction. Combs lost, but Martin won and faced an uneasy relationship with the victorious Chandler—especially because he had asked Butler for his support and had promised him a job should he win. But when Butler asked Martin for the job, Chandler warned Martin that he would have to get rid of Butler or face slim pickings at budget time. Martin didn't want to back down on his promise, yet he knew he had to protect his department. He tried to explain to Butler, but Butler reminded him that a promise was a promise; when Martin failed to deliver the promised job, the two men became nonfriends if not outright enemies.

The coolness continued through the Combs years, when Dr. Martin became president of Eastern Kentucky University. When word hit the grapevine that Butler, after having served as superintendent of public instruction, was going to run for commissioner of agriculture, Martin surprised friends by declaring his support. "I'm all for him," Martin explained. "He can do the hogs of Kentucky less harm than he can do the children." Butler's reply is not recorded.

Combs's commission on public education had proposed that the constitution be amended so that the superintendent of public instruction would be appointed by the state board of education and subject to removal for cause. The commission also thought that the Council on Public Higher Education should include more lay members and should concern itself with matters other than teacher-training programs and the division of funds among the colleges—such matters, for example, as duplication of graduate programs by the colleges, tenure and qualifications, and the question of individual colleges' lobbying in the legislature for budgets.

The commission also proposed that the state superintendent should be removed from the state board of education, that the state board should be able to recommend that local superintendents or board members be removed for misconduct or to remove them if the state superintendent failed to do so, and that the state board should have power to order audits of local boards.

The commission's proposals outraged the educators, especially Wendell Butler, who was said to be "mad as hell and ripe for a fight." The college presidents, too, were said to be ready to bolt Combs in the legislature if he backed the commission's recommendations. Their threats, of course, underlined the old axiom that you don't necessarily help state educators by helping state education. And vice versa. Especially vice versa.

Combs didn't relish the thought of having the education lobby against him. He needed their help to hold the line on the sales tax, and he would need them, too, when the candidate of his choice began running for governor. He went to a meeting of the Kentucky school administrators and made peace. He embraced Butler's view on the limited role of the state board of education in local school matters. He said he would not push for an appointive superintendent. Butler, in the audience, smiled broadly. "Sounds almost like I wrote it, doesn't it?" he said to a reporter.

That galled Combs, but he wasn't one to let pride bring about a legislative fall. "After all," he said, "I got just about what I wanted. You can't have everything."

13

The Delicate Balance

Ideology tends to be a vague commodity at the state level. The terms liberal and conservative, radical and reactionary, have less distinct meaning in the governor's office than in the president's—though since the days of Franklin D. Roosevelt's New Deal, liberalism at the state level, as at the federal, has indicated a willingness to tax and to spend for social purposes; conservatism, the restriction of governmental social activity and thus less need to impose taxes. But it is risky to attach these tags to Kentucky parties at any particular time, partly because factions are most often to be built around personalities rather than policies. Like the national party of New Deal days, the state Democratic party tends to be a conglomerate, and its philosophy is that of the reigning governor, if indeed he has a philosophy. The Republican party is something of a conglomerate, too, though it usually presents itself as a conservative monolith.

It is also often hard to categorize a party by the conduct of administrations. Democrats are expected to be more willing to intervene in the private sector on behalf of the less privileged, Republicans on the side of business, if at all. In Frankfort, such stereotypes are frequently misleading. Happy Chandler pleased conservatives when he sent the National Guard into Harlan County, where they curbed union pickets and allowed mines to reopen; he cheered liberals when he sent the Guard to Sturgis to quiet anti-integration forces. Democrat Wendell Ford cut the sales tax; Republican Louie Nunn raised it. Chandler, nominally a Democrat, made a career of opposing taxes, though he quietly enacted more tax bills than he vocally opposed.

Since the Civil War, eastern-southeastern Kentucky, which was strongly pro-Union, has been the stronghold of the Republican party, while pro-Confederate western Kentucky has been the "Gibraltar of Democracy." Yet eastern Kentucky produced liberal Democratic Congressman Carl Perkins, while western Kentucky produced conservative Democratic Congressman Carroll Hubbard. And western Kentucky produced conservative Democratic Congressman William Natcher, while eastern Kentucky produced liberal Democratic Governor Bert Combs.

Goebel may be said to have been the first to carry the liberal banner, opposing as he did the L&N Railroad and its limiting effect on state progress. Beckham carried on the liberal cause against the conservative Cantrill, who served the interests of the Jockey Club and later the bipartisan combine. Cantrill's mantle fell to the Johnson-Talbott-Klair faction, just as Beckham's fell to the Laffoon-Rhea faction. In turn, Chandler fell heir to the conservative faction, and Clements wrested control of the liberal wing from the Laffoon-Rhea remnants. A strict alignment did not always exist, of course. Clements was considered more conservative than his 1947 opponent for governor, Harry Lee Waterfield; Waterfield later became allied with Chandler, thought to be in the traditional conservative mold. John Y. Brown, who considered himself a liberal and probably deserved the designation more than most others, was widely seen as a maverick. Interestingly, these three important figures in Kentucky's political drama were born a few miles apart in western Kentucky: Chandler and Brown in Henderson County, Clements a few miles away across the Union County line.

For the purposes of practical politics, the Chandler wing collapsed with Chandler's loss to Breathitt in 1963. The Combs faction remained dominant throughout the Breathitt administration, faltered with the loss of Henry Ward to Louie Nunn in 1967, and fell from power when Combs, attempting a return to the governorship, lost to Wendell Ford in 1971. Since then there has been no clear conservative-liberal delineation within either the Democratic or Republican party. By the same token, there has been no dominant Republican figure since the retirement of John Sherman Cooper, nor any wing within the party that could reasonably be called liberal. Very generally speaking, Republicans from eastern Kentucky have been considered more conservative than those from Louisville and Lexington, also centers of occasional GOP strength, but such geographical classification should be regarded with caution.

There is a measure of irony in that Combs's liberal image stemmed in part from his taxing and spending for schools, which has historically been viewed with suspicion by the very people that liberalism is supposed to serve. It also stemmed from his support by liberal newspapers and intellectuals; from his pro-labor actions, specifically passage of laws calling for higher unemployment benefits, worker's compensation, and a prevailing wage; and from his pro–civil rights stance. But it is worth noting that he incited no conservative revolt and throughout his administration remained on relatively good terms with the Republican minority and with the business community—even though after the first legislative session a spokesman for Associated Industries of Kentucky called him a labor lobbyist.

Perhaps the secret to much of Combs's success lay in his ability—partly intellectual, partly instinctive—to balance idealism and practicality. Though he knew that only a small fraction of a 3 percent sales tax would be needed for bonus payments, he had bulldozed it through the legislature, thus gaining money for his own programs on the patriotic pretext of doing something for the veteran. He managed to enact a liberal program and survive in a basically conservative state by taking care not to sound too liberal, to be down-to-earth in his pronouncements, and to balance populist policies with laws and programs designed to aid business, sensitive to the fact that healthy business and industry were necessary for the economic soundness of a modern state—not to mention the vital importance of the tax revenues involved. Wilson Wyatt's drive to attract industry and encourage business softened (though it did not dissipate) the AIK's dislike of the liberalized labor laws. When Combs picked his second highway commissioner, he chose Henry Ward, general manager of the Louisville Area Chamber of Commerce. His strip-mine control law worried coal operators more than it hampered their operations. He failed to disturb the cozy arrangement under which Kentucky bankers lent at 6 percent interest the state deposits on which they paid 2 percent. And there is some evidence that much of Combs's success was due to his habit of saying no more than necessary and keeping a firm rein on his temper.

Racial policies and politics posed a special problem for Combs. Kentucky has never been racially progressive. It has seldom degenerated into the meanness that has often characterized other southern states, but it traveled the path of integration only about as fast as federal law and court decisions required. The Republican sectors of the state—especially the eastern, southern, and southeastern counties that remained strongly pro-Union during the Civil War—had been antislave, but they were fairly southern in their attitude toward blacks. It was at the Harlan railroad depot, as James Jones pointed out in his novel *From Here to Eternity*, that a sign allegedly read "Nigger, don't let the sun set on you in Harlan County."

Neither have central and western Kentucky been noted for liberal attitudes toward integration. During the 1950s and 1960s, sporadic resistance to school integration erupted throughout western Kentucky, where farmers were already racially sensitive because of the departure of black labor for better-paying industrial jobs during the two decades following World War II. Just as conservative administrations in Washington have managed to enact liberal racial and foreign policies, so did the Republican administration of Louisville Mayor William O. Cowger manage to push through a public-accommodations ordinance without serious opposition. But even in Louisville the city's progressive image in race relations rested largely on the pronouncements of the two daily newspapers, as the social explosion over forced busing for racial balance in the schools would later show. Thus Combs chose to emphasize his creation of a Human Rights Commission but was hesitant to involve the governor's office in the Louisville controversy over the right of blacks to public accommodations. Not that he was antiblack, but he doubted the ability of Frankfort to change attitudes greatly by law, and he did not want to lose—by the injection of racial issues into the legislature—support that he would need during the eight weeks of the second session.

Like a successful president, a governor must be able to compromise as well as to lead, especially in his relations with the legislature. He enjoys an advantage of sorts in that the legislature is in session only four months of his four-year tenure, and he is able to govern most of the time without legislative interference. But it is all the more important that he be able to exercise considerable influence with, if not control over, the legislature during the time it is in session, for he has only those eight weeks in which to win passage of the program on which his reputation and place in history depend. He must enact his program during the first session so that he will have time to put it into operation and produce results, and he must protect it against attack and supplement it during the second session.

Legislators, political scientists, and political writers have for generations deplored the fact that Kentucky's governor has so much power in relation to the legislature. Calls go up each year the lawmakers are in session for "independence of the legislature from control by the governor." As a matter of historic fact, legislatures not controlled by the governor are usually not controlled by anyone, or led by anyone. If the governor doesn't tell the legislators what to do, they often spend their time arguing aimlessly, talking endlessly, engaging in factional politics, trying to pass specialist and ripper legislation, and accomplishing very little.

The legislature, as well as the governor, is the victim of the constitution. Efforts have been made during the past two decades to increase the power of the legislature by creating interim committees to study and prepare legislation for approaching sessions, and the Legislative Research Commission has been expanded and given considerable latitude to help them. But the Legislative Research Commission has been curtailed by the courts to keep it from becoming something of a fourth branch of government, and the legislators are still in session too little of the time to develop a considerable body of expertise. Nor is there any compelling evidence that the interim committees have produced much in improved legislation or anything tangible other than rather generous expense accounts for their members and only occasionally necessary offices furnished at state expense.

Combs approached the 1962 session with reasonable optimism. He had only to hold the line to be regarded a success, and with his majority in both houses he had reason to believe he could do it. There was broad speculation in the press that he could not. The Chandler forces were going to try to organize the Assembly, and with this advantage they would try to repeal or amend the sales tax. Even if they failed, their publicized assault on the tax would boost the chances of Chandler, who on January 3, 1962, opened headquarters in Frankfort for his "ABC in '63" campaign for governor, pledging to repeal or weaken the sales tax once he was in office. (It was typical of Kentucky that the race for governor should begin almost two years before the election, reflecting not only the importance of the factional division of the Democratic party but the state's preoccupation with politics.)

Combs's State of the Commonwealth message to the joint houses was a low-key recitation of progress made in his first two years and a declaration of his determination to fight to keep that progress. He acknowledged that "there are those who want to make this Assembly a testing ground for missiles designed to be launched in 1963," an obvious thrust at Chandler, adding "But if the schemers insist on injecting politics of 1963 . . . we will have no choice except to meet the challenge." A few Chandlerites commented caustically that he had taken credit for the sun coming up every day without accepting blame for its going down. Combs did not expect to set the woods afire with his speech. Rather, he used the occasion to list the measures he would ask of the session, and to test both public and political reaction to them in advance of their introduction. Broadly, the list included:

> Reorganization of state government.
> Creation of a community college system, including new community colleges.
> Acts to clarify the strip-mine control laws.
> Approval of bonds for the establishment of vocational education schools.
> A law banning auto junkyards near highways or requiring them to be screened from view.

Revision of absentee voting laws.
Expansion of the state crafts program.
A redrawing of congressional district lines, reducing districts
   from eight to seven.
Passage of a record budget.

Administration Democrats then proceeded, with almost no difficulty, to organize the legislature. If the Chandlerites seriously hoped
for a ruling majority, they were quickly disabused. From the time
Senator Alvin Kidwell of Sparta was chosen Senate majority leader by a
20 to 7 vote, it was obvious that there was no contest. The only
difference in the administration lineup was in the House, where previous floor leader Tom Ray, a bright and ambitious young Jefferson
County lawyer, had decided he could better build a power base for
himself by running for sheriff. His place was taken by the experienced,
wily, humorous Richard Moloney of Lexington, a thin-haired, cigar-
chewing Irishman given to rumpled vested suits and a crafty smile; his
casual manner and confidential tone concealed the political mind of the
expert poker player. Moloney was not as direct or open as Ray had
been, but he was able, and he and Combs were on good if not intimate
terms.

Frankfort has seldom seen a more complex, competent, or interesting man than Richard P. Moloney. Even those who regarded him with
caution or suspicion found it hard to resist his charm. Yet he could be
subtle and devious; his eyes could sparkle one moment and turn flat
and hard in a second. It is not surprising that he was reputedly one of
the best poker players in Kentucky; his face did not necessarily reflect
what he was feeling.

The son of an Irish policeman, Richard Patrick Moloney was born
in Lexington's tough Irishtown, attended parochial schools, joined the
Navy at 16, came home for a while, then went back to sea as a merchant
seaman for two years. In 1924 he passed the state examination to
become a druggist and practiced that trade, making 60 cents an hour,
while he attended law school. By 1926 he was practicing law in Lexington and playing a little politics, which came naturally.

"Politics was just a part of life when I was a boy," he said later.
"There was always shooting around the polling places on election day,
and I loved to hang around. My mother always threatened to skin me
alive if she caught me; she used to pray all day long on election day. My
father was a cop and the cops had to patrol the polling places."

In 1944, Moloney was elected to the state Senate, and was known
for the rest of his life as "the Senator from Fayette," though he later
gave up his Senate seat and came back to be elected to the House. After

serving as Combs's House majority leader, he was expected to continue in the same capacity under Governor Edward Breathitt, but he died of a heart attack in December 1963.

It is likely that no man in the history of the state was ever more loved by legislators, politicians, lobbyists, and the press than Dick Moloney. In the legislature his reputation was that of the total Irish politician, yet he was also the champion of many of the more liberal and idealistic proponents of the public welfare who came to Frankfort to lobby *pro bono publico*.

Perhaps one of the strangest examples of this side of the Moloney personality was his relationship with Dr. Gladys Kammerer, a professor of political science at the University of Kentucky, who began her career believing that Moloney was in league with the devil, or worse. Moloney, she declared, was the spokesman for slot-machine interests in the Bluegrass and for gambling interests generally. Then Dr. Kammerer came to Frankfort to lobby for several causes—a merit system, election law reforms, and funds for mental health. (She was generally regarded as author of the Youth Authority Act of 1952, which created the Youth Authority eventually dismantled by Chandler.) She was obliged to call on Moloney. To her surprise, he proved not only extremely informed but helpful. She also found him philosophical and liberal to an extent that she had not imagined. Almost against her will, Dr. Kammerer became a staunch Moloney supporter.

Moloney also became something of a hero to Mrs. John Serpell of Louisville, a longtime crusader for mental health. He teamed with Louisville's William Childress to push through a bill creating the state Human Rights Commission, and was credited with the maneuvering that freed the University of Kentucky and the regional colleges from the jurisdiction of the Department of Education and the state Division of Personnel.

Yet the idealist in him never overcame the practical—and at times whimsical—politician. Once, in 1944, he introduced a bill prohibiting wives from engaging in spring housecleaning without the express consent of their husbands. He was a great favorite of the Frankfort press corps; reporters loved even to hear him rake the press over the coals, which he did whenever he felt that journalists were uninformed or unrealistic. "For the press had learned," editorialized the *Courier-Journal* at his death, "that when the chips were down Dick Moloney would be found on the side of good government. And the beginning reporter learned, as the old ones knew, that he told the truth."

Even when they were opposed, on such occasions as the Combs-Wyatt rivalry, Moloney and Earle Clements enjoyed each other's company and the tough politics of which both were capable. Few people were more saddened than Moloney by the split between Combs and Clements. Not surprisingly, Moloney's son Michael became a power in the legislature during the 1980s as senator from Fayette County.

In his initial address to the second session Combs had asked for a moratorium on politics. That sounded nice, but he probably didn't expect it; if he did, he was doomed to quick disappointment. It proved to be a tense, raucous, ill-mannered session, shrill and ugly with political charges, countercharges, and factional maneuvering. The Senate had usually been dignified and deliberative, while the House had often been rowdy, but the Senate of 1962 lost its dignity; within a week its sessions had degenerated into shouting matches. There were delays, a filibuster, loud accusations from the floor, and threats of censure. The noise and dissension, fomented by the Chandlerite forces, didn't amount to much and didn't produce much, but it gave the public a damaging view of the legislative process.

In the midst of the session, House Speaker Harry King Lowman dealt Combs and Wyatt a mild shock when he announced that he was a candidate for the U.S. Senate. It was generally known that Wyatt was waiting only for the end of the session to announce his candidacy, and that he would be strongly supported by the governor. Suddenly Combs had two presiding officers running for the same Senate seat, and a House speaker who was now aligned with and supported by Happy Chandler and by Earle Clements, who had jumped angrily (and uneasily) into bed with Chandler. (Combs always believed that Clements lured Lowman into the race primarily to complicate things for Wyatt.) To Lowman's credit, his candidacy made no apparent difference in the functioning of the House or in his handling of the Combs program. But as soon as his hat was in the ring, antiadministration Democrats in the Senate stepped up their attacks and accusations against Combs and Wyatt, in boisterous mockery of Combs's call for a holiday from politics.

In the Senate, Cap Gardner gave notice of the strategy to be anticipated from the Chandler camp in 1963 when he attempted—and failed—to exempt food, medicine, and fuel from the sales tax. It was a lukewarm effort, apparently intended to keep the issue hot rather than to weaken the sales tax. Actually, Chandler didn't want the tax repealed. He intended to run on the issue.

Combs showed that he was probably going to get the heart of his program when the House passed his $1,104,041,713 budget, $80,000,000 larger than the original 1960-61 budget, and $5,770,000 larger than the budget eventually spent. It was an indication of the tenor of the Assembly that the budget breezed through the House and got only the expected four opposing votes in the Senate—from Republican Nick Johnson and three Chandler Democrats. But Rex Logan kept the kettle boiling by denouncing the budget across the board and declaring that "the Combs administration is littered with broken promises and disgraceful extravagances."

Chandler forces in the House then launched a fight that showed they couldn't win floor victories even with unanimous Republican support: they challenged the House "gag rule," Number 12 of the rules under which the House operated. Rule 12 permitted adoption of the previous question by a simple majority of representatives present; once the previous question was voted, no amendments could be offered to the bill being considered, and debate was limited to ten minutes for each side. Chandlerites behind Representative Fred Morgan of Paducah wanted to change this to require a vote of 51 of the 100 House members. They lost, 64 to 30, with 23 Republicans and only seven Democrats in favor. Their failure was seen as a bad defeat for the Chandler forces and as evidence of their weakness.

Nevertheless, Combs tended to walk softly and to flourish a stick only when necessary. He wanted, above all else, to protect the sales tax, and he did not want to alienate enough people in fights over other issues to give Chandlerites the muscle to pass exemptions to the tax. In his opening address, he said that he would ask later for bonds to finance a system of two-year community colleges. This was in line with the report by the commission to study public higher education headed by Dr. Otis C. Amis of the University of Kentucky. The Amis Report, issued in the fall of 1961, had proposed a master board of control for higher education (the Council on Public Higher Education that was eventually established was only advisory to the governor, and in the 1980s proponents of higher education were still hoping for a board with power). It was one of several proposals that had immediately drawn the fire of college presidents. Now Ted Gilbert, director of the Council on Higher Education, gave warning that the educational establishment was ready to oppose the community college plan when he said, "We're more concerned about adequate financing of the [colleges] we have."

Indeed, the reaction of the school people to Combs's proposals showed why true school reform in Kentucky has been so slow and hard-won. Wendell Butler and his subordinates in the Department of Education were perfectly willing to let local school boards raise taxes without voter approval, as Combs proposed. But while Butler had promised to support a constitutional amendment to make the superintendent of public instruction appointive, neither he nor most county superintendents actually worked for it. Butler also raised the battle flag against a proposal to let the state auditor audit school board books.

In all, it was one more demonstration of the fact that professional educators have historically been more intent on keeping control of their little kingdoms than on improving the education of Kentucky students. They declare that their stand is necessary to protect the schools against the schemes and wiles of politics—one of the most heart-wrenching examples of the pot-kettle juxtaposition in history. County boards and superintendents defending students from politicians can be compared to the efforts of wolves to defend the sheep against foxes. But the governor was not likely to persuade or force the educators to accept improvements that infringed on their turf.

Combs ran into the same provincial attitude when he introduced his plan to reorganize state government. Several proposals for shifting agencies from one umbrella department to another drew sporadic fire from some of the agency people involved, but a major outcry arose when it was announced that the plan would combine the Department of Fish and Wildlife Resources with Parks, Conservation, and Mines and Minerals. Using state money to thwart the governor, warning notices went out to the 301 sportsmen's clubs, and Combs was inundated with snarls from hunters and fishermen, decrying this threat to the independence of Fish and Wildlife. They demanded that nothing be done to disturb the setup under which the Fish and Wildlife Department got state funds but was under the control of the "sportsmen" whose activities it was supposed to control. It was, and had long been, a highly questionable if not blatantly unethical arrangement, but it was one issue on which the thousands of sportsmen or their representatives in the Assembly were prepared to fight. Combs, not one for windmills, sidestepped—affording another small example of how progress is nitpicked to pieces in Kentucky.

Still, the Assembly went into the second month of its session with the Combs forces firmly in control. The administration bill to create a joint Senate-House investigating committee ran into some oratory but passed, 69 to 16 and 26 to 8. A move to delay a vote on the governor's budget appropriations bill flopped, the administration prevailing by 69 to 21, with nine Democrats voting with Republicans to delay. In a Louisville speech, Combs said he expected trouble on his plan to realign the state's congressional districts and was prepared for a tough fight on the sales tax, but his leaders in both houses seemed not to take his remarks seriously. From all indications, he had major matters well under control.

14

The Kingmakers and
the Candidates

A governor must always govern with an eye out for politics, like a pioneer plowing with one eye peeled for Indians; in 1962, gubernatorial politics were not about to wait for the legislature to finish its business. Chandler had his "ABC in '63" race well underway, and his activities were beginning to concern "kingmakers" of the Combs wing (Bill May, Louis Cox, Lawrence Wetherby, Doc Beauchamp, Smith Broadbent), who felt that they should get a horse on the track before the unopposed Chandler made too much political headway. On January 21, 1962, newspaper stories in Louisville and Lexington reported that the kingmakers were fairly solid in their support of Highway Commissioner Henry Ward for governor, though Cox was reportedly backing Sixth District Congressman John Watts.

This didn't bother Combs too much; he was leaning increasingly toward Ned Breathitt but he thought the kingmakers would eventually support his choice. What concerned him more was the prospect of Earle Clements supporting Chandler. It was not just that he knew Clements could hurt; the thought of Clements in the Chandler camp was painful. He and Clements had been personally close. They had worked together, campaigned together, had taken abuse from Chandler and come back to beat him. He knew that philosophically, ideologically, the liberal Clements did not belong with the conservative Chandler. So on January 24 he flew to Washington and had lunch with his former mentor and friend. He tried to sound Clements out on the idea of Breathitt as the candidate, but Clements was chilly and noncommittal. Neither would he agree to stay out of the race, or not to support Chandler. Beneath his old familiar surface politeness there was a marked strain of barely concealed bitterness. It was apparent to Combs that he had done the one thing that Clements could never forgive or forget—he had hurt the Clements pride.

The lunch produced nothing, but Combs did not return to Frankfort dejected. Instead, the meeting cleared his mind. He had done all that could be expected of him, he felt. His first obligation was to protect his program. If Clements was beyond appeal, Combs had no choice but to follow his own policy judgment.

The day after he returned, Combs announced that he would ask the Assembly to start action leading to a vote on a limited constitutional convention in the elections of November 1964. The next day he introduced his school-reform package, which contained four principal points: independent audits of local school systems; state power to oust local school officials; removal of the superintendent of public instruction from the state board of education after 1964; and a professional practices commission to help police the conduct of teachers and administrators. The bill also set up procedures for having special judges hear local school controversies when there were charges that local judges were not impartial, and it set a minimum of 185 school days a year. Combs said he was still thinking about a constitutional amendment to make the superintendent appointive; he admitted that his school bill was not as strong as some legislators had urged, but said that he thought it was the best he could get through the legislature without hurtful fights. He and Wendell Butler had differed on ways to finance education of the mentally retarded, but Butler now told the press that he would support the bill.

It was the practical Combs, willing to give on minor issues in order to win major ones. His bill did not go down well with a group of House members who had served on the committee investigating state education. There were reports of meetings, a possible rebellion, but Combs decided to stick his ground and hope for time. A few days later he announced that he favored two constitutional amendments: one to make the state superintendent of public instruction an appointive office, one to make it easier to amend the constitution and call a revision convention.

While Combs could hope to escape a school rebellion, he could not escape the injection of politics into the session. On February 6, Clements met with Chandler, Treasurer Thelma Stovall, Frankfort attorney Clifford Smith, attorney and Chandler adviser Joe Leary, attorney James Gordon, and Louisville labor official Eulick "Mike" Walsh—at the same Standiford Motel where Clements had arranged the Wyatt-Combs merger—and agreed to support Harry King Lowman for the U.S. Senate. The next day Lowman made his formal announcement for the race. It didn't surprise anyone and seemed to have little impact, except to give notice that the Chandler campaign was in full swing, and to warn Wyatt that he could probably expect the same people to be against him in the general election.

On February 8, Combs launched an effort on which he had been working since the beginning of his administration, an effort brought close to home by the fact that his son Tommy was mentally retarded: he announced his "New Deal" for the mentally retarded in Kentucky. The program carried a two-year budget of $4,405,200, construction of a $750,000 building at the Frankfort Training Home, new programs of field service, new rules on foster home care, and a study of possible local centers for the care of 350 to 500 patients. The next day he went to Washington, where he and Glenn Seaborg, chairman of the Atomic Energy Commission, presided over a meeting at which it was announced that Kentucky had become the first state to take control of most of the nuclear activities within its borders. At the time, hopes for peaceful development of nuclear energy were running high, and Kentucky had optimistic plans for becoming a leader in the field.

On February 15, Earle Clements told a reporter that he had intended all along to reject the trucks acquired from Thurston Cooke on a lease basis in the famous "truck deal." He added that he knew the state could not legally acquire the trucks without competitive bidding. He said he had never met Cooke until the latter became finance chairman for the Combs-Wyatt campaign, and that he had signed the truck lease only after Highway Department attorney Jack Reed had said it was legal. He said he could not answer other questions because the joint investigating committee had the matter under study.

Clements' statement left once more an air of suspicion around the whole matter of the truck deal, which seemed to have more lives than a cat. If Clements had known that the lease arrangement was illegal, and that he could not acquire the trucks without competitive bidding, why had he defended the noncompetitive lease before the Louisville Chamber of Commerce the day after Combs canceled the contract? If he knew the contract was illegal, why had he signed it? And why had he accepted Jack Reed's opinion that it was legal if he knew that it was not?

Clements' blast, however, was only the first of what appeared to be a well-planned attack designed to cast suspicion on Combs and Wyatt. On February 21, Senator Rex Logan delivered a fiery speech in the Senate, in which he accused Combs and Wyatt of direct participation in the truck deal. In a tirade delivered on a point of personal privilege, Logan charged that Combs and Wyatt discussed the truck matter with Cooke weeks before they took office; that Combs and Wyatt or their representative persuaded Cooke to plead guilty to fraud charges arising from the collapse of his auto business after the truck deal was exposed; that Combs promised to pardon Cooke at the end of six months but reneged on the promise; that Cooke took the Fifth Amendment in hearings before the joint investigating committee as a result of an agreement between Wyatt and Cooke's attorney, Robert Grubbs; that Cooke, then a prisoner at LaGrange Reformatory, was afraid to testify before the legislative committee because he was under the penal custody of the Combs administration and was afraid he would be murdered in prison if he talked and jeopardized the governor; and that the interference of Combs in the investigation was grounds for impeachment.

Logan added that the events before the investigating committee were worth 50,000 votes for Happy Chandler, a bit of very wishful thinking. Rex Logan might have been an effective legislator under different circumstances. He was a good speaker, with an impressive voice; he wasn't afraid to tackle any subject or opponent. But he was intemperate; he let his emotions and perhaps the sound of his own voice destroy his perspective. He went too far in personal attacks, became vituperative, at times preposterous, amusing those he might have impressed. In the course of his attack on Combs and Wyatt, Logan, as quoted in the Lexington and Louisville papers, referred to his fellow senators as puppets and "hoop dogs." He called president pro tem Alvin Kidwell "Robot Kidwell, who is wound up every morning so he will know what to say." Speaking of Cooke's reliance on the Fifth Amendment to keep from testifying, Logan said, "If I were in his place I would not want to divulge the truth of the truck deal . . . because I think he probably would come out of there [prison] in a box," implying that Combs would have had Cooke killed had he told the truth. "And," added Logan, "I'll say that outside of the Senate chamber, too. At the time Cooke was involved in this trouble . . . either Combs or Wyatt . . . went to him and told him that if he didn't plead guilty they'd keep him there as long as they had political influence in Kentucky . . . they also told him they would give him a pardon at the end of six months. That's another Combs lie. . . . If the . . . legislature had the backbone, there's enough here to condemn Combs and to impeach him from office."

Wyatt retorted that "I am not going to indulge in a daily alley-cat fight with the raving henchman of Happy Chandler." Alvin Kidwell, shaking with anger, swore he would never give Logan the floor under a point of personal privilege again. Combs said nothing and reportedly discouraged friends in the Senate who wanted to censure Logan.

How much damage, if any, the Clements and Logan attacks achieved is questionable. Chandler, of course, made much of the matter, charging that it proved what he had been saying about the bad moral tone of the Combs administration. The truck charges were apparently in retaliation for what opposition forces saw as a Combs plot against the Chandler forces. On the day before the legislature convened, Senator Tom Raney, a former United Mine Workers official from Pike County, had called Combs and told him that he had been offered $5,000 and a job for his wife by Pikeville businessman Zach Charles Justice if he would vote with the antiadministration forces next day to organize the legislature. Justice, he said, had told him the offer came from A.B. Chandler. Combs, reluctant to "put my dog in that fight," urged Raney to tell his story to the newspapers. Raney did. Chandler denied knowing anything about the bribe offer, which was then referred to the investigating committee that was also probing the truck deal. It was shortly afterward that Senator Logan began making headlines with his truck-deal attacks on Combs and Wyatt.

Combs tried to regard these attacks in the context of their real, rather than their apparent, effect on governmental process. They irritated. They stung. But while they titillated the legislature, they did not materially change its operation. It was necessary to answer the more serious charges, so that they would not be useful in future election campaigns. Otherwise, the best thing to do was to let the accusers scream until the screams became monotonous.

Weeks before, Combs had pushed a bill through the legislature forcing operators of auto junkyards to screen their roadside eyesores from public view or move them away from public highways. It had been a more bitter battle than might have been expected over what seemed to be a minor matter, but Kentucky was dotted with sprawling auto graveyards, and most of them were profitable because, the operators protested, they could be seen from the road by potential customers. A considerable lobby came to Frankfort to fight the bill, and it took work to get it passed. But on Feburary 17, Combs accepted the "Keep America Beautiful" award at the annual meeting of the National Advisory Council of Keep America Beautiful, and his junkyard law was cited in the award.

This pleased him more than he admitted, for he had devoted a lot of time and attention to beautifying the state. His parks program, his roadside planting and small lakes programs, his drive to get junk cars off roadways and out of creek beds, his efforts to beautify the capitol grounds with the floral clock, the extensive planting of the median on Capitol Avenue, and his rose garden around the mansion—all had helped to restore the state's natural beauty and lure tourists.

As a part of the capital city's renovation, Combs launched a program to beautify the Old Capitol, a project that had at least one humorous result. When the rock wall around the Old Capitol grounds was restored, metal spikes were placed on top of the new walls, not only for their decorative function but to keep away the loafers who had been sitting there as long as anyone could remember. The loafers complained bitterly, and in time the complaints filtered through to the governor's office. Combs investigated. Yes, said the Buildings and Grounds people, the spikes had been put there to fend off the loafers, adding, "Governor, those people have been sitting there for 50 years." "Well," said Combs, "if they've been sitting there for 50 years, they've probably got squatters' rights by this time. And remember, loafers have an interest in the place, like the rest of us. Let's let them sit for another 50. There are too few places in the world where a man can do any decent loafing." The spikes came down, and gradually the loafers came back.

But Combs was by no means out of the woods. Significantly, the Senate beat his proposed amendment to make it easier to amend the constitution. This shook him. He had known he would have trouble with the bill but thought he had done his homework well enough to ensure close passage. Yet once more the strange affection of Kentuckians for their outmoded constitution showed itself. And the incident showed also that while failure to support progressive measures can often be blamed on poor leadership, Kentuckians cling to their past shackles even when their leaders try desperately to tug them into the present. In the end, Combs was obliged to settle for two lesser amendments: one to remove the salary limit, the other to provide for carrying on state and local governments in case an atomic attack wiped out major officials. (Tensions between Russia and the United States were creating a great scare at the time, with people rushing to create shelters of one type or another, stocked with food and water and presumably safe from fallout. The president of the University of Kentucky, Dr. Frank Dickey, had gotten one of the first shelters in Lexington but explained that it was proof against only fallout, not blast. Combs refused to dig a shelter at the mansion.)

That Kentucky was not champing at the bit to lead the way into the second half of the twentieth century was demonstrated by the passage of a bill that would have reduced the working age from 14 to 12; Combs vetoed it. However, with little heated opposition, the Assembly adopted his plan redrawing congressional district lines. This had to be done because the 1960 census showed that Kentucky had fallen behind the national average in population growth and would have to reduce its congressional districts from eight to seven. Under the plan, the Fourth and Fifth Congressional Districts were lumped together, the First,

Second, Sixth, and Seventh were changed slightly, and the Third was left largely untouched. It was a painful step in one sense, forcing Joe Bates in the Fifth District and Frank Chelf in the Fourth to fight it out. But in a more long-range sense it was one more reminder that Kentucky was losing people, not keeping pace.

Finally, on March 14, the joint legislative investigating committee released its report on the truck deal and on the Raney bribe charge. Raney, said the committee, had volunteered to take lie-detector tests which showed he was telling the truth; he had indeed been offered a bribe by Zach Charles Justice, but there was no proof that the bribe had come from A.B. Chandler. Similarly, there had been some sloppy handling of the aborted truck lease by Highway Department officials, but there was no evidence that any illegal or unethical instructions had come from Combs or Wyatt or that they had known of the nature of the truck deal prior to the time Combs canceled it.

When the report was released, Rex Logan threw the Senate once more into turmoil with a shouting, fist-shaking attack on Wyatt, this time adding a new charge: that a lease-purchase contract for the trucks had been drawn up by Ed Prichard. Prichard denied it, calling Logan's remarks "the products of a sick mind." And while the anti-Combs forces were occupied with accusations, the leadership was methodically enacting the major portion of the Combs program.

On March 7, Combs signed the bill creating a system of nine community colleges, including five then constituted as branches of UK and four more scheduled for construction. This marked a definite change in the nature of junior colleges, as they had been known previously. Before, they had been founded when and where the legislature could be persuaded to finance them. Combs made them a unified system, with uniform requirements and standards, fees, and tuition. And he placed them under the University of Kentucky, which had the power to enforce performance standards and to recommend new community colleges.

There were immediate protests from the presidents of the regional colleges, who would have preferred to see the individual community colleges placed under the control of the closest regional college, or under an independent board. They lost the fight, but there have been repeated efforts through the years by presidents and boards of the regional universities to get such control. All such efforts have failed, and it has been so generally agreed that the University of Kentucky system has worked well that in 1985 the Council on Higher Education voted to put the vocational education schools also under UK jurisdiction.

The system has been the target of other political pressures, however. In the 1960s, as the postwar baby boom began to hit the colleges, expansion of the community college system was hailed by college officials and enabled the state to handle the student flood. As the boom subsided, however, empty dormitory rooms and classrooms became a financial burden, especially as city students chose to attend community colleges, where they could live at home and continue to work while attending classes. Strangely, instead of producing pressures to reduce the number of community colleges in order to force students back to the universities, it increased pressure for the more convenient community colleges, to the point where the issue became almost ridiculous. For example, in 1986 the legislature approved a community college for Owensboro, despite the fact that there was a community college a few miles away in Henderson. The only pretense at justifying such an expenditure was the fact that Owensboro's downtown needed an economic shot in the arm.

There was the usual flurry of bills during the last week of the session, and then on March 17 it was over. Asked what his feelings were on the occasion, Combs said, "Whew!" then added, "I feel like I've been rode hard and put up wet."

But he had gotten out of the session much of what he had wanted. If there is any substance to the legend that governors always have trouble with their second session, it was not evident in 1962. During the session, 371 Senate bills and 583 House bills had been introduced. The legislature had passed 298 bills and 18 resolutions. Combs had signed 278 bills, vetoed 8, and allowed 12 to become law without his signature.

For all intents and purposes, Combs was over his roughest road. Barring special sessions of the legislature, he had all the laws and all the authority to start programs and spend money that he was going to get. He still had about 19 months in office, but his duty would be largely administrative. Politics, of course, would be a major concern during the coming year: the imprint that he would leave on the history of Kentucky depended to a great extent on how well he influenced the elections of 1963. A victory by Happy Chandler would mean, he knew, the dismantling of much of the program he had built.

Combs felt, in this regard, a certain sense of mission. He had been a young law student when the Democratic party of Kentucky was split into the Rhea and Chandler factions. He was a young veteran just home from the wars when Earle Clements had taken control of the Rhea faction and the Clements and Chandler factions had divided the state. Now Clements had gone over to the enemy, and the contesting camps were the Combs and Chandler factions. He deeply wanted to see his wing of the party triumph and survive, not only for the power it would give those who had fought at his side but because it would mean, or so he hoped, an end to the Chandler influence that he felt had helped so materially to keep Kentucky backward. He wanted to elect people who would carry forward his programs and effect the plans he had not completed. And he knew that this depended to some extent on how well he managed the affairs of state in the meantime and what kind of image he and his administration could fashion.

One pleasant aspect of a governor's last months in office is that during that time he begins to see the results of some of his programs. For example, Conservation Commissioner J.O. Matlick announced on April 13 that the small-lakes program had 14 projects completed or underway: seven small lakes had been formed by highway fills, three were nonhighway dams, and four were being planned. A week later the Garden Clubs of Kentucky, Inc., hailed Combs's moves to keep billboards off interstate highway rights-of-way, his roadside beautification and parks programs, his law to screen junkyards, his program to get junked cars off the roadsides and out of creek beds, and his efforts to beautify the capitol grounds, including construction of the floral clock. The club members made Combs their first honorary male member. ("I don't know how this is going to work out," Combs said.)

And as Derby Day of 1962 approached, interest in politics heated up as much as interest in the horse race. Marion Vance, a Glasgow Democrat, announced that he was in the race for the U.S. Senate and immediately charged that Combs had added 5,000 people to the state payroll to help Wyatt's Senate campaign. Harry King Lowman, now that the session was over, felt free to begin his own Senate effort and charged that Wyatt had failed miserably in his effort to bring industry to the state.

But what worried Wyatt was not the charges of Lowman or Vance. Though the governor's race was more than 18 months away, he was afraid that Ned Breathitt was going to announce his campaign for the governorship before the fall Senate elections. This, he feared, would take the attention of Democrats away from his Senate race against Thruston Morton and divert it to the 1963 governor's race. Although most state politicians tend to consider the U.S. Senate a better post than that of governor, both politicians and voters are usually more interested in the run for the state house; governors control more jobs and programs than do senators. Wyatt knew, too, that if Democrats started dividing their ranks between Breathitt and Chandler, some would drop away from him, since the Combs-Wyatt administration was pro-Breathitt and anti-Chandler. Wyatt wanted to keep his campaign and the governor's race as separate as possible.

It wasn't to be. "I asked Bert not to launch the campaign for the

1963 gubernatorial primary until after the 1962 Senate election," Wyatt wrote later. "I was convinced that the simultaneous running of both races in 1962 would alienate the Chandler wing of the party from my candidacy and could easily spell a Morton victory. Bert listened, but I could see that he was determined to defeat Chandler for governor, and felt that an early start would help his candidate."

That was precisely the case. On May 2, Breathitt announced in Louisville that he would be a candidate for the Democratic nomination for governor. The announcement did not create tidal waves of enthusiasm. Chandler ridiculed it. The leaders of the Jefferson County Democratic organization openly expressed doubt that Breathitt could beat Chandler, suggested that Henry Ward would make a stronger candidate, and proposed a Ward-Breathitt ticket. The kingmakers also continued to support Ward over Breathitt.

Partly for these reasons, Combs came out on the same day with a strong endorsement for Breathitt, designed to head off further criticism or party division. "I consider it my first duty to concentrate on being governor for the remainder of my term," he said, "but I will support Ned Breathitt within the limitations of that job." Breathitt quickly added that he would not campaign or open a headquarters but would "donate all my energies to the election of Wilson Wyatt." But the damage, Wyatt thought, had already been done. Later, in his autobiography, Wyatt wrote that when he heard of Breathitt's announcement and Combs's endorsement he told Combs, "Bert, that will cost me 50,000 votes."

Combs remembers the incident differently. "Wilson and Barry Bingham came to the mansion to see me one night," he recalled. "We sat in the little study off the hallway and talked. They asked me if I could support Wilson for the Senate. This didn't surprise me because there had been some speculation, I knew, that I might want to run for the Senate. I was glad to put a stop to those rumors—I had no intention of running—and told them I would be glad to support Wilson. But I told them that night that I was primarily interested in defeating Chandler, and that he was making a lot of waves, and that I felt that we had to get our man into the race as soon as possible in order to keep Happy from making too much headway. And I said specifically that we could not delay the governor's race until the Senate race was over. I am confident that they left that night knowing that I was going to announce for Ned as soon as he got into the race."

Combs's action showed how vital he considered the election of a suitable successor and the defeat of Chandler, who, he feared, would dismantle much of what Combs had accomplished. Many party wheelhorses still regarded Breathitt with misgivings: he was too young, he was unknown, Happy Chandler would "eat him alive, head, tail and pinfeathers" once they faced each other on the stump.

There was a story at the time that Dick Moloney and 19 other people interested in the governor's race called on Combs at the mansion to talk about a candidate. Moloney, like most of the others, was for Henry Ward and made a strong case for his candidacy. It turned into a considerable session. Moloney later reported to a friend, "Well, we talked it over with Combs, and the vote was 18 for Ward, and one for Breathitt." The friend said, "Good! Then Ward's our man." "No," said Moloney. "Breathitt's our man. The one vote for him was that little blue-eyed mountain governor of ours." Some say he did not use the term "governor." Highway Department employees, not believing the decision was final, continued to campaign for Ward until he passed them the word to quit.

In retrospect, it is doubtful that Breathitt's early announcement hurt Wyatt's campaign. The Chandler people had already gotten the word that Happy was going for Morton. Everyone knew that Happy was against Combs-Wyatt, and that Combs—no matter who he was for—would be against Happy. In western Kentucky, Breathitt supporters tried to soothe the feelings of Wyatt and his headquarters by running prominent ads in the local papers assuring the voters that Breathitt and Breathitt people were solidly behind Wyatt. "A vote for Wilson Wyatt for U.S. Senator will be an endorsement of Edward T. Ned Breathitt for Governor," the ads declared. Pro-Chandler Democrats saw this, or pretended to see this, as proof that Wyatt was allied with Breathitt and against Chandler. It gave them an excuse, if they needed one, to stay at home or vote against Wyatt.

"Happy," said Combs, "tried to stir trouble in the Wyatt camp by telling Wyatt people it was disloyal of us to back Breathitt while the Senate race was on. That was typical of Happy. It was wrong for us, who were backing Wyatt, to run the race for governor, but it was all right for him, who was backing a Republican, to be running his race for governor. In any event, Chandler and Clements would have opposed Wilson regardless of Breathitt's candidacy. Breathitt's running did not make them any stronger against him."

Whether or not it was essential for Breathitt to get the early start, there is no question that a lot of his backers were afraid that Chandler was making too much headway, and that only with an announced candidate in the field could they begin to form the organization they were going to need.

15

A Party Divided Once More

Wyatt won an easy victory in the primary (Harry King Lowman, his only serious opponent, became ill and withdrew) and prepared to face U.S. Senator Thruston Morton in the fall election. He knew he was in for a fight. Chandler was against him, though he continued to say that he would support the ticket in spite of all the slings and arrows he had suffered at the hands of Combs. Clements had never been warm toward Wyatt, and now was reported to be making common cause with his old enemy Chandler. As Wyatt wrote in his autobiography, *Whistle Stops*: "Since Clements and Combs had become estranged it soon developed that Clements would support his long-time political enemy Chandler rather than a candidate supported by Combs. Clements' antipathy toward Combs carried over to me as well. Early in the preparation for the Senate race I visited Clements at his apartment in Washington and asked for his support. He came quickly to the point and asked how I stood with Combs and with the *Courier-Journal*. I told him that, as he well knew, my relationship with both was entirely friendly. He responded sharply, 'Then how can you expect me to support you?' "

Even without the help of the Democratic bolters, Thruston Morton would have been a formidable opponent. Tall, handsome, urbane, and articulate, Morton was—like Wyatt—a wealthy and successful Louisvillian. Yale educated, he had assumed direction of his family's Ballard mills and had engineered their sale to the Pillsbury Company, leaving him with time and money to spend on politics. He had served as assistant secretary of state and as chairman of the Republican senatorial campaign committee, and had surprised the political soothsayers by defeating Earle Clements for the Senate, with the help of Dwight Eisenhower and Happy Chandler.

Morton found himself at home in the inner circle of Republicans in Washington. He was usually considered a moderate on fiscal policy and sturdily anti-Communist on foreign policy. He was a conservative candidate running in a state that had been voting Democratic in state races and Republican in national races with increasing frequency. Republican Senator John Sherman Cooper had become almost a Kentucky tradition. Eisenhower had carried Kentucky over Stevenson by 95,739 votes in 1956, and Nixon had carried it over Kennedy by 80,752 in 1960. In 1961, Republican Marlow Cook had been elected Jefferson County judge, while Republican William O. Cowger had won the race for mayor of Louisville. There was an apparent Republican tide running, and many of Wyatt's friends urged him to run for governor instead of for the Senate. His reply was curious.

"All aspects of the Combs-Wyatt program had been launched," he said in his autobiography, "and I felt that I had done probably all I could in that area. Certainly it was not worth four more years just for a better title."

Actually, as Combs pointed out in a speech to the Kentucky Education Association in September 1962, a staggering amount remained to be done. State teachers still received $2,000 a year less than the national average; illiteracy was widespread; unemployment continued high; industrial development was lagging; and the economic problems of eastern Kentucky were as stubborn as ever. The truth is that Wyatt enjoyed the excitement and high stakes of government in the world's most powerful city more than the hard, bitter, and often unrewarding struggle in Frankfort.

Combs's role in the fall campaign was fairly active. He made more than a dozen speeches for Wyatt, and did what he could to help with organization and strategy. Indeed, he did more than some of his and Wyatt's friends thought he should, believing that his participation in the campaign would only give Chandler cause to stage an open bolt. From the start, Wyatt had tried to avoid more factional clashes and had gone out of his way to make it plain that he wanted to represent all members of the Democratic party. That included Chandler. But, in retrospect, this attitude was unrealistic. Chandler was not to be wooed. He wanted not only to become governor, with the power over the party that the office carried, but to crush the opposing wing of the party. Clements, for so long his major obstacle, was no longer a factor. If Chandler could crush Combs and Wyatt, there would be no effective opposition on the horizon.

Meanwhile, Combs had his hands fairly full with the flood of small duties that occupy a governor between sessions. He had been thinking for some time of moving the statue of assassinated Governor William Goebel from the drive in front of the capitol to the lawn of the Old Capitol across the river. It was a logical idea, since Goebel's statue would then stand within a few yards of the spot where he was shot. Furthermore, at the top of Capitol Avenue the statue constituted something of a traffic hazard. But Combs had hesitated to move it for fear that Frankfort citizens, people from northern Kentucky, garden clubs, and historical societies might object. Now he gave the order, and the statue was swiftly and quietly moved at daybreak. He waited for the protests. They never came. On the contrary, the move prompted several people to suggest that the statue of Daniel Boone be moved from the Frankfort cemetery to a spot more easily accessible to tourists. "One statue at a time," Combs told them. "Let's let old Daniel rest for the time being."

Not all his problems were so easily handled. Early in the summer the American Automobile Association (AAA) had charged, in a bulletin sent to its seven million members, that "Kentucky has become far and away the worst [state] for speed traps in the nation"—not exactly the kind of publicity the state, in its drive to develop tourism, was seeking. Combs had quickly denied the charge, but the AAA responded by naming the offending towns: Bedford, Bonnieville, Crofton, and Hanson, all small towns on north-south U.S. highways. And there was nothing Combs could do about it, since the governor has no control over speed laws in towns. He can spend millions on parks and tourist facilities, build highways and spend other millions to promote the state's attractions. But a handful of small towns willing to fatten their own treasuries by shaking down outsiders can ruin the image and hurt the tourist trade. Combs called in the mayors of the offending towns and tried to be the diplomat. The situation gradually improved. (The police chief of Bedford, for example, was once reported to have suggested, when the city was criticized for its speed trap, "Why don't we just arrest them till noon and knock off the rest of the day?")

Combs then did a curious thing. While dedicating the new lodge at Jennie Wiley State Park near Prestonsburg, Combs praised Andrew Jackson May, the former congressman for whom the lodge was named (and uncle of Bill May), and then deliberately poked a stick into the political hornet's nest with a joking attack on critics of his parks and road spending: "They ran to tell the king the sky was falling, but they found it was merely an acorn falling from a tree beside a pool in Versailles."

This was too much for Chandler, the only Democratic politician in Versailles with a famous swimming pool. The pool was famous because it had been built during World War II, while Chandler was in the U.S. Senate, with wartime-scarce steel and concrete; and the job had been done by Ben Collings, a wealthy Louisville contractor who had been awarded considerable work for the state. Happy had repeatedly fought off the allegations of favoritism and corruption leveled by newspapers and political opponents, and now he charged into the fray with a roar. Combs, he said, had broken the truce that he, Chandler, had tried so hard to keep, and was trying to divide the party. Combs rubbed more salt into the wound when, on his birthday, August 13, he announced at an eastern Kentucky ceremony that he had chosen the name Mountain Parkway for the toll road—which, he reminded his listeners, Chandler had ridiculed as "that road that starts nowhere and goes nowhere. If you get on it, you can't get off. If you get off, you can't get back on."

"It was apparent by that time," he said later, "that Chandler and Clements were working against Wyatt in every way possible. It would have been silly to court them at that stage, and I thought it was better to call their hand than to permit them to work behind the scenes undetected. Wyatt never had a chance to get their support; everyone knew that but Wilson."

Actually, there was another reason for Combs's attack, one that showed the extent to which he had matured as a political strategist. He had discovered, the hard way, the secret of campaigning against Chandler. Happy was a master of attack but was vulnerable when put on the defensive. He was brilliant in ridicule, sarcasm, abuse, and accusation; but when the same tactics were turned on him, he reacted ineptly, losing his composure, becoming visibly angry and unimpressive. During the days of the "crippled goose," "Castro," and swimming pool charges, Chandler had found himelf on the defensive and had lost the charm, assurance, and ebullience that made him such a crowd pleaser. Combs felt that Breathitt had to avoid the mistake that he, Combs, had made in his first campaign, the mistake of letting Chandler keep him on the defensive. Instead, he was testing Chandler, finding out what bait he would rise to, showing Breathitt the effectiveness of attack. Breathitt later used the tactic brilliantly in his charge that Chandler voted to begin World War II and then resigned his army commission. The charge threw Chandler into a fury. He was never able to answer it convincingly, nor was he able to regain his old fighting balance.

Combs also faced the task of redrawing the legislative districts of the state. Section 33 of the Kentucky constitution demands that every ten years, or within two years of each federal census, the legislature divide the state into 38 senatorial and 100 representative districts of approximately equal population. The realignment was overdue, not having been done since 1942; officials in the counties that had gained population, and were thus entitled to additional representation in the legislature, were demanding that Combs call a special session and get the redistricting over with. But Combs, like every governor before him, did not relish the job. In every redrawing of district lines some counties gain representation, and some lose; the gainers are seldom grateful, and the losers are always resentful. Combs knew that he was going to have to call a special session to deal with the matter before he left office, but he knew that to call the legislature into special session and hand the lawmakers a plan would signal a fight. He was hoping that someone would sue to force him to call the session so that he would not be blamed for what happened. In September, Louisville Mayor William O. Cowger obliged. His district stood to gain representation.

To stall for time and to develop a plan as nonpartisan as possible, Combs appointed a 13-man committee to study various redistricting suggestions and come up with a proposal for the legislature. Although there are few better ways to avoid taking action than appointing a committee, the federal court to which Cowger's suit was referred ruled that Combs was acting in good faith. By the time the special session came up on January 28, 1963, several plans had been formed, and no one seemed to blame Combs for the unavoidable.

Meantime, back on the campaign trail, Wyatt was having an even rougher time than he had anticipated. Thruston Morton had apparently decided to take not only the rough road but the low road, which is to say that parts of his campaign did not reflect on him favorably. Morton was a social if not a political friend of Wyatt, and the two men had a considerable regard for each other. Further, Morton was a personal friend of long standing to *Courier-Journal* and *Louisville Times* publisher Barry Bingham. Yet as the summer wore on and the race for the Senate became tougher, Morton's attacks on Wyatt, and on the Bingham newspapers that supported him, became reckless; they contained statements Morton knew were not true and for which he later expressed regret.

He began, in a free-swinging speech in Lexington, to imply that Wyatt was in league with, if not an outright supporter of, people who were friendly to the Communist cause. He did this at first by tying Wyatt (accurately enough) to Adlai Stevenson—who, he claimed, had been "soft on Communism." This approach apparently did not sell too well. So, beginning with a speech in Louisville, he alleged that Wyatt had shown his true colors by becoming the first chairman of Americans for Democratic Action, which, Morton said, was the favorite hiding place for Communist fellow travelers. That caught on; the ADA had always been suspect, largely because few people had ever understood exactly what it was or why it had been formed in the first place. This was in a day when Communist China referred to itself as a "people's democratic republic," Communist East Germany was "democratic," and various other totalitarian governments chose to wrap themselves in the robes of democracy.

Actually, as the *Courier-Journal* immediately pointed out, the ADA had been formed in 1948 to help Harry Truman's presidential campaign by keeping liberal Democrats from following Henry Wallace off into the extreme left fringes of the party. The ADA red herring had been dragged across the campaign trail once before by none other than Chandler, who wrote to Truman—when the president came to Paducah to speak for Combs and Wyatt—that he could not share the stage with people who bolted Democrats, and reminding Truman that Wyatt had tried to defeat him by helping found the ADA. It is possible that Morton took his cue here from Chandler, who was again proving helpful, as he had been when Morton defeated Clements in 1956.

Speaking to the chamber of commerce in Louisville, Morton took what was, for a man of his caliber, a surprising step: he fabricated a charge against his old friend Barry Bingham. Earlier in the summer, he charged, Bingham had called a meeting at Louisville's Pendennis Club of the reporters and editors involved in the campaign, and had laid out instructions on how news of the Morton-Wyatt race was to be covered, ignored, or slanted. Bingham at once denied angrily that any meeting had been held by himself or any other official of his companies, or that any instructions to slant or distort the news had been given to anyone by anyone. News and political reporters, some of them admirers of Morton, appeared more hurt than angry. But a small seed of suspicion had been planted.

Wyatt fought back, and in a statewide Democratic rally in Louisville on August 25 (which neither Clements nor Chandler attended), he tore into Morton as the representative of the rich in Washington and as a man more concerned with the success of the Republican party than with the problems of Kentucky. Combs, speaking to the Democratic Women's Club of Lexington on September 28, tolled off a list of Morton's sins, which included his opposition to federal funds for teachers, his vote against creation of a Department of Urban Affairs, his vote against Medicare, and votes against increased funds for old-age pensions and dependent children. Morton wound up his campaign in Louisville on November 4 with an attack on the Combs administration for supplying, with taxpayers' money, a publicity machine for Wyatt. The same day, Wyatt barnstormed through the First Congressional District with what one reporter termed "the oratorical vigor of the great Alben Barkley."

It didn't help. On November 7, 1962, more than 800,000 Kentuckians went to the polls and elected Thruston Morton by a margin of 45,208 votes. It had been a campaign that both parties should have been glad to forget.

The next day Happy Chandler was out in full voice, blaming Wyatt's loss on Combs, the sales tax, Combs's mismanagement of state government, and his disloyalty to other Democrats. Combs fired back with a list of the times Chandler had bolted the candidates of his party. Chandler returned the fire with a charge that Combs was hysterical and needed a rest. "He must face up to the terrible mess he has made," Chandler said in a press statement. "The escape hatch to the federal bench has been closed. I predict that Breathitt will be dumped just as Clements was dumped. The evidence is persuasive."

In this statement are contained many hints to the remarkable resiliency of Happy Chandler the politician. His ability to rationalize his own conduct and to condemn with great indignation others engaging in the same conduct; his habit of interpreting as sin actions which, committed by him, became virtue; and his willingness to state as fact things that the record showed were made up out of whole cloth—such tactics, employed consistently, stood the man in good stead throughout a long career.

Combs had now taken his second painful defeat. He had lost his appeal for a constitutional revision, and he had failed to help Wyatt to the Senate. What chance did he have, he wondered, to elect Breathitt as his successor with a divided party in a state that was voting Republican, and against a Chandler who seemed to rise from each political fire like a phoenix, denying that the fire had singed a feather? The final weeks of 1962 were not very enjoyable ones.

On December 18 Combs greeted his final year in office by announcing two major programs and several smaller ones that he hoped to get underway before he left the mansion. Penal reform and better housing for the elderly headed the list. Others were an increase in tourist promotion, an expansion of educational television service, a wider highway cleanup and beautification program, more roadside parks and small lakes, more treatment for alcoholics, and a program to enrich higher education.

On December 23 he issued the call for a special session on reapportionment of the state's legislative districts, to convene January 28, 1963. The call seemed to silence his critics, and some, such as Louisville's Mayor William O. Cowger, had kind words to say. The next day station WHAS of Louisville presented its fifteenth annual "News-Man of the Year Award" jointly to Combs, Cowger, and Jefferson County Judge Marlow Cook. In presenting the award, Barry Bingham praised Combs

for his educational achievements: expansion of the vocational education system, creation of the educational television network, and establishment of the community college system.

At a small cake-and-coffee party in the state reception room of the
capitol, Combs said he would rather look forward to 1963 than back on
the year passing. "Although we got a lot done," he said. "We took some
licks. You don't find a possum up every tree. I face 1963 with two
resolutions," he went on. "First, I intend to work as hard next year as I
have the first three years. Second, I intend to keep my sense of humor,
and not get mad at anybody."

"You mean you're not going to get mad at ABC?" a newsman asked
(referring to Albert Benjamin Chandler).

"I said everybody," he said, "and that includes ABC."

"Are you going to campaign for Breathitt?" he was asked.

"Well," he said, perhaps thinking of the Wyatt race, "I have a
feeling Kentuckians don't want to be told how to vote. I'm for Breathitt,
and I want him to win for the sake of our programs. But just what I'll do
about it remains to be seen. I'll play that by ear."

Combs had by that time become rather famous for his preference
for "playing it by ear" rather than staking out in advance a hard and fast
policy. Some saw this as a shrewd way to keep from committing
himself on tough issues; others saw it as ducking. Ed Prichard was fond
of telling a story in which the Lord "looking down upon this great
spinning globe with its burden of sinful humanity, decided that the
time had come for Judgment Day, when every man should be called to
account and the pure separated from the impure, the godly from the
ungodly, the good from the evil. And so he spoke, and the world was
wracked and torn, and the seas were dried to their beds and the
mountains brought down, and the earth was shattered and the graves
gave up their dead. And as the great wailing, cringing mass of mankind
gathered quivering and fearful before the throne of God, the Lord
looked down and at the edge of the great mass he saw this little white-
haired figure in a white raincoat, and he called for him to come
forward, and he spoke, in a voice that was the great rumbling of
thunder, and said to him, 'Judge Combs, in your life you have been a
leader and a judge of men, and now I want you to help me to decide
how I shall judge these people before me, separating the good from the
bad, the sheep from the goats, deciding which shall be hurled into
outer darkness to suffer eternal damnation and eternal suffering, and
which shall live with me in bliss in paradise.' And Combs looked at the
Lord, and he shuffled his feet, and he scratched, and then he sort of
grinned and he said, 'Lord, why don't ya just play this by ear?' "

As it turned out, Combs did quite a bit of campaigning for Breathitt between the first of 1963 and the primary election on May 28, but a lot of it was rather indirect. Most of his speeches asked voters to defend the sales tax or the road program. He had several opportunities to get in his political licks without scheduling a political talk because he spent much of the first part of 1963 at dedications, occasions where as speaker he was expected to say a few kind words for his administration, his friends, his policies, or other agencies responsible for the structure being dedicated.

For example, during January he cut ribbons opening a stretch of Interstate 75 between the Kentucky River and Richmond, portions of I-64 around Frankfort, Lexington's New Circle Road between U.S. 60 and U.S. 421, and parts of Kentucky 52 between Richmond and Irvine. Much of the money for these roads came from Washington, of course, but it is customary for state officials to take credit, and Combs was not about to let the voters forget whence came their blessings.

During February he dedicated projects at Eastern Kentucky State College costing $6,750,000, and evaluation and admission centers at Outwood Hospital and the Frankfort Training Home. He took advantage of school meetings to ask teachers, school administrators and parent-teacher groups to support his program of increased aid to schools—which, he pointed out, depended on the sales tax. During his term, he reminded them, 3,595 new classrooms had been built, and $71,500,000 spent on new buildings. But Kentucky teachers were still paid less than the national average, and the state still had 890 one-room or one-teacher schools. With Chandler ranging the state, promising to slash the tax and blasting Combs for wasting money, Combs didn't have to spell out his message. If you want to keep the state moving, he was saying, keep Chandler out of office.

A great deal of time and effort—and patience—was consumed during February by the special session of the legislature called to reapportion the state's legislative districts. It was a fight from which Combs could hardly gain; on the contrary, there was a danger that voters displeased by the final reapportionment plan would react against him and his candidate, Ned Breathitt. So he kept as aloof from the routine pull and haul as possible. In his opening address he reminded the legislators that other states failing to produce fair districting plans had been forced to accept plans produced by the courts, and urged them to settle on a plan acceptable to everyone. He also gave them alternative plans devised by three University of Kentucky professors—Malcolm Jewell, Jack Reeves, and Max Milam—and one by Mayor William Cowger of Louisville, then left them pretty much to their own devices.

It took the legislators the entire month to grind out a law. It did not please everyone, including Combs. He thought it "a little bit rough" to lump all four far western Kentucky counties—Ballard, Carlisle, Hickman and Fulton—into one House district; he questioned the suitability of combining Clark County, in the Bluegrass, with coal-mining counties farther east; and he criticized the political judgment and fairness that put Democratic Warren County into a Republican district. But, in all, he thought the law would stand up in court.

And he was satisfied that he had done right to refuse a request from Louisville to include in the special session a move to change the state's 161-year-old Sunday closing law, which was causing a storm of controversy in Louisville and Jefferson County. No one seemed to know exactly what the law would and would not permit; passed at the beginning of the nineteenth century, it specified that only those establishments whose services were "essential" could open on Sunday, but changing times had made this criterion a source of endless confusion. Were filling stations essential? If so, could they sell candy and soft drinks? Food was obviously a necessity, but did this mean groceries could remain open? If so, could they sell tobacco? Beer? Razor blades? Could restaurants open? Movies?

Combs decided, and probably wisely, to postpone action on that one. He had gotten past one potentially damaging hurdle and had garnered reams of praise from the press for his "progressive" attitude in acknowledging the "right of the legislature to independence." And there were a handful of other pitfalls between him and the all-important primary election.

Combs had other ceremonial duties—indeed, he welcomed them—such as the long-awaited dedication of the Mountain Parkway, and the dedication of Herndon Evans Lodge at Pine Mountain State Park in Pineville, named for the Lexington *Herald* editor who had once been editor of the Pineville *Sun* and who, as a member of Combs's Parks Board, had worked tirelessly to expand and improve the beautiful park near his old homestead, even donating land of his own.

But the primary hung over everything like a funnel-shaped cloud that threatens constantly without ever quite touching earth. Always Combs had to come back to the race for governor. Breathitt, considered inexperienced and unimpressive at the start of the campaign, was beginning to change the minds of a lot of his detractors. Far from being shy or awkward on the platform, he was showing a flair for speaking and for platform theatrics. With Ed Prichard lending his touch to the speeches, Breathitt was starting to lay into Chandler with gusto, and the natural process of politics began to take its course—the better the performance, the bigger the crowds; the bigger the crowds, the better the performance—as the electricity began to flow between candidate and public.

Chandler was still trying to ignore Breathitt and center his fire on Combs. But Breathitt was tearing into Happy in Chandleresque fashion, ridiculing him, imitating him, polishing tricks and tactics of his own, while Prichard and his claque shouted in the background, "Pour it on!" "Tell them the truth about Happy!" and (for some reason) "He's clean! He's clean!" And there was a fresh, energetic group of campaign workers around Breathitt, men able to work days at a time and willing to take chances on new ideas—men such as Foster Ockerman, a Lexington attorney who was his campaign manager; John Y. Brown, Jr., son of the Democratic warhorse; Thomas Carroll, Don Mills, Field McChesney, William Biven, advertising man William Beam. They offered a rather striking contrast to the familiar, aging faces around Chandler.

On May 1, Combs addressed the Law Day ceremonies at the University of Louisville law school, encouraging the students to work toward returning some semblance of dignity to political campaigns in Kentucky so that the public could hear, and even think about, the issues in the election—a good idea that no one seemed ready to practice. No one involved in the primary campaign was discussing the growing argument about the purpose of the Council on Higher Education, the relative roles of state colleges and the university, and the proper place of the community college system. The Amis Report on higher education had recommended that the presidents of the state colleges be removed from the council and that it be reorganized to operate without the political catfights over appropriations that occurred every time the state budget was considered. The proposal made sense, but the college presidents were not likely to adopt a reform that would deprive them of power, especially the power to horsetrade for appropriations and new construction funds, control admission standards that might restrict enrollments, and decide who should be able to establish graduate schools. And they were rigidly opposed to giving the council these powers.

Eventually, the council would, indeed, be given limited powers and placed under a professional director and staff, sparking an idea for a similar agency to bring order, honesty, and uniformity to the state's system of elementary and high schools. But Combs, in the meantime, was engaging in a battle with a powerful figure within the college hierarchy—University of Kentucky Vice-President Frank Peterson.

Frank Peterson seemed at first an unlikely target for a reform move. Easygoing, quick to smile, quietly efficient, Peterson had come to the university through Frankfort, where he had been a key finance

man in Chandler's first administration, 1935-39. He remained in Frankfort during the Keen Johnson administration following Chandler's and
came under fire from the press, especially from Howard Henderson of
the *Courier-Journal*, for his purchasing practices. He was given a post in
the UK administration as a reward for his service, and for years seemed
to be nothing more than an affable financial administrator, gradually
rising to become the almost indispensable comptroller of the university. In the process he had made friends, including many in the political
arena, by doing small favors here and there. He had also developed a
following within the university. (Both President Frank Dickey and
former President Herman Donovan came to his defense when he was
charged with irregularities in financial matters, though trustees later
complained that they did so because Peterson had had work done on
their farms gratis.) He also had some very stubborn critics who charged
that he had used his position to feather his own nest. For example, on
March 4, 1963, the *Courier-Journal* reported that Combs had told the UK
board of trustees that Peterson

> bought property near UK, then sold it to the university at a
> whopping profit;
> used his position to have the university buy soap and de-
> tergents in quantity and then sell them to a laundry he
> partly owned;
> owned part of a tire company that sold tires to vendors doing
> business with the university;
> and owned, with his wife, half interest in a vending company
> having 130 vending machines on the UK campus.

"I didn't pick that fight," said Combs in a 1985 *Courier-Journal*
interview. "It was forced on me. Peterson's shenanigans, especially his
involvement in the vending machine business, was common talk in
Lexington. It was said that he gave his company the best locations for
machines on the UK campus. There were other serious charges. Two of
the trustees were demanding an investigation. At least one reporter,
Kyle Vance of the *Courier-Journal*, was becoming interested. When all of
these accusations came to me, I knew that if I didn't take the initiative I
would be accused of a whitewash. As governor, I was chairman of the
board of trustees. And I didn't want another truck deal on my hands.
So I took the initiative. It is significant that Peterson didn't fight his
ouster. He was clearly guilty of some of the charges."

After reading the accusations against Peterson, Combs called for a
report from a committee of three trustees he had appointed on January
25, 1963, to study the matter. To his surprise the committeemen—

Judge James Sutherland of Bloomfield, Dr. Harry Denham of Mays-
ville, and Dr. Lewis Cochran, a UK professor—said that in their opinion these facts were not sufficient grounds for preferring charges
against Peterson. This brought cries of "whitewash" from trustees Sam
Ezelle and Clifford Smith. The board finally voted five to four to
suspend Peterson until the allegations could be further studied. On
April 27 the trustees voted unanimously to bring formal charges of
misconduct in office against Peterson (though it was never explained why
the three trustee-committeemen had changed their minds). And on August 25, after a UK audit had questioned Peterson's methods, he was given
a year's leave of absence with pay, and his office was abolished.

As might have been foreseen, Happy Chandler insisted that Peterson had been punished for being a Chandler supporter, but it is not
likely that Combs would have gone so far out of his way to expose such
a relatively unimportant political figure. His action did, however, serve
to leave the impression that many of the coterie of minor officials
faithful to Chandler were cynical, if not corrupt, and create some
suspicion of Chandler himself at a critical time.

At any rate, it was good to have the case out of the way. In the
summer of 1963, John Oswald, a vice-president of the University of
California, was chosen as the new president of UK, succeeding Frank
Dickey. The Oswald appointment was not without critics in both the
Combs and Chandler camps. "I took some heat from some of my
friends for recommending Oswald," Combs admitted. "They thought
there were some deserving Kentuckians from whom a new president
should be chosen. But UK needed a fresh face, and a man of Oswald's
caliber."

The muttering against Oswald—and it continued as long as he
remained in Lexington—reflected not only resentment of his policies,
which many people both on and off campus considered harsh and
unfeeling, but the view that in choosing him Combs had violated
political tradition. With few exceptions, the presidency of UK and of
the state colleges had gone not only to Kentuckians but to Kentuckians
of the proper party alignment, men enjoying the approval of local
politicians and civic powers. It has not been unusual to find former
superintendents of public instruction, senators, and representatives
becoming heads of regional universities. Membership on the board of
trustees of the University of Kentucky has always been a political plum,
as have posts on regional boards of regents. This injection of partisan
politics into the university system has had a deadening effect. During
the middle 1980s, two regional presidents were driven off by regents
who charged not that they were incapable or ineffective, but that they
"just moved a little too fast for folks around here."

16

Tale of a Fate Foretold

Oswald was able to take over as president of the University of Kentucky on September 1, 1963, for perhaps the most exciting and expansive period in UK history, without the embarrassment the Peterson case might have caused. He also avoided fallout from the May 28 primary, which was just as well, because the primary got rough. So rough that Happy Chandler lost his composure when Breathitt charged that Chandler had voted to declare World War II and then had resigned his reserve army commission. Happy blew up. "I hate to hear a dirty, stinking little liar impugn my patriotism," he told a Whitley City crowd on May 16. He did not deny that he resigned his captain's commission shortly after voting to declare war. He insisted, however, that he had called Secretary of War Henry Stimson and told him to "pull my card" (place him on active duty) but that Stimson had said "he would rather have a senator than a captain." So he, Chandler, had resigned the commission.

Breathitt continued the charge. He and his corps of speakers, Ed Prichard in particular, charged that Chandler's son-in-law, James J. (Jimmy Jack) Lewis, was collecting money for Chandler's campaign, some from people desiring favors from the state. This was surely no novelty in Kentucky, but the charge took on a comic character when Prichard shouted that Chandler was riding the state insisting that people "fill the sack for Jimmy Jack!" It became one of those campaign gimmicks which—like Chandler's "$20,000 rug" of 1955—could be counted on for a laugh, and the Breathitt speakers never missed a chance to bellow "Fill the sack for Jimmy Jack!" Breathitt, in brief, was pulling a Chandler act on Chandler. It was part demagoguery, part buffoonery, part hyperbole, as it had been when Chandler used it; it was also, as it had been for Happy, effective.

"We were interested in the legislative races," says Combs, "but primarily we were concerned with Ned. He was a good candidate, but he had little to do with financing, headquarters work, schedules, press, that sort of thing. We financed his campaign, just as Wetherby financed mine. We obtained our money mainly by these dinners. We had passed a law against assessing state workers, but we could give these dinners. It wasn't mandatory that state employees come to them, and we tried to make that plain, but I knew that department heads were suggesting pretty plainly that they come. It was the better part of valor. Buy a couple of tickets at $250 each. Good insurance."

The campaign was not without its painful moments, chief among them the appearance of Earle Clements on the platform with Happy Chandler at a rally in Morganfield in which Chandler charged that the truck deal had been engineered by Combs to discredit Clements—an evil scheme which, he implied, had been hatched at least in part by the *Courier-Journal*. Clements seemed uncomfortable, and some of his longtime supporters and friends stayed away from the rally or left early. But Chandler pulled good crowds in his western Kentucky swing, causing some worry in the Breathitt camp.

May 28 dawned, like the proverbial day of battle, fine and clear, and Kentucky voters streamed to the polls. Chandler, casting his ballot in Versailles, told reporters that he would beat Breathitt "world without end," a favorite expression of his; and he stuck to his optimism when, late in the afternoon, the early returns showed Breathitt doing well in places where he was not expected to do well.

At Breathitt headquarters in Louisville, campaign workers began getting their first phone calls, chiefly from eastern Kentucky, in late afternoon; as each favorable report came in, wild cheers went up. And the reports were good. Surprisingly good. Foster Ockerman and his lieutenants, watching the incomplete returns, began to wonder if their people were not gilding the lily. At the Frankfort Chandler headquarters, equally rosy reports were going up on the board, to similar cheers from the campaign staff.

But as the dinner hour passed and the polls closed across the state, it became obvious that Chandler had a real scrap on his hands. Usually Chandler and a group of supporters would listen to returns in the log cabin on the lawn of his Versailles home, waiting for the victory trend to become comfortable, at which time they would march to his brick home and from there drive to Louisville for the celebration. But this time the calls were not telling him what he wanted to hear. He was not carrying the First Congressional District as he had predicted. He was getting shellacked in the Third, though this was no real surprise; he had talked about carrying it, but few people in his organization really expected him to. His dependable home district, the Sixth, was coming through for him, but elsewhere the balloting was taking a strange turn.

By seven o'clock, according to Associated Press and Lexington

Herald reporters, the enthusiasm and optimism among the Chandler officials were beginning to wane, and looks of surprise and worry began to appear on faces around the room. No one who has ever been in a campaign headquarters when the bad news starts coming in can forget that feeling of dread, that premonition of disaster that seeps into the workers, though they continue to cheer and try to smile and turn increasingly to the candidate for reassurance. The uneasy feeling slowly yielded to serious concern. Things were not going the way they should have gone. Breathitt was running very strongly in the mountains. He was doing well in the Second District. Louisville was going more heavily for him than anyone had predicted or even imagined.

By nine o'clock it was obvious to everyone that a major, smashing upset was in the making. Breathitt entered the hotel ballroom where his returns were being tabulated to a wild uproar. Nothing was heard from Chandler or his headquarters, but that was not necessary. The story was written in the figures on the board. Breathitt had won, and he had "won big."

The returns not only shook the Commonwealth; they wrote an end to one of its most colorful political careers. Ned Breathitt, 43, had defeated the 64-year-old Chandler by a shocking 60,000 votes. Chandler had prepared to drive into Louisville for a riotous victory celebration. Instead, he retired to his home, surrounded by his family and a few friends, and heard with disbelief the returns come thundering in. And while he sat, trying to accept the unacceptable, the incredible end of his time, the Breathitt headquarters were bedlam. Time and change had caught up with Happy Chandler. To show the devastating extent to which the election had been a personal rebuff, his running mate Harry Lee Waterfield easily won nomination for lieutenant governor. The results were a painful handwriting on the wall for Earle Clements, too. His home county, Union, went for Breathitt 2,528 to 1,913. His home precinct went for Breathitt 317 to 274.

It was not until the following day that Chandler could bring himself to concede defeat. Even then he would not admit that it was the end of the line; that just as he had, more than a quarter of a century before, brushed aside those who had referred to him as "that boy," now he had been brushed aside by a young man he had called "this little fella." Two weeks later, on June 11, he told Bill Neikirk of the Associated Press, "This faction is not dead. It's lively. Any faction that can get 264,000 votes isn't dead." Asked if he would support Breathitt, he snorted, "I haven't any high opinion of that fellow. They were responsible for that scurrilous campaign. I won't be a party to that. I'm not going to be counted out of anything."

But he had, of course, already been counted out, set aside by the voters. He had not known it at the time, but he had delivered his own valedictory the night before the election when he quoted for reporters the lines from Kipling's "Recessional": "The tumult and the shouting dies; the Captains and the Kings depart." Now, in his last hurrah, the words had a painful, personal ring. It was, as *Courier-Journal* reporter Ben Reeves wrote, Kentucky's final break with the nineteenth century.

And when the voters sent Happy off into history they sent with him another great of the old days: Earle Chester Clements, the big man from Morganfield, a man who had denied himself the better farewell that he had earned.

"Yesterday," Reeves wrote, "seems to have been Kentucky's day to say goodbye to the days of William McKinley. . . . Chandler is more than a typical Kentucky politician. He is part of a larger American genre that included such famous political names as Cotton Ed Smith, Tom Watson, Theodore Bilbo, Earl Long, Michael James Curley, W. Lee Pappy O'Daniel, Ole Gene Talmadge. They were all colorful, dynamic, forceful political personalities who were admirably geared by nature to their eras and their areas. Time caught up with them, too.

"The effect of Breathitt's victory over Chandler creates a whole new political climate and environment for Kentucky. It seems to establish Governor Bert T. Combs, who has been called by friends and foes alike the worst politician ever to occupy the governor's chair, as an eminently shrewd and successful politician after all."

And it is likely that for no one, Breathitt included, were the election results sweeter than for Bert Combs. He had spent election evening at the mansion watching the returns on television. According to those present, he gave no outward sign of the tremendous stresses he must have been enduring. When the outcome was announced, he made a statement to a few reporters watching with him, congratulating Breathitt on his victory. "Ned has made an unusually good candidate and run a great race," he said. "Mabel [Mrs. Combs] and I extend to him and Frances [Mrs. Breathitt] our congratulations and very best wishes." From Louisville, Breathitt called to ask Combs, who had chosen Breathitt over the advice of his closest advisers and had stuck to him through months of adverse reports and predictions, to come to Louisville and share the celebration. But Combs said, "This is your night. We'll watch you on television, and Mabel and I will come by tomorrow afternoon."

Significantly, Combs called and talked with his daughter Lois at Randolph-Macon College in Virginia. The two were extremely close, and he knew that she would be waiting to hear the results, in itself a measure of his concern about the election and his relief over the outcome. He worked for about an hour on a commencement speech he was scheduled to deliver next day at the Kentucky School for the Deaf; then he and Mabel took a walk around the mansion grounds. It was a soft, late spring evening, and the scent of early flowers from the gardens he had planted around the mansion was pleasant on the air. He felt a little tired, as the tension and uncertainty of months drained slowly out of him, and deeply satisfied. He went to bed shortly before midnight and was asleep almost at once.

17

Hard Times Now Are Gone

As far as crises were concerned, the hard days were past for Combs. Not that he could rest on his accomplishments. June 16 found the legislature in special session for the second time in 1963, and for an unusual reason.

In 1956 the Welfare and Retirement Fund of the United Mine Workers of America opened ten hospitals, five of them in Kentucky, financed by the royalty of 40 cents collected by the union for each ton of coal mined. The hospitals, big and modern in a region desperate for modern hospital facilities, cost about $27,000,000. These hospitals, spread across the coalfields of Appalachia, had long been a dream of UMW boss John L. Lewis and represented his determination to improve the medical care available to his union miners.

But the cost of operating the hospitals was greater than anticipated. Furthermore, the shaggy-maned Lewis had provided his beloved hospitals with their own Achilles' heel. In the years following World War II, he had forced on the soft-coal operators a contract requiring such increases in miners' wages that the operators had been obliged to mechanize the mines, digging coal with machines instead of men. Slowly, the number of miners decreased, and the decrease in union miners and union families was cutting demand for the hospitals' services and reducing hospital income. By 1962 officials of the Welfare and Retirement Fund had decided to jettison the drain on their treasury by selling or closing the hospitals.

This was of painful concern to the state, for five of the hospitals were in eastern Kentucky—at Middlesboro, McDowell, Hazard, Harlan, and Whitesburg. The asking price was $7,732,000, and Combs knew there was not that much excess in the treasury; nor had the legislature voted any money whatever for such a purchase. Yet officials and doctors throughout the coalfields warned that if the hospitals closed, the situations in the eastern counties would be acute.

To its eternal credit, the United Presbyterian Church's Board of

National Missions stepped in to offer its services in an effort to keep the hospitals open. The Rev. Gordon Corbett of Lexington had studied the situation for months, calling on Combs, members of Kentucky's congressional delegation, UMW officials, and officers of his own church, trying to find some way to finance the purchase. It is doubtful whether the hospitals could have survived without him. But the mission board put its weight behind the effort because, as Dr. Kenneth G. Neigh, its general secretary, said, "I believe we need to do this. I believe we can do the impossible."

On April 22, Combs went to Washington and, with Seventh District Congressman Carl Perkins, called on Josephine Roche, former assistant to John L. Lewis and then secretary of the Welfare and Retirement Fund, to see whether the price of the hospitals could not be negotiated. "That was the coldest woman I ever ran up against in my life," said Combs. If we can't get our money out of them, Roche said in effect, we will close them by July 1. Take it or leave it.

Combs and Perkins then went to see Bill Batt, head of the Area Development Administration, but were told that while the administration wanted to help, it would be setting a dangerous precedent to do so, and that only President John F. Kennedy could make such a decision. The Hill-Burton Act (for financing hospital construction in poverty areas) could finance only new construction, Batt reminded them; if he used Hill-Burton money to bail out the miners' hospitals, he would be deluged with demands that he bail out other hospitals in financial trouble. But eventually, with the personal intervention of Kennedy, the ADA committed itself to an initial grant of more than $3,000,000. With this encouragement the Presbyterian board began negotiations to buy the hospitals, which it proposed to turn over to an independent board.

But an annual operating deficit of $700,000 was expected, and Kentucky, or the agency assuming responsibility for their operation, would be required to pick up that amount. Combs knew that the state could not forever carry the burden; he also knew it could not afford to let the hospitals be closed. Doctors and administrators assured him that with tighter management, the Kentucky hospitals could operate without the deficit, and on this assurance he called the legislature into special session on July 16 to implement the federal grant that would enable the Presbyterians to buy the hospitals. It was his fifth special session, more than called by any other Kentucky chief executive.

The lawmakers responded quickly. "I was impressed," Combs said later. "I thought it showed a lot of good will on the part of members from other parts of the state, voting money like that for eastern Kentucky counties, people from Louisville, for instance. We don't always pull together like that." The legislators also approved a constitutional amendment outlawing Kentucky's poll tax, an anachronism that had been defunct for years because of federal prohibitions but needed removing from Kentucky's cluttered books. Two weeks later Combs also signed into law the special session's bill providing a considerable measure of parole reform, giving the Parole Board the right to say when a prisoner is eligible for parole rather than requiring a set minimum of time to be served, and enlarging the board from three to five members. Said Combs, "It's a start." But national corrections officials called it "a great credit to Kentucky."

Now Combs could feel his time as governor getting short. In some respects, he looked forward to his last day eagerly; in others, he felt that he was leaving too much undone. There were many pleasant occasions in the final weeks—dedications, speeches before admiring and appreciative audiences. He took his final governor's tour and got a good reception at just about every stop. He dedicated General Burnside Island State Park. He opened the 127-mile Western Kentucky Parkway and unveiled a statue of Alben Barkley in the rotunda of the capitol. Earlier, he had received the first payment of an eventual $3,000,000 that Kentucky would receive from the Federal Highway Administration for banning billboards from the interstate rights-of-way.

But there was one critical area to which he still had to address himself. Louisville Mayor William Cowger had gone out on a limb to pass an ordinance forbidding racial discrimination in public accommodations. He was taking a lot of heat for it and had urged Combs repeatedly to propose to the legislature a similar law. When Combs failed to include it in his call for the second special session of the year, black leaders as well as members of the Human Rights Commission and officials of the Kennedy cabinet in Washington began putting pressure on him to amend the call. On June 19, 1963, Combs met with President Kennedy in Washington, and while he avoided a commitment to a state public accommodation law, he did pledge to support expanded minority rights. This didn't please anyone.

Combs was already on record concerning civil rights. In October of 1962, at a southern governors' conference in Hollywood, Florida, he was one of the few governors willing to stand up and approve President Kennedy's speech earlier that week insisting that Mississippi obey the ruling of the Supreme Court and admit a black man to the University of Mississippi. Mississippi Governor Ross Barnett condemned Kennedy and the court for violating the rights of his state, declared he would not preside over the involuntary integration of the university, and in effect defied federal authorities to enforce the court's edict. But while Deep South governors rushed to deplore the Kennedy speech, Combs said: "I can sympathize with the chief executive of any state whose traditions and customs have come into conflict with the law of the land. All governors, however, have taken an oath to support the constitution . . . for the sake of himself and his state, Ross [Barnett] should stop playing Custer's Last Stand and join us."

"But," he said later, "I had already sampled the legislature, and concluded that in view of the civil rights fight going on, and all the emotions involved in it, I'd have no chance at all of passing an accommodations bill through the legislature. I had already asked them for a lot, and that was a very touchy issue just then. So I decided on an executive order [issued on June 26, 1963] prohibiting any state-regulated establishment from discriminating against blacks.

"That was my response to the civil rights leaders. At first, some of them didn't think it amounted to much. But then they realized that this included eating establishments, hotels, motels, state parks, all state facilities, in fact any facility that some state agency regulated or licensed, and they thought better of it.

"It had some strange twists to it. For instance, we decided that, under it, we had to close Cherokee Park, down near Kenlake, because it had been an all-black park, and since they now had access to all parks, there was no need for it. But a lot of blacks wanted their own park, objected to closing it."

Naturally, not everyone stood up and cheered the executive order. Though he was now a lame duck, Combs had plenty of political enemies who had not forgotten. On June 28, Rex Logan rose in the special session of the assembly to blast Combs for the executive order. He asked the Senate to adopt a resolution condemning him and predicted that the order would prompt at least 100,000 Chandler Democrats to bolt to Louie Nunn, the Republican gubernatorial nominee, in the fall general elections. It was a case of *déjà vu*—Logan's last blast. Nunn also attacked the order as "a dictatorial edict of questionable constitutionality" and charged that it had been dictated by U.S. Attorney General Robert F. Kennedy, brother of the president. From his home in Versailles, Happy Chandler—like an old Confederate soldier who could not accept Appomattox—declared that the "illegal act" showed that Combs knew that Breathitt was going to lose the race for governor, and that the two of them were "desperate."

As a matter of fact, it is hard to see how Combs (and/or Breathitt) had anything to gain politically from the integration issue one way or another. Either way he went, special session or executive order, Combs was bound to catch abuse and arouse strong feelings and possible reprisals in the governor's race. In all probability, he took the less dangerous way out. With Republicans possibly trying to make hay for Louie Nunn and such Democrats as Rex Logan hungry for one more shot at the hated target, the introduction of civil rights at the special session could have made it a madhouse. The executive order got the issue settled quickly and attracted all of the fire toward Combs, rather than letting legislative oratory include Breathitt.

Actually, the Antidiscrimination Order was one more way in which the reticent, wryly humorous governor from Appalachia resembled the outgoing, openly emotional Boston Irish president. Combs had forfeited his chance of becoming close to Kennedy when, out of loyalty to Earle Clements, he backed Lyndon Johnson for president over Kennedy in 1960—a bit of loyalty later ignored by Clements. But Combs and Kennedy had felt and acted alike in their concern for Appalachia, in their feelings for civil rights, in their desire to ease the blight of poverty. After he issued his executive order, Combs received from Kennedy a short but expressive note: "Thanks, Bert," it read. "We need more governors like you."

Of course, the resulting situation posed something of a problem for Happy, who had claimed all along to have the ear and support of his friend President Kennedy. And it was something of a touchy political matter for Nunn. Louisville's Mayor Cowger—who, with Jefferson County Judge Marlow Cook, represented a huge bloc of Republicans—openly differed with Nunn on the executive order. Indeed, the issue seemed to split Republicans all over the lot. Thruston Morton sent a letter to Nunn, agreeing with him and criticizing Combs for issuing the order. Meanwhile, the *Record*, the Catholic newspaper of the Diocese of Louisville, carried a strong editorial endorsing Combs's action.

Finally, however, Franklin Circuit Judge Henry Meigs dismissed a suit by the Louisville Tavern Operators Association challenging the legality of the order. There was no controversy existing, said Meigs, since nothing had been done to enforce the order. Nunn switched tactics to attack Combs on the cost of groceries for the mansion, an issue whose time, apparently, had not come. He then attacked Combs for allegedly ignoring bootlegging in Floyd County. That didn't make much impression, either, but Nunn followed it with a charge that Combs had permitted the parks to sell gift dolls that had been made in East Germany. Combs promised with a straight face that he would see that the parks were not infiltrated by Communist dolls.

Nunn's was not the first criticism of merchandise sold in state parks. Members of his own administration and some newspapers had complained that much of the merchandise in park gift shops was flimsy, imported junk; they had urged that more Kentucky items be stocked. As a result, the shops soon blossomed with Kentucky-made cornshuck dolls, woven baskets, books by Kentucky authors, and rustic furniture produced in the mountains of eastern Kentucky. But, as proprietors of the shops complained, many of the best-selling items still came from Japan. And, apparently, Germany.

Combs interpreted these assaults as evidence that the Republicans were having a hard time finding issues. He was right. Nevertheless, Nunn was a good candidate and ran a strong campaign, for a man who had been little known outside his home county of Barren until a few months earlier, and who represented a party long accustomed to a minor role. His criticism of Combs's executive order was aimed at the method rather than the purpose of the order, though the *New Republic* called his attack racist. Generally, however, the campaign was conducted on a fairly high level.

On November 5, Breathitt won the governorship by 13,055 votes (449,551 to 436,496), a much smaller margin than he and the media had predicted. Harry Lee Waterfield waltzed in on a 65,000 margin, indicating that Chandler had been of considerable value to Nunn. Even conceding Chandler's help, however, the Nunn showing was very impressive for a man who, ten years earlier, had been a total unknown. He had gained attention when he became the first Republican in half a century to win the post of county judge in staunchly Democratic Barren County. And his showing against a young, popular, and rising Democrat was clear warning that he would be heard from again, as of course he was, coming back four years later to win the governorship.

A final special session remained, called by Combs to raise the pay of state judges and to require periodic inspections of automobiles in an effort to get dangerous clunkers off the highways. Without hesitation, the lawmakers passed the pay bill on December 4. The next day, just as expeditiously, they defeated the auto inspection bill and went home. This was all right with Combs, who had not expected the bill to pass but had pleased some constituents by having it introduced. As House Majority Leader Richard Moloney explained, had the bill been passed, it would not have gone into effect until the following July, and by that time it could be brought before the next regular session and get more thorough consideration without damaging the inspection program. A dozen or more legislators came by the office to say goodbye, since it would be the last time they and the governor would meet in their current roles.

Now Combs became aware of a strange but unmistakable feeling around the executive offices and around the mansion. He was still governor, he still had a job to do, but now the hours and days seemed to rush upon him and past him. Each time he sat at his desk in the big executive office, he was aware that he would feel a twinge of regret when he took the last pictures from the walls and the last mementos of his administration from the desk.

Later he recalled that each time he walked into the mansion and spoke to the trooper on duty and the trusty at the door, it seemed that he was seeing them in a somehow different light. He found a curious pleasure in sitting in the small office to the left of the southern doorway to the mansion, where he had sat so many times—with small groups over coffee or a drink, making telephone calls, studying speeches, writing notes. A pleasant room.

"I found myself reflecting," he wrote to a friend, "on the role in my life that these rooms, these places had played, and about the twists of fate that had brought me from my modest home in the hills to this building of large and imposing rooms, with its graceful furnishings and chandeliers, its white-jacketed servants. And I thought of how my time in the mansion was somehow symbolic of the transient nature of my role in the state of which the building was itself a symbol."

There were times during the final days when he admitted that it would be good to get away from the unrelenting burden of responsibility and go back to an ordinary house and an ordinary law office to pursue a more ordinary life—if life could ever again be ordinary. Still he knew that he was going to miss much of it, miss the smiles that greeted him in so many places, miss the feeling of having been part of life on a meaningful scale, miss the feeling of satisfaction at having done something of which he could be proud—things that he would remember when the details of life as governor began to blur and only the broad memories remained. And he knew that he would miss, too, the feeling of power that was part of what he had achieved. And he would miss the feeling almost of pleased surprise at having come face to face with himself, as though he had had the chance to look into a magic mirror in which he could see his inner self.

He had a few details left to take care of. He had already pardoned Newport Police Chief Harry Stuart, restoring his rights and allowing him to run for office again if he wanted to. Now he pardoned Campbell County Sheriff Norbert Roll so that he could run, too, or at least live without the stigma hanging over him. It seemed a good way to end the rather messy affair of Newport and to avoid needless or permanent hurt to those involved, now that the town had been cleaned up to the satisfaction of the reformers—though probably not, he realized, for all time. There'll always be a Newport, he thought wryly.

On November 30, Combs was the guest of honor at a special gathering of the Kentucky Education Association in Frankfort, and the attending teachers thanked him for having done more for the education of Kentucky's children than any governor in the state's history. He could not, he said, have asked for a finer tribute. On December 7 he gave Shakertown, at Pleasant Hill, $50,000 toward its restoration project; in a speech to state employees, he asked them to look after the floral clock when he was gone. Friends knew that Combs had always had a warm spot for the clock; it had been his idea, and he had stuck to it when all around were saying it was a bad idea. On December 10 he followed tradition, and issued pardons to 11 of his mansion trusties, commuted the sentences of five others to time they had already served, and reduced the sentences of the remaining five. This, too, he told a friend, was a rewarding experience. He had gotten to know these people and to like them. They had made mistakes; they had paid; and it had been interesting, as well as touching, to watch the nervous determination and uncertainty with which they viewed their days and their duty, on which depended their futures.

On December 10, Bert Combs walked for the last time from the mansion to his office in the capitol. Two reporters fell in step with him, asking him how he felt. In the chill winter air that turned their breath to mist, workmen were hammering and sawing away at the big platform taking shape where, four years earlier, had stood the platform on which he had taken the oath of office, and where on the morrow he would close a chapter of his life.

Nodding, speaking now and then to familiar faces, he entered the capitol through the familiar eastern doorway and walked past the guard and down the marble hallway, noting the people rushing in and out of offices, laughing, shaking hands, carrying things back and forth, conferring on the matters that had for the past three weeks occupied members of the team of men and women who helped accomplish the transition from one administration to the next. Around the executive offices there were new people, eager to get to the task ahead.

There was not much to do—some papers to sign, people to speak to, people to thank, brief ceremonies. In the afternoon there was a little party, and some gifts which, again, touched him. Among the secretaries and clerks in the offices around the waiting room, there were some tears.

He turned from the office, emptied of the mementos that had marked the room as his, and walked for the last time as governor down the corridor, out the great bronze doors and into the dusk of the wintering day. The next morning he rode in the inevitable parade with his successor, Edward Breathitt, shared with him the shouts and plaudits of the crowd, and sat with him on the inaugural platform. The scene was much the same as it had been four years earlier, and yet it was different, as he himself was different. The four years between had changed his life, and had brought change to the state and those about him. He wondered how well history would judge him. Then it was time for him to speak his valedictory.

"I do not expect to stand here again," he said,

and being only human, I look back today and wonder how . . . Kentucky has fared under our stewardship. I have not done all that I hoped to do when I stood here four years ago. Perhaps no man ever does. But when I addressed you four years ago, full of new plans and bright hopes, I said, "The only thing I can hope for is to leave the governor's office four years from now with the respect and perhaps the affection of the people I serve." My hope then is my hope now, and to the extent that I have earned your respect and perhaps a little of your affection, to that extent I have been successful.

When I look back on what has been done, it seems that we have done well, that our progress has been great. But then I look at the problems that remain, the terrible difficulties that face our successors, and I realize again how small an impress a man makes upon his world, how long and trying is the road we travel, how few are the victories, how elusive the answers we seek.

These have been years of great change in the world and in our state; years also of great tragedy, great sorrow, great hope. So, undoubtedly, will be the years ahead. Yet there is reason to believe that we face better things. For governors and their works and their little hour upon the stage soon pass. It is the spirit that survives, and the spirit of Kentucky is strong. We may change her laws, we may alter her lovely countryside, but the spirit of Kentucky endures. And if during my stay in office I have helped to keep intact our faith in ourselves, if I have added a bit to the heritage we pass on to our children, if I have helped to keep proud the spirit of Kentucky, then I am content.

To all of you, I say thank you for permitting me to serve as your governor.

Then Bert Combs stepped to one side, and Edward Breathitt stepped forward.

How It Can Be Done

Three men—Combs, Clements, and Chandler—have dominated this brief survey of Kentucky gubernatorial politics in the middle years of this century. They were, or are, interesting men, men of personal strength, intellect, and ambition. Each left an impression on his state. There was for each of them a measure of glory; there was also a degree of pathos.

It is symbolic that A.B. Chandler, who epitomized his state in so many ways, wrote a record which, like that of Kentucky, was less than it should have been because of missed opportunity. Yet he remained true to his own ideal of limited government, of an individual independence the virtue of which is perhaps greater than its practicality in today's world. He symbolized a time, a mood, that was essentially Kentucky. If he had been more willing to risk the danger of today for the gain of tomorrow, he might have written the brightest pages of Kentucky's history, for he enjoyed the power that comes with immense popularity. But, through the basic reserve of the southern conservative, he failed to take the steps that might have brought Kentucky into the American mainstream. Yet that conservatism should be borne in mind. He represented, as Allan Trout once said, the Republican wing of the Democratic party in Kentucky. Many Chandler critics have tended to blame him for a failure to be something he never pretended to be—a liberal Democrat whose liberal policies might have benefited Kentucky more than his cautious ones. At the same time his career reminds us that great men take great risks.

Earle C. Clements had attributes of greatness—strength, courage, and intellect. In fact, he may well have been the greatest political intellect of this century in Kentucky, and it is significant that there were close and strong ties between him and another outstanding political mind, Ed Prichard. Those who watched Earle Clements move through the political milieu commented frequently on his ability to foresee not only the result of each action but the results of that result. He made few false moves except when he moved through temper or injured pride.

He was also the victim of ill fortune. He did much for his state and might have done still more had he not run afoul the combined forces of state Republicans and errant Democrats at a time when Republicans nationally were in the ascendant. The loss led him into the series of events that culminated with his involvement in the Highway Department troubles of the Combs administration, and his subsequent break with Combs and his awkward alliance with Chandler, an alliance of differing philosophies. His last years, most of them spent in lingering bitterness and ill health, were less than he deserved. Let it be of comfort to the many who loved him that as hard pride softened in his last days, the warmth of the inner man emerged once more.

It may be presumptuous to attempt here a precise assessment of the administration of Bert Combs or of his contribution to his state. Time will place a value on his work, as on the work of his predecessors. But a generation has passed now since he held the office, and in the flat light of more than 20 years, his record seems to be sound.

He was unusual, and in this no flattery of him or derogation of others is intended. When we contemplate the difficulty and often the pain of the governorship of Kentucky, it would seem that we owe a measure of admiration to any person who attains it and holds it to the benefit of his state, and nothing in this brief and incomplete account should be permitted to cast an unintended shadow on any of those who have played their parts in it.

The four years of Bert Combs were good years. He did well. He paved the way for the administration of Ned Breathitt, and that too was a benefit to the state and its people. Combs has always believed that the election of Breathitt, who endorsed without exception the particulars of the Combs program, was proof that his program, his reforms, were accepted by the people of Kentucky. He is probably correct in this, although it is also likely that by 1963 the people had simply tired of old faces, old tactics, and wanted a change to men younger than Happy Chandler. The gratitude of the electorate is as brief as its memory.

The Combs administration, and the Breathitt administration that followed, saw Democratic factionalism in Kentucky begin to ebb. This was probably due in part to the slow shift of population from rural to urban, in part to the modest Republican resurgence that made factionalism more likely to cost Democrats general elections. Some of the decline may have been due to television, which dramatically increased the cost of campaigning, forcing candidates to look to sources other than courthouse organizations, and which made an appealing camera appearance more important than issues or organization.

But until his defeat by Wendell Ford in 1971, Combs was the

undisputed leader of the last strong faction. He may also be called the last of the strong governors. He was able to enact an almost revolutionary program of laws because he held the legislature in tight control. There were two reasons for this: he had strong and loyal leaders in both houses, and he had enough money to propose programs that the people, and therefore their legislators, wanted. Money—specifically money yielded by the sales tax—that was the secret. Without it there would have been no university expansion program, no community colleges, no broad teachers' raises, no park facilities construction, no mental health programs, no welfare-payment increases, no tourism programs, no industrial promotion. That is why every move Combs made, every political tactic he devised was made with the protection of the sales tax in mind. Without it his program could not have been financed; without it his program could not have been continued by a successor. That is why the defeat of Chandler was his primary goal, why it was more important than the election of Wyatt or the passage of any single piece of legislation.

The sales tax and the improvements it made possible had the effect also of encouraging succeeding governors to attempt similar moves; Edward Breathitt withstood Chandler's promises to repeal the tax, and defended it successfully throughout his administration. Louie Nunn had a precedent for his courageous move to increase the tax from 3 to 5 percent in order to finance his school and parks programs. The temptation to lure votes by cutting the tax will always be there, of course. Nor is there anything magical about the tax. It has not yielded enough money to keep Kentucky education in step with that of other states. At this writing the state ranks somewhere between 43rd and 46th among the states, and no candidate for governor has dared to admit the obvious—that it is going to take an increase in the sales tax, in personal and corporate taxes, and probably the imposition of a substantial state property tax to get Kentucky into the educational mainstream.

Some of Combs's success can be traced to simple self-control. Unlike Chandler, he controlled his tongue. The tirades of Rex Logan, the needling of Cap Gardner, the obstructionism of Wendell Butler rankled him, as they would rankle any sensitive man, but he refused to get into name-calling contests. He would not trade insults with Chandler. Like Clements, he was a tireless worker. Like Clements, he believed in the dignity of the office. But he brought his own style to the governor's office, and left his own mark on it.

Like other governors before and since, Combs improved the operation of state government through his reorganization. Whether this was a major accomplishment is debatable. Government and governors respond to changing conditions, changing needs. When roads were the great need of the state, the Highway Department was the weapon and the measure of a governor. Evolving social needs and the growth of federal programs forced a shift of emphasis to welfare functions. Combs altered, expanded, and tuned the agencies and functions of government to meet the pressing demands for better education, broader welfare services, and multi-lane, limited-access highways. He was the first to use the state's bonding power in a creative way, as in his financing of the Mountain Parkway, basing support not on existing traffic but on traffic the road would stimulate. He was, in a sense, the state's first modern governor, a break with the political past of sectionalism, patronage, and exploitation of state employees, though the radical change probably came with John Y. Brown, Jr., the first of the television candidates, the first intentionally weak governor, who tried neither to organize nor to dominate the legislature.

Combs tried his best to drag Kentucky into the modern era, with modern roads, modern education, modern parks, modern welfare services. But he could drag the people of Kentucky only so far; he could not persuade them to create conditions for truly modern, efficient government by revising the state constitution. He showed them that while taxes are not painless, neither are they unbearable, and that it is probably less painful to pay a little more now than to wait until accumulating needs require the payment of a great deal. But he could not convince them that sensible taxation is necessary for progress, that taxes can be creative, that individual goals can often best be achieved through social action. He gave the people a taste of progress. But, as the record shows, Kentucky remains a backward, poorly educated, technologically deficient state. As of this writing, yet another high-level statewide committee, this one appointed by the lieutenant governor, has recommended revision of the constitution and steps to raise the educational level of the state. But it makes no mention of the essential ingredient of this improvement—taxes. Kentucky still has a way of turning its back on tomorrow.

One reason Bert Combs did well is that he could and did take risks. He could take risks because he aspired to no higher office, unlike most of the men who have held the governorship; he could therefore chance the unpopularity that must at times be the portion of those who would lead along a hard but upward path. He had opportunities to run for Congress or the Senate, during and after his term. He had, and took, the opportunity to be a federal judge, but found that he did not like it much and quit it to come home to Kentucky.

Bert Combs liked being governor of Kentucky. He tried once more for the office, in 1971, and failed. That failure has generally been attributed to lingering resentment of the sales tax, though the tax had proved the salvation of Kentucky's government. Combs rejects this theory: "My failure in that second race was a personal one," he says now. "As long as I was on the scene and in a position of leadership, I could win; I did win, and people I supported won on the strength of my policies. I have reason to believe, and do believe, that I could have won had I run when Henry Ward ran. I was strongly urged, and refused; and people, including many close to me, accepted my refusal as a sign of my withdrawal from active political life.

"I had long been inclined toward the judiciary, and it was gratifying to attain the federal bench. To my surprise, it proved a disappointing experience, possibly because I had become too accustomed to, too fond of, the clash and excitement of public life and the satisfaction of achievement and accomplishment that came with the governor's office. But by the time I removed myself from the bench and returned to Kentucky, other forces had been at work, people had made other alignments. Many did not understand why I wanted to give up a judgeship paying $42,500 a year for a chance at a governorship paying $30,000, and were suspicious of my motives. I never managed to get my message across. And I must admit that I did not run a good race. Perhaps I had been away too long. That had created a vacuum, and [Wendell] Ford moved into it."

It is true that his resignation from the federal bench in order to run again for the governorship hurt Combs. As he says, people could not believe that any man without ulterior motives would resign the higher-paying office of the federal circuit bench to be a more modestly paid governor. This is especially true in a poor state, where the idea of seeking a lesser-paying but more satisfying job is suspect. We demand dedication on the part of our politicians, but when they demonstrate dedication, we become suspicious of their motives.

It cannot be denied that Ford made excellent use of the sales tax issue without putting himself into a position where carrying out his promises involved damaging the state very greatly. He promised merely to reduce it, but that was enough to give him the initial spark needed to ignite his race. Yet we cannot ignore the fact that the man who defeated Combs promised to reduce the sales tax. And the people responded, as they have for long responded to the siren song of the easy way. That too was an echo of the tragedy that has been historically a dark cloud over the land of Kentucky.

Curiously, for a state that has produced so many statesmen, Kentucky has suffered from wayward leadership. It is true that the divisive circumstances of their early years made Kentuckians suspicious of and resistant to progress, but in this they were little different from the people of other developing states. The tragedy was that they lacked progressive and unselfish leaders, public officials who would take political risk in an effort to inspire and lift the people. On the contrary, Kentucky has suffered too many pseudo-leaders who were willing to play upon their fears and resentments, their opposition to taxes and individual sacrifice, in order to gain political power. Political leaders have played to the weakest nature of Kentuckians and have too often brought forth the worst.

It is hoped that these pages have shown how divisions have hampered Kentucky's drive toward excellence. Political factions were one aspect of that division, but not the only one. Since the defeat of Chandler, the death of Clements, and the defeat of Combs, there have been no true factional leaders, yet there has been little enlightenment or progress in the government and welfare of Kentucky. At this writing, it is still far down the list among the states in the quality of its services and the education it offers its young. It did not maintain the forward movement begun under Combs.

Since his departure from Frankfort, Happy Chandler has attained something of the stature of a folk figure, appearing at athletic events and other public functions, singing "My Old Kentucky Home," and waving to people, many of whom no longer recognize him.

Combs has retained an interest and a measure of influence in state politics, especially since the death of Clements, but the days of his ambition are past. Nor has anyone risen to mold a dynasty, a dominant faction. John Young Brown, Jr., might have done so, but his personality does not seem designed for the often tedious chores of political organization. He is by nature a great salesman rather than a political philosopher. As Chandler was the great showman of the courthouse lawn, so Brown appears to be a television candidate.

Kentuckians have long been drawn to the showman rather than the statesman. More's the pity, perhaps, and that fact too casts a kindly light on the four years of Bert T. Combs.

_____ SELECTED BIBLIOGRAPHY _____

PRIMARY AND SECONDARY WORKS

Baylor, Orval. *J. Dan Talbott: Champion of Good Government*. Louisville: Kentucky Printing, 1942.

Blakey, George T. *Hard Times and New Deal in Kentucky, 1929-1939*. ⭐ *ILL* Lexington: University Press of Kentucky, 1986.

Bodley, Temple, and Samuel M. Wilson. *History of Kentucky*. 4 vols. Chicago and Louisville: S.J. Clark, 1928.

Chandler, Albert Benjamin. Papers. Special Collections, University of Kentucky Library, Lexington.

———. Interviews with A.B. Chandler, 1972-73. Special Collections, University of Kentucky Library, Lexington.

Channing, Steven A. *Kentucky*. New York: W.W. Norton, 1977.

Chinn, George M. *The History of Harrodsburg and the Great Settlement* ⭐ *Area of Kentucky, 1774-1900*. Harrodsburg: Harrodsburg Historical Society, 1985.

Clark, Thomas D. *Agrarian Kentucky*. Lexington: University Press of Kentucky, 1977. *F4 35C55*

———. *A History of Kentucky*. Rev. ed. Lexington, Ky.: John Bradford Press, 1950.

———. *Kentucky: Land of Contrast*. New York: Harper & Row, 1968. ⭐

———, and Albert D. Kirwan. *The South since Appomattox*. New York: Oxford University Press, 1967.

Collins, Lewis, and Richard H. Collins. *Collins' Historical Sketches of Kentucky: History of Kentucky*. Rev. ed. 2 vols. Covington, Ky.: Collins, 1882.

Coulter, E. Merton. *The Civil War and Readjustment in Kentucky*. Chapel Hill: University of North Carolina Press, 1926.

Coward, Joan Wells. *Kentucky in the New Republic: The Process of Constitution Making*. Lexington: University Press of Kentucky, 1979.

Eller, Ronald D. *Miners, Millhands, and Mountaineers, 1880-1930*. Knoxville: University of Tennessee Press, 1982.

Evans, Herndon J. *The Newspaper Press in Kentucky*. Lexington: University Press of Kentucky, 1976.

Fenton, John H. *Politics in the Border States: A Study of the Patterns of Political Organization, and Political Change, Common to the Border States*. New Orleans: Hauser Press, 1957.

Friendly, Fred W., and Martha J.H. Elliott. *The Constitution: That Delicate Balance*. New York: Random House, 1984.

Gipson, Vernon. *Ruby Laffoon, Governor of Kentucky, 1931-1935*. Hartford, Ky.: McDowell, 1978.

Harrell, Kenneth E., ed. *The Public Papers of Governor Edward T. Breathitt, 1963-1967*. Lexington: University Press of Kentucky, 1984.

Harrison, Lowell H. *The Antislavery Movement in Kentucky*. Lexington: University Press of Kentucky, 1978.

———, ed. *Kentucky's Governors, 1792-1985*. Lexington: University Press of Kentucky, 1985.

———, and Nelson L. Dawson, eds. *A Kentucky Sampler: Essays from the Filson Club History Quarterly, 1926-1976*. Lexington: University Press of Kentucky, 1977.

Ireland, Robert. *Little Kingdoms: The Counties of Kentucky, 1850-1891*. Lexington: University Press of Kentucky, 1977.

Klotter, James C. "Clio in the Commonwealth: The Status of Kentucky History." *Register of the Kentucky Historical Society* 80 (Winter 1982): 65-88.

Jewell, Malcolm E., and Everett W. Cunningham. *Kentucky Politics*. Lexington: University of Kentucky Press, 1968.

———. *Kentucky Votes*. 3 vols. Lexington: University of Kentucky Press, 1963.

Kleber, John E., ed. *The Public Papers of Governor Lawrence W. Wetherby, 1950-1955*. Lexington: University Press of Kentucky, 1983.

Klotter, James C., and John W. Muir. *Ben Johnson, the Highway Commission and Kentucky Politics, 1927-1937*. *Register of the Kentucky Historical Society* 84 (Winter 1986).

Lee, Lloyd G. *A Brief History of Kentucky and Its Counties*. Berea, Ky.: Kentucky Imprints, 1981.

Libbey, James K. *Dear Alben: Mr. Barkley of Kentucky*. Lexington: University Press of Kentucky, 1979.

Lofaro, Michael A. *The Life and Adventures of Daniel Boone*. Lexington: University Press of Kentucky, 1978.

Ogden, Frederic D., ed. *The Public Papers of Governor Keen Johnson, 1939-1943*. Lexington: University Press of Kentucky, 1982.

Pierce, Neal R. *The Border South States*. New York: W.W. Norton, 1975.

Robinson, George W., ed. *The Public Papers of Governor Bert T. Combs, 1959-1963*. Lexington: University Press of Kentucky, 1980.

Schacter, Harry W., ed. *Reports of the Committee for Kentucky, 1943-1950.* Louisville: The Committee for Kentucky, 1950.

Schulman, Robert. *John Sherman Cooper: The Global Kentuckian.* Lexington: University Press of Kentucky, 1976.

Sexton, Robert. "Kentucky Politics and Society, 1919-1932." Ph.D. diss., University of Washington, 1970.

Share, Alan J. *Cities in the Commonwealth: Two Centuries of Urban Life in Kentucky.* Lexington: University Press of Kentucky, 1982.

Stone, Richard G., Jr. *A Brittle Sword: The Kentucky Militia, 1776-1912.* Lexington: University Press of Kentucky, 1977.

Syvertsen, Thomas H. "Earle Chester Clements and the Democratic Party, 1920-1950." Ph.D. diss., University of Kentucky, 1982.

Tapp, Hambleton, and James C. Klotter. *Kentucky: Decades of Discord, 1865-1900.* Frankfort: Kentucky Historical Society, 1977.

Webb, Ross A. *Kentucky in the Reconstruction Era.* Lexington: University Press of Kentucky, 1979.

Wright, John D. *Transylvania: Tutor to the West.* Rev. ed. Lexington: University Press of Kentucky, 1980.

Wyatt, Wilson W., Sr. *Whistle Stops: Adventures in Public Life.* Lexington: University Press of Kentucky, 1985.

INTERVIEWS

Note: The dates for these interviews are imprecise because over the years I have lost or discarded many of my notebooks and have been obliged to judge dates by articles resulting from the interviews.

Clements, Earle C. Frankfort: November 1947; February and March 1948. Madisonville: 1956. Morganfield: 1957, 1969, 1980.

Combs, Bert T. June 1956; June, August, and November 1959; February and March 1960; June 1961; March, August, and June 1962; November and December 1963; June, August, and November 1971; March, May, June, July, September, November, and December 1984; March, June, October, November, and December 1985; March, April, June, July, and August 1986.

Farris, Edward. Frankfort: June and November 1985.

Matlick, J.O. Frankfort: May 1955; November 1956; November 1961. Louisville: 1961; March 1962; May 1964.

May, William H. Frankfort: 1957; August 1959; March 1960. Louisville: June and July 1971. Frankfort: March and May 1986.

Munford, Tyler. Frankfort: February 1948; March 1950. Morganfield: May 1986.

Wetherby, Lawrence. Frankfort: March and May 1948; July 1955; June 1959.

INDEX

Wells, Rainey T., 31
Western Kentucky, 3, 30, 44, 51, 78, 81, 126
Western Kentucky Turnpike, 172, 175, 220
Westpheling, Jo, 88
Wetherby, Governor Lawrence, 53-54, 56, 58, 59, 63, 73, 83; as lieutenant-governor, 35; as governor, 48-49, 52; and Combs, 60, 61, 79, 106, 189, 214; and Chandler, 66, 75, 116; 1956 defeat of, 74
Whallen, Colonel John, 29
Wheeler, Patton G., 156
Whisman, John, 98, 173
Whitaker, John, 47
Williams, Charles, 77
Willis, Governor Simeon, 47, 55, 59, 155
Willis, Sally, 155
Willson, Governor Augustus, 22
Wilson, Woodrow, 28
Winston, Dix, 5, 89, 154
Wittenberg, H.G., 146

Wooten, Bailey, 31, 33, 36, 43
Works Progress Administration (WPA), 44, 45
World War I, 41, 53, 82
World War II, 47, 50, 53, 58, 75
Wyatt, Wilson Watkins, 30, 110, 142, 148, 168; and Chandler, 78, 80, 96, 192; and Combs, 79, 81, 82-83, 91, 93, 94, 97, 123, 138-39, 172-73; *Whistle Stops*, 79, 200; campaign merger with Combs, 84-86, 190; as lieutenant governor, 100, 101, 105, 153; and Clements, 107, 200; and income surtax, 117; and constitutional revision, 156, 158; and campaign for U.S. Senate, 159, 172-73, 186, 191, 204-5; promotion of industry, 162, 175, 181; and Breathitt, 197-98; on running for governor, 201

Young, Allie, 32, 72
Youth Authority, 54, 66, 116, 185
Youtsey, Henry, 22